DISCOVERING SWALLOWS & RANSOMES

*An autobiography inspired by Arthur Ransome
and his real-life characters*

JOHN BERRY

Edited and introduced by Jim Andrews

Published by Sigma Leisure – an imprint of
Sigma Press, 5 Alton Road, Wilmslow, Cheshire SK9 5DY, England.

British Library Cataloguing in Publication Data
A CIP record for this book is available from the British Library.

ISBN: 1-85058-814-7

Typesetting and Design by: Sigma Press, Wilmslow, Cheshire.

Cover picture: The Secret Harbour – an oil painting by John Berry

Copyright materials used in this book:
Quotations and illustrations by Arthur Ransome © The Arthur Ransome Literary Estate
Photographs © John Berry; Asadour and Rahel Guzelian; The Brotherton Library; Arthur Lupton; Roger Stephens; Hugues Villard; Dave Stewart; John Sanders; Ian Constantinesco; Michael Webb
Illustrations (except those by Arthur Ransome) © John Berry; Roger Wardale; Dick Kelsall

Printed by: Bell and Bain Ltd, Glasgow

Foreword

This is a tale of enthusiasm – initially, a boy's real-life enterprise, formed in the mould of his literary heroes, then later, carried through with his wife Judy to manhood and an enriched 'middle age'. What John discovered can now be shared in this remarkably readable and enthralling document.

Ransome's *Swallows and Amazons* series became an example and initial driving force from the moment John and his twin sister Juliet first opened those magical pages. But John yearned to go further – to seek out Arthur Ransome himself and find out if those children in the books were as real as they seemed. The author was aged 12 when he set out on his battered old bicycle, for 26 miles along those winding country lanes, towards and around Coniston Water.

John and Juliet Berry were born (remarkably after a miscarriage and a still birth I'm told) on a Friday 13th July 1928. He is now a portrait artist but suffered dismal days at school and in ill-matched employment, due, in part, to what is now recognised as a form of dyslexia. Only a happy personality, grit and unwavering determination got him through what became unique situations.

As a writer, yachting journalist and very keen Ransome enthusiast myself, I first met John in the early days of The Arthur Ransome Society ('TARS'), home to a diverse selection of kindred spirits. To no-one's surprise but his own, he followed me with a stint as the Society's North Regional Chairman.

When John asked me to supervise his 'tail' [sic], I was flattered and editing it has proved a thrilling and delightful task.

There are already many excellent books about AR, his life and works, but here, in the form of a fascinating memoir, is a very different, concise and remarkably unclichéd insight into the unusual character of Arthur Ransome – and his not-altogether-fictional characters.

There are also thousands of Ransome enthusiasts of all ages about the world, but this book is not intended just for them. It is going to be of absorbing interest to others too.

Discovering Swallows and Ransomes is a succinct and accurate title – of a true story full of humour and verve. Turn the page and join John in his unusual adventures . . .

Jim Andrews, Windermere.

Acknowledgements

The Brotherton Library in Leeds is an enthralling environment and I'm grateful for access to their Special Collections, and for allowing the quotes from Arthur (and Evgenia's) diaries, a delightful study in themselves. Allowing me to include Arthur's characteristic letter to Col. Busk, Clifford Webb, the letters from Arthur to me, a 'Hollywood', family pictures and so much else. Not least the patient guidance from Ann Farr and Christopher Sheppard.

Similarly, the A.R. Literary Executors in the shape of Vice President Christina Hardyment (also John Bell and especially Dave Sewart) for allowing 'Permissions'. Wearing another hat, Christina's own *Arthur Ransome and Captain Flint's Trunk*, reveals mountains of research – and herself as a latter-day 'Nancy Blackett'. Her Obituary for Brigit Sanders in *The Independent* was a revelation!

My sincere thanks to all those who have provided photographs and granted pictorial permission. Most especially Titty's 'children', Asadour and Rahel Guzelian, Taqui's Roger Stephens, Susie's Hugues Villard. Also, John Sanders.

I owe very much to the late Tony Colwell. As a publisher's editor for Jonathan Cape Ltd, it is hardly surprising that after launching the likes of Ian Fleming he was alarmingly frank over many years. But he *gave* all his help as a friend – even in his last few days of agonising illness. If, as a new boy, I appear the least bit professional, I owe much to Tony. Margaret, his widow, reminded me of the families own love for the Ransome books and told how, in happier days, they even rented "Hullabaloo-type" boats on the Broads and "waded across the Red Sea" as in AR's *Secret Water*.

Of course, huge thanks are owed to Jonathan Cape, courtesy of Catherine Trippett, Permissions Manager at The Random House Archive & Library, for allowing certain book illustrations and quotations, all celebrating the Ransome ambience – and being the vehicle of so much joy!

It was Victoria Slowe and Liam McDowall's accounts of Dora Altounyan and family, as contained in the Abbot Hall's Exhibition catalogue for *Through Women's Eyes* that gives a precious insight into dear Dora's somewhat stifled career in art and her not fully recognised exceptional portraiture and landscape paintings – followed by political trauma in Syria and the family's return to Coniston and undeserved poverty. Thank you Abbot Hall, and for permissions too!

Other helpers in order of batting are: my sister Juliet for recollections and corrections, our mother Enid (née Moore) especially, for her own book *Seven Dogs and a Berry*. The so-part-of-it Arthur Lupton for inside knowledge and the fireside photo of Arthur & Evgenia; Diane McAnulla; Peter

Smith; Janet Gnosspelius; Hugh Brogan; Thomas Macan; Margaret Ratcliffe; Cicily Ledgard; Judy Andrews; Danny Darnborough; Ruth Skye; Peter and Jill Blackburn. Especially, Dick and Bibby Fowkes; Hugues Villard, Geraint Lewis and Ted Alexander. Not least son-in-law, David Pickering, for computer help and scanning illustrations onto CD. *Classic Boat*; *Lancashire Life*; *The Westmorland Gazette*; *The Manchester Guardian* (with much still lurking) *The Observer* and *Huddersfield Examiner* too.

Among the most inspiring years of my life, were courtesy of Ernest's "invitation" for me to have tea with the famous inventor, George Constantinesco. Our subsequent marketing attempts led to nothing and I feared that scientific advances were being jeopardised forever. Then, 45 years later, I relocated his son, Ian, who having retired from the UN Food and Agriculture Organisation (FAO) in 1974, continued as a Consulting Agricultural Engineer, including writing about his father's inventions and demonstrating, often with Meccano models, the vital validity to his father's priceless legacy. Ian has enhanced my background knowledge, corrected and given credence to my own account! I thank him very much indeed!

I have been long and markedly helped by Roger Wardale and he must sometimes regard me as a pilfering pupil. The so-professional drawings in his own book *Nancy Blackett* – of *Amazon* and of *Swallow* show how they really were constructed around 1928 – and he now allows me to include! It was also via Roger that I heard again from Richard Pierce, the builder of Beachnut boats – and his unique sailing experience in *Mavis*. I thank Richard too.

Once more it was Wardale, this time as Editor of (TARS) *Mixed Moss* who allowed me the abridged version of *Tea with the Ransomes*. I'm so indebted to the late Ellen C. Tillinghast for the account of her visit to Hurlingham Court with her three girls (whom I'm unable to locate). In addition, from *Mixed Moss*, I was allowed bits of the *North Polar Expedition* in which Jim Andrews describes how, by extraordinary dowsing, he locates The Old View House as in *Winter Holiday*.

What a compensation it was when Judy and I met Tania Rose, almost as if dear Titty had planned it at her funeral reception! Tania's memories of visiting the Ransomes at Hurlingham Court, were another, very different, insight. Then, dear Brigit Sanders, her last years devoted brilliantly to The Arthur Ransome Society (TARS) helm. With typically kind awareness, she prompted me to "confer" with Philippa Ryan, and learn of her cousinly adventures on Coniston Water with Roger Altounyan during the war. It was the equally kind nature of John Sanders to whom I owe the account of Roger's fishing for char, permissions, and so much more.

Only after endless challenges was the real-life Roger recognised for his unique aid to asthma sufferers. I'm so indebted to Fisons for allowing me the comprehensive accounts of what he accomplished while in their employ – and, even more for Roger's INTAL and its derivatives, as are many thousands of fellow sufferers with extended lives! Then, on the very last official day before publication, I was granted, via Dave Sewart, pictures from Rodney Dingle's excellent book about 'Roger' – and the record of John Prichard's own prime memories of Roger. Thank you all!

The Altounyans generally, spent little time contemplating their unsought *Swallow* images. Each was a sterling character anyway. It is to Ernest and Dora, Titty and Melkon, Roger and Hella particularly that we owe most. But then Taqui Stephens' own books emerged and her so-helpful openness and that of her son Roger remain.

As a lifelong admirer of Clifford Webb's illustrations in ARs two earliest books, I had never expected to know something about *him*. Then came (TARS) *Mixed Moss Vol 3/6 – An Artistic Coincidence* by Robin Anderson, and gripping disclosures from his son, Michael!

Quite apart from being a TARS instigator and Vice President in later life, Dick Kelsall, accompanied by elder brother Desmond and family, helped Ransome's first awakening and emergence as a major author. It is for Dick's vital and creative contributions revealed in Chapter 11 – an invaluable addition to that from the Swallows. I feel so privileged and indebted!

I must mention AR himself! Arthur Ransome was a main influence from early life and frequent absorption ever since. With an exceptional and complex nature, his outlook was not without anomalies and I marvel at his wide achievements, service to this country and the joy he continues to give to thousands throughout the world. Without Arthur (and Evgenia), life would not have been so rich. I trust this book is worthy of them, all those who feature in consequence and his enhusiastic followers!

Arriving at the Broadland last chapter, I asked Patricia Mockridge, being on the spot and an ex-schoolmarm, if she would help to check the reality of things. She got drawn in and contributed more detail and severe proof-reading than ever expected. I could not have managed "quite so splendidly" without her!

Of all those who have helped over the years, it is Jim Andrews who bore the brunt. As a reformed industrialist, established author, national yachtsman, archaeological dowser, vitamin authority and TARS devotee etc. – living on the banks of Windermere – he really did not need diversions but responded with such relevance to one radically flawed draft after another. Jim became my Editor from the nineties and I still dream of a crippling invoice in the post. I hope it is not too late to say "thank you Jim, thank you very much indeed!"

Little of this would have taken place without Judy. Our intrinsic interests provide the material, her extraordinary memory and our joint enthusiasms found fulfilment. From very separate childhoods, we have been uplifted and remain strengthened by the Swallows and Ransome-type sway. Then came The Arthur Ransome Society (TARS) – and more kindred spirits than we ever knew existed – with whom we feel so at home.

It is to Judy that I dedicate this book!

John Berry

Contents

Chapter 1

An Irresistible Urge

My twin sister, Juliet and I, count ourselves fortunate in having had a mother and two adoring maiden aunts, all of whom read English at Oxford, and steeped us in good literature from the start. It is to their introduction of childhood classics that we owe, among many other things, a lasting joy of books.

When we were six, one of these good things was to stay at Mr Walker's farm in Colthouse in the Lake District. We travelled up in the open dickey of an adopted aunt's Morris two-seater. As we reached Lakeland, I was heard to exclaim "I like the shape of this country" – and have been repeating much the same thing ever since.

Later, we stayed opposite the farm at a delightful house leased by yet another aunt. This had a lane along the back and next door lived 'Lovina' who kept the place in order and was a lovely character. Beyond the lane was a chuckling beck and a walled-in vegetable garden belonging to her husband, Mr Christopherson, who gardened for Mrs Heelis (Beatrix Potter). We naturally took him to be 'Mr McGregor' and when Juliet once saw them chatting there together, she wore one sack round her shoulders and another round her waist.

Nearly seventy years later, while invited to lunch at the lovely house, we heard how Christopherson's general cultivating skills made him an invaluable member of Beatrix Potter's loyal band of assistants. However, unlike the rest of them, he could be outspoken – and was regularly 'sacked' in consequence. That he invariably turned up for work the following day seemed to go unnoticed.

What happened after the delightful Beatrix Potter books reign is, for me, even more timeless and memorable, a book which brought even Father into

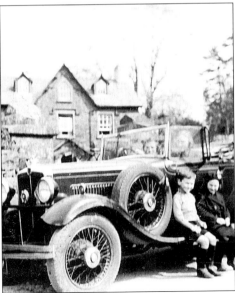

When we were six

our enthusiastic panel of bedtime readers, gave flight to unimagined but achievable aspirations and cement to our love of 'The Lakes' forever. It was, of course, *Swallows and Amazons* and the eleven books of an expanding field which were to follow.

Of all the children in the books, it was initially the exemplary boy, 'Captain John Walker' and suggestions of a future naval career which, initially, I most wished to emulate – but the charitable phrase 'late developer' seemed to follow me about.

On leaving preparatory school, aged ten, my parents, after reluctantly considering a Training Ship, wisely decided in 1939, to compromise with a boarding school on the East Coast. This had a harbour nearby and I looked forward to it for months.

What I had not anticipated was the near-starvation diet and I assumed my first helping of breakfast porridge to be a dirty plate. Then there was what in those days passed for discipline. Introduction to our ape-like dormitory prefect went well until my refusal to call him 'sir'. It may have been in consequence of this, that the following morning I was so savagely beaten in his study by a huge gym shoe that I nearly passed out and, for the first week could not sit down on the three raised foot marks which covered my seat.

It was 'John Walker' whose example of fortitude in *We Didn't Mean To Go To Sea* got me through that first and only term. A further twelve beatings were to follow but these, by masters, were mild in comparison and I certainly never asked Matron (she who cut our nails far below the quick) for

Fishing catches

'counselling' as might be today's convention. We never questioned authority in those days and it would have been quite out of character for 'Captain John' anyway.

Most weekends were spent with close friends down by the harbour where we swam, fished and chatted to local seamen and the crews of visiting yachts. What we most wanted was to go to sea – but this was confined to occasional voyages in a robust sea-going pleasure steamer, *The Girl's Own*, and sea-fishing during parental visits when we hauled in phenomenal catches.

Fine evenings meant cricket at the nets, but even more enjoyable for me was helping to dig the school's Air Raid Shelter. This was in the turnip field which ran along behind the school, a six-foot deep trench with parallel sides. It became about fifty yards long and lined with gleaming corrugated iron sheets on a light wooden framework. The whole effect was finished off with the immaculate duck boards which we had helped to turn out at 'woodwork'. It was an inspiration of aesthetic beauty and I secretly yearned for an air raid!

Mercifully, war had still not been declared and we had no opportunity to try things out before a bout of heavy rain caused the sides to close up for the whole length, like the jaws of a gigantic vice. We relied on the cellars from that point on!

The two-hour Art lessons were what I most looked forward to but I had an unfortunate tendency to share my opinions. Mention of draughtsmanship and composition were taken rather personally by the art master on two occasions. The first resulted in an afternoon spent stuffed with knees to chin in a large wastepaper basket under a drop-leaf table covered with a green baize cloth. I think he wanted me to stop talking and I certainly took the hint.

The Art department was on the top floor and only three weeks later, I was dangled by the seat of my pants, far enough outside the window to see the receding view of window frames and hard tennis courts far below. This was to teach *me* "perspective".

In retrospect, I think the staff were bracing themselves for call up and regarded us already as a conflict zone. Unfortunately, the Art master had haemophilia and, being unfit for service, had found some redemption in designing and creating our short-lived Air Raid Shelter. What must have been the final straw, after the shower of rain incident, was his and my attempt to pull out untidy bits of corrugated iron which protruded from the turnip field. He cut himself and ended up in hospital.

Our tuck-shop allowance was sixpence (2.5p) a week and, being ceaselessly ravenous, I sometimes wondered why my parents were having to *pay* for such privations. I used to garden for the Head Master for 'chocolate money' and will always remember our last meeting. This was on the last day of Summer term and I was looking forward to the arrival of my parents as never before. The Head Master had just acquired an early form of lawn sprinkler and I, placed in charge of the tap, was told to turn it on.

But nothing happened and he twiddled the sprinkler head and examined its jets more and more closely until the sudden release of built-up water pressure wet him spectacularly through. Meanwhile, thirty yards away, imagine my feelings as I ran forward 'to help' – and carefully conceal the fact that I had been standing on the hosepipe!

* * *

In August 1939, our parents hired a thirty-foot gaff-rigged sloop, named *Mavis*, from Herbert Woods of Potter Heigham. The hire charge was little over £5 a week as I remember and we spent fourteen of the happiest days of my life on the Norfolk Broads, little aware of any lasting consequence.

I feel that holiday was a special tribute to our parents as it was half-way through it that Father, already a First War naval participant, received his RNVR call-up telegram. This was from the tiny village post office in Barton.

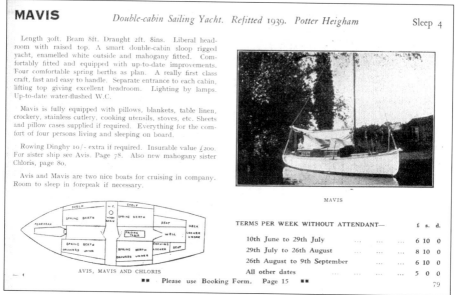

MAVIS   *Double-cabin Sailing Yacht. Refitted* 1939. *Potter Heigham*   Sleep 4

Length 30ft. Beam 8ft. Draught 2ft. 8ins. Liberal head-room with raised top. A smart double-cabin sloop rigged yacht, enamelled white outside and mahogany fitted. Comfortably fitted and equipped with up-to-date improvements. Four comfortable spring berths as plan. A really first class craft, fast and easy to handle. Separate entrance to each cabin, lifting top giving excellent headroom. Lighting by lamps. Up-to-date water-flushed W.C.

Mavis is fully equipped with pillows, blankets, table linen, crockery, stainless cutlery, cooking utensils, stoves, etc. Sheets and pillow cases supplied if required. Everything for the comfort of four persons living and sleeping on board.

Rowing Dinghy 10/- extra if required. Insurable value £200. For sister ship see Avis. Page 78. Also new mahogany sister Chloris, page 80.

Avis and Mavis are two nice boats for cruising in company. Room to sleep in forepeak if necessary.

MAVIS

AVIS, MAVIS AND CHLORIS

TERMS PER WEEK WITHOUT ATTENDANT—				£ s. d.
10th June to 29th July	...	...	...	6 10 0
29th July to 26th August	...	...	...	8 10 0
26th August to 9th September	...	...	...	6 10 0
All other dates	...	...	...	5 0 0

■■ Please use Booking Form. Page 15 ■■

79

Catalogue of Yacht MAVIS

In her book, Mother wrote:

> The storm was brewing. We had been lying a few days at Ranworth and I walked along the little quay in the evenings listening to radios in other yachts. The news from Europe was grave. One night we had the most spectacular thunderstorm we had ever seen, the heavy rain drops splashed on the Broad like small fish leaping and the lightning zigzagged across the dark expanse of sky. World affairs seemed reflected in nature.
>
> A few days earlier we had moored in Barton Broad and collected our mail and scrumptious new-made bread from Barton Post Office which we had given as our poste restante. A telegram for Charlie had been waiting there a week "Report Admiralty forthwith". Charlie sent a telegram there and then and said he would wait for a reply at Barton. While we waited, we watched an old man making baskets, beautiful baskets made from willows, rushes and reeds growing in profusion all around him. The reply from Admiralty was quick in coming. The former message was cancelled. Charlie was asked to await events.

It was after this voyage through northern Broadland that I wrote, with Juliet's help, to Arthur Ransome, through his publishers, Jonathan Cape Ltd, giving a graphic account from our ship's log which she had carefully written up each day.

I told him how we had run hard aground in the middle of Hickling Broad and how Father, holder of a Yacht Master's Certificate, but whose mind must have been on other things, had tried to quant us off while still under

The Skipper and crew

The Mate and crew

full sail! Somehow, this had the effect of swinging *Mavis'* stern right round through the wind and catching her mainsail flat aback as in a fierce gybe.

What happened next, as I described to Mr Ransome, was very sudden indeed. The hefty boom whipped round and caught poor Father a fearful blow across the head and shoulders which would surely have killed a lesser man. Indeed, for awful seconds, we feared the worst as he sailed through the air, quant and all, to land head first a boat length away. So, thankfully, he emerged, though inky black, and stood forlornly in the shallow water – to acknowledge our cheers and relieved guffaws.

* * *

The unexpected response from Mr Ransome came twelve months later. This was a card enclosed in an envelope postmarked 'Coniston 1940' and it must have been just after he acquired 'The Heald' on the east side of Coniston Water. Its border of familiar book illustrations was so kindly complemented by writing on both sides and marked a high point of early life and cemented my regards forever. He wrote:

> Thank you for a very jolly letter. I think you and Juliet were a bit young to start these books at eight. You see they are really written for moderately grown up people, like your father and me. By the way, he must have a grand hard skull. I was knocked out for nearly three days when I got a whack on the head from the boom. Now then, secrets are secrets, and I mustn't let out more than is in the books, but I will tell you this much, that most of your guesses are about right. Walton-on-the-Naze, for example & Bowness.

Your father was quite right to have strong views about Windermere. It is much more tricky sailing than at sea.

If I waste time writing letters I won't have any for writing books.

Good luck to the skipper, mate & crew of the Mavis and Best wishes for fair winds!

Arthur Ransome

Best wishes to the Blood Brothers too.

I like your sign.

Card from Arthur Ransome

Fifty years after receiving his postcard, I had an excuse for reading Ransome's Diaries at the Brotherton Library in Leeds, and was painfully amused by the following extracts, referring to his whack on the head by the boom:

2nd Nov 1936 ... I got a frightful crack on the noddle. Headache.

3rd Nov Headache.

14th Nov Head still funny after crack on Nov 2. Seems to have fallen in a bit on the right side and is pressing on whatever stuff I have instead of brains.

The beautifully drawn eel at the foot of his card was a generous acknowledgement of the one I had drawn for him, which in turn was a copy of one in beautiful blue and red ink that I had painstakingly, very painstakingly, tattooed on the back of my left hand with the sharpened point of my school compasses.

This was intended as a lasting tribute to Arthur Ransome but may sound rather sinister nowadays, as it was achieved while under the influence of his *Secret Water*.

Over lunch that day, Mother and Father – who was on leave – asked what had happened to my heavily bandaged hand and if they might see. By this time the eel had swollen and glistened wetly with fetching realism. I always remember the pride with which I unveiled this artistic triumph, and the silence of my parents as they gazed in stunned admiration at its sheer beauty.

I also remember my dismay when it transpired that after all, on balance and with due consideration, they preferred my hand in its former blank state. Incomprehensibly, I was asked to remove it with equally painful nail-brush and soap.

'The Blood Brothers', to whom Mr Ransome wrote his best wishes, were an equally gory manifestation inspired by a Chapter in the same book, and *The Blooding* illustration which again, he could hardly have anticipated in his young disciples. One wonders if any other young reader subjected his best friend to reluctant Blood Brotherhood, with a blunt penknife, as I did!

That he and I were to adopt exactly the same obscure profession, in his case a celebrated artist, I'm sure is pure coincidence and has nothing to do with shared genetics.

*   *   *

Soon after war was declared, Father found himself as First Lieutenant in a German-built armed trawler chasing contraband off the Orkneys. With a small crew in a whaler, his job was to board and search all foreign merchant ships. As this was an open boat in which it was unsafe to wear oilskins, he never fully recovered from being continually wet. No sooner had he been invalided ashore than his ship had occasion to tow a suspect towards Kirkwall. On the way, the merchant ship was torpedoed and sunk. The U-boat, thinking herself alone, surfaced for a breather. At this, *Northern Duke* managed to hit the bow with her 4-inch gun and the base of the conning tower with a second shot. The U-boat was sunk and Father was lastingly saddened by his "missed participation".

At some point, it was decided that Juliet and I should be evacuated to Canada but then came the tragic torpedoing of the Atlantic liner and the prospect of a very different upbringing was abandoned.

Quite unnecessarily, Father became concerned for our safety and persuaded Mother to evacuate all of us to the aunt's house with Beatrix Potter associations. It was here that Juliet and I, aged eleven, spent twelve months of almost pure joy.

Alas, we lost Granny that year but there were infrequent visits from Auntie Winnie and Uncle-in-law William Clifford Crook, who leased 'our' lovely home. They were sterling characters and Uncle Clifford kept us enthralled, in an almost Ransome-like role.

His father had manufactured leather driving belts but died, with debts of

Northern Duke

£200, when Clifford was thirteen. To feed his mother and self, he tried to sell belting himself and remembered pushing the heavy steel-wheeled truck laden with samples to a mill in Marsden, eight miles away. There, the buyer told him he had no time to see him – and so began another low point in life as he struggled back to Huddersfield, gazing at the leather samples in front of him – and remembering a friend in Leeds who had a machine to cut segments to make footballs.

With only hope and the borrowed assistance of unemployed labour, twelve footballs were made and these 'samples' he showed in Norway where, embarrassingly, he had to overrule being booked into the best hotel. There followed an unwitting order for 'two hundred' (two hundred dozen, as it subsequently turned out) "if up to sample". So started, what was gradually to become one of the largest manufacturing companies of footballs, tennis rackets, golf clubs and billiard tables etc. in the world. We gained by it too.

For Uncle, Lakeland mornings started with ceremonial deep breathing before the open little bay window which hung over the back lane of the house. One such ritual was marred by a gigantic sneeze, which projected his teeth across the lane and into the wood beyond. It took Juliet and me ages to find them in the powdery leaf mould.

The Crook family engaged in all manner of macho adventure and this appealed to me enormously, almost taking over from Ransome at times. Unfortunately, boating was not one of these as John, the youngest had capsized their grossly-over-canvassed 18-footer in Bowness Bay and it has remained on the bottom there ever since. Instead, the boys became expert rock climbers and skiers and on one occasion, with their father, were caught in a Swiss avalanche. Fortunately, the middle son, Paul, had the presence of mind to raise his ski stick far overhead and the tip of this was discovered the following day.

Juliet and I suspected that it was in competition with his athletic sons that, each year in St Moritz, Uncle would vainly try to break the Cresta Run record. All had gone well until the third year when, kitted out with helmet and goggles he waited on the sledge for the signal to 'GO'. This was no formality as, between Shuttlecock and Battledore Corners was a substantial level crossing. Unfortunately, a foolish spectator (or was it a wilful competitor?) gave him a 'good luck' pat on the shoulder and Uncle, thinking it was 'GO', set off far too soon for the crossing gates to be open.

Head first he went down the icy slope between the grandstands, reaching over 100mph before, in excess enthusiasm, he took Shuttlecock Corner far too fast and spun over the top into forgiving straw – just yards before the less forgiving crossing gates.

It was in response to just such upbringing, that I strove to emulate and all our cousins, even one as a 'conscientious objector Friends Ambulance Driver', who distinguished themselves in WW2, whether on ground, sea or air. Uncle Clifford's offspring alone included one son in the army and two sons and a son-in-law as Spitfire pilots, two in Rhodesia. The daily news broadcasts were rivetting for us all.

It was the eldest son David [Flt Lt D.M. Crook DFC, author of *Spitfire Pilot*] who especially caught my imagination. He was to become involved in long and heroic achievements throughout the Battle of Britain. For a time, he was the only surviving original in Yorkshire's 609 Squadron, surrounded by youngsters whose average life expectancy was fourteen days. By David's bedside, along with a well-thumbed Bible, was found a copy of *The Wind in the Willows* and I liked to imagine him finding some easement in the trauma of those desperate days.

Barbara, their beautiful sister, inspired us with Chopin waltzes on the piano and climbed with me up bits of Latterbarrow – on her hands!

All too soon after our arrival, Mother cycled via Wray into Ambleside and climbed up part of Wansfell to see the headmaster of the then Kelsick Grammar School and arrange for our attendance. Later, she wrote:

> The school bus was also the shopping bus. It allowed two hours in Ambleside. I had arranged with Mr Airey, the bus driver and owner in Hawkshead, that the children might leave their bicycles in his garage. John sat by Mr Airey or immediately behind him if he could. One afternoon the bus was ready to return to Hawkshead and the weary shoppers eager to be home. "Why don't we start?" they asked. "Mr Berry is not here yet," explained Mr Airey. Then John, a small boy, arrived and climbed in, unaware of having kept the bus waiting.

Going to and especially returning from school was a joy. Juliet and I cycled into Hawkshead and left our unlocked machines against the outside wall of the garage. There and at various points along the route, we picked up school chums in Mr Airey's always-immaculate 25-seater Commer.

Never having taken a driving test (but with an unblemished record) any skills I now possess owe much to Mr Airey's example as we zoomed and twisted along those leafy lanes, safely 'opening up' each blind but familiar bend and maintaining a calm momentum with consummate skill and economy.

At Ambleside, we trudged up Wansfell to the School and, for me, the low point of each day as an undiagnosed dyslexic, with spelling and some learning difficulties retained to this day. I pirated all day from my so-patient and clever sister sitting at our shared desk – and thought only of other things.

These distractions were invariably Ransome-orientated and all I wanted was kindred spirited friends with whom to share robust adventure.

Resources were limited but Juliet and I managed to explore quite widely on our bicycles. Happy hours were also spent on Claife Heights, getting to know the craggy fells, woods and tarns. I remember gazing down on Windermere with our tiny telescope and deciding that Ramp Holme must be 'Wild Cat Island' in the books.

We wandered everywhere and in those days, just as Ransome depicts, there was nothing unusual or considered unsafe about children exploring on their own.

We joined the troop of Hawkshead scouts and guides. These were run, with exceptional interest and zeal, respectively by Dr T. T. (Kit) Macan and his wife Zaida. The whole countryside seemed made for our Ransome-like adventures as we pushed a heavily laden *Pigeon Post*-type hand-cart to our camp in the hills above the village. Here we made camp and a practical turf-roofed lean-to beside the rushing beck and learnt the rudiments of self-support. The use of semaphore using hand-held flags, though imperfectly learned from *Winter Holiday*, I like to think helped our group to rendezvous near Ferry House and swim in Lake Windermere. All this following instructions received from Dr Macan's home above Colthouse, a mile away across the valley.

Dr Macan, awaiting call-up, was an outstanding freshwater biological researcher (and author of *Life in Lakes and Rivers*, by Collins) then working at Wray Castle, where he kept *Navicula*, his 14ft gunter-rigged sailing dinghy. There too, in the boathouse was a lead-walled 'diving bell' which he had built. This was box-like and designed to rest on the shoulders, complete with a small downward-facing observation port. On top was a valve connector which was intended to provide ventilation via its rubber hose and car pump. All six of us eagerly volunteered to try it out and were a little hurt when he failed to accept.

However, he did tow us for miles on our bicycles, clinging one-handed to a huge box on the back of his Ford 8 as we scooted along twisty country lanes, collecting literally tons of waste paper for the war effort. Fortunately, there was hardly any traffic and the thought of danger never crossed our minds. Mother once said that "awareness and concern for danger is something we develop in peace time, and lose in times of war". She was right as always!

The shimmering beck behind Auntie's house tumbled from high in the wood and fells above. Its path in places was too steep to follow and this, coupled with the volume of water, seemed to cry out 'Hydro Electric Power'. Making a water wheel was the easy part. How to drive a non-existent electric motor was beyond resources.

High at the top of the garden was an ancient yew tree and in it we fixed a platform. This was to provide a comfortable lookout with views across the valley towards Hawkshead and beyond. It would have made a grand signal platform. Another tree, beside the lawn, was some unusual fir. It had a wealth of frond-like branches. At mealtimes, the trick was to fling oneself from the top and be carried gently down twenty feet onto the lawn, to smell gloriously of pine for the rest of the day.

Leaf mould lay deep in the wood and did much to lighten the soil in the much-needed vegetable plot we made in the orchard. Nuts were everywhere and our three resident red squirrels kept us in hoots of laughter with their antics on the kitchen windowsill.

We revelled in everything about us, not least the fragrant blue wood smoke to an almost Wordsworthian appreciation of woodland smells after rain. There were few distractions except from nature and it was owls and foxes which kept us entertained at night. Much of our awareness was owed to Ransome and with windows, nearly always open wide, as seemed normal practice in those days, we could just imagine sleeping under the stars.

One favourite book was *Pigeon Post* and what I really needed, especially with Juliet so often reading in the house, was the scientific 'Dick Callum' with whom to expand into astronomy and so much else. I thought his story-writing sister 'Dorothea' would have been just right for Juliet. But no one, still less either of 'the Ds', seemed to be about.

I had just one regular school friend in the village. He was two years older but not my type. It was his abundance of pocket money and lack of scouting and Ransome-like inclinations which really divided us.

However, his family had a rowing dinghy on the north west bank of Esthwaite Water and this suggested something of a panacea. As we rowed to the northern basin, we could see large eels snaking through the reeds and water lily roots on the bottom. Gradually, we moved upstream into the mouth of Black Beck and into a blissful world that I could never have imagined. We rowed between grassy banks as the river bent excitingly between overhanging woodland trees. All at once we came into the dappled sunlight of Priest Pot with its wonderland of natural wildlife, a freedom and enchantment of breathless beauty.

I only shared this brief voyage once because, in this magic place, my associate suddenly made a quite unexpected stab at a flotilla of baby ducklings with the blade of an oar. Fortunately he missed the lot and their mother, in her innocence, seemed unaware of any danger until, I threatened to strike ... rather noisily with the other oar. Everything went sour and we hardly spoke for weeks.

Further upstream, about level with Hawkshead, Black Beck runs through open fields and is crossed by an indirect footpath from Colthouse. The river bank here has a walled section and, some time later, the same acquaintance, seemingly reformed, found some atonement in teaching me to tickle trout.

In this, I was given to understand that trout find certain gaps at the base of the wall a convenient lair in which to wait for unsuspecting 'food' swimming by. Lying on the bank, we gradually lowered gently undulating hands into the prescribed position, palms uppermost, fingers constantly wafting and moving hypnotically upstream, close to the bed.

I had not moved far when, quite astonishingly, I felt the strong wafting motion of fins and was able to shift gently up-stream into the 'cuddling' position, the fish virtually within my grasp. I could even imagine feeling its little heart beating yet seemingly unperturbed. But what a live and wonderful creature this was! I had never consciously killed anything. We were a family of relative townies, sometimes eating, when we had the chance, what someone else had killed. As always, this seemed normal, safe in the knowledge that many creatures would simply not exist without our perceived needs. But this was quite different, here was something so alive, more beautifully designed than any modern submarine, probably with devoted friends and relations and obviously enjoying itself enormously. Feeling rather foolish, I gave it one last tickle and withdrew my hand.

At the same moment, my instructor flung a silvery object high into the air and away from the water and home – to thrash and gasp helplessly in the long grass. As we had no plans for its consumption, I think we put it back.

Had I known it, this was a foretaste of the legitimate practice of 'Jacky', Ransome's farm-boy, of "guddling in t'beck" as described in *The Picts and the Martyrs*. I suspect 'guddling' derives from 'cuddling' in local dialect. Anyway, I would hate to inform 'Jacky' that it has since been made illegal.

*   *   *

There was a severe drought during the second of those idyllic summers. It was tragic to see quite large fish gradually becoming stranded and gasping all along the path of our beck for hundreds of yards towards the village. It would have been quite easy to lift out numbers of live fish; and there were some very hungry people in the village but, though it was hard to understand, I never remember seeing anyone taking that unfair advantage. Still, it seemed an awful waste and pollution in those days of rationing and relative poverty.

Typical was a friendly farm boy from nearby. His cycle had no brakes, mud guards or saddle and, instead of air-filled inner tubes, he had packed each tyre with straw – as could be seen from bits poking out. He was clearly proud of this desperate measure and I was deeply impressed.

During the exceptionally hard winter of 1939/40, the second coldest January of the century, the little beck and our household pipes from which they fed froze solid. Initially we were obliged to break up lumps of ice to melt and drink, safe in the knowledge that no pollution, except perhaps the odd dead sheep, could threaten from upstream.

Deep incessant snow lay pristine white and, best of all, school was closed for weeks, not for reasons of 'quarantine' as in *Winter Holiday* but just as effectively in our case, from snow-filled roads and the steep Wansfell approaches.

During a brief thaw, Juliet and I built a large and creditable *Winter Holiday*-type igloo on the lawn, except that ours was far more authentic than that in the book. It was carefully made of concentric blocks and had a short tunnel entrance. With the return of biting frost we thought it would last for ever and squeezing inside on a rug with a single candle, we were able to read from the book itself.

Like most children in those days, Juliet and I had very few possessions but felt we had everything we could possibly want. Then, one morning Mother told us that something awaited us at 'the sawmill'. With no idea what it could be, we trudged across those billowing fields and took delivery of the most perfect 'Dick and Dorothea'-type sledge, which then followed us everywhere.

The sawmill which made it, lay somewhere through the arch of the ancient Hawkshead Courthouse where, in the full-width upper room, we held our weekly scout meetings and stored a growing tonnage of waste paper which we continued to collect. I still remember how some of it, notably photographs of unclad ladies in *Lilliput*, was a glorious revelation to the sheltered mind.

After a vain scouring of Colthouse Heights for a Cresta-like run, Juliet and I continued with our 'War Effort' purpose in life. We pulled our sledge for miles in our quest for paper to recycle. On one excursion, we called at the home of Mrs William Heelis (Beatrix Potter) in that rather humble cottage she illustrated along the side road in Near Sawrey.

Sadly, she was failing and not well enough to search out waste paper. Instead, she sent down a metal cigarette box full of coloured animal photographs, with her blessing. Looking through these, we thought some bore a resemblance to her illustrations and we treasure them still.

The stack of paper and books roped down on the sledge made all the weight we could pull. Our rubber boots slid and our breath shot out in long plumes in the dry cold air. Walking back for tea along the waterside road, the scenes of brilliant yellow and complementary mauve shadows from lowering sun were quite breathtaking, and so was the temperature.

Day after day, the whole atmosphere of that exceptional time was of *Winter Holiday* and made the book entirely believable. For us, the most evocative lines will always be:

Softly, at first, as if it hardly meant it, the snow began to fall.

* * *

After Wordsworth's stay with Ann Tyson during his school days in Hawkshead, Beatrix Potter found that Ann had moved to a cottage with a beck running through the garden in Colthouse. We had friends there but, at the time, the breast-feeding wife of a Lancashire head master seemed to know little of any Wordsworth connections.

From there, as we now learn from Hunter Davies, William was allowed complete freedom outside school hours and, aged ten onwards, roamed the same fells as we did though sometimes at night. He frequently fished and even skated on Esthwaite Water during the much colder eight years he was there.

In our day, 160 years later, though global warming had hardly started, seasons had changed and the six inches of black ice on Esthwaite was a precious rarity. It took day after glorious day of bright freezing weather, the glass-clear ice getting gradually thicker and reliably supportive just as in *Winter Holiday*.

A younger generation Mrs Heelis rather boisterously ran her car on it and, as she was a friend of Mother's, I felt rather hurt that I had not been included. Days later, we saw a horse and cart taking a short cut right across the middle.

One day remains especially in mind as we walked down the lake. In the blinding sunlight was an endless filigree of white frost-covered branches, dazzling against the deepest of blue skies. There too was the crackle and tinkle of icicles and brittle vegetation as we shuffled along the north east shore. It was one of those rare occasions when I thought we must be in heaven!

We put our skates on and found firm ice everywhere except where water still flowed into the lake. These were the places where we were particularly wary as the ice became sculptured and could be wafer thin. Any trickling sounds along the shore were as warnings to keep clear. Elsewhere, the ice was clearly immovable, like clear unblemished glass until we arrived. I even imagine seeing a small fish frozen in the ice but now think this may have been in the book.

We only had company once and this was a spectacular athletic blonde, a short-skirted lady in red, an accomplished skater who never saw us on the woodland shore as she spun, twisted and turned in an enchanting way we had never seen before.

On such a day we decided to turn our sledge into an ice yacht and this proved a far greater challenge than expected. With two planks of wood, three skates, some rudimentary hand tools, recycled nails and screws, and lots of time, I believe we could have made something far more dramatic and manoeuvrable than that in *Winter Holiday*. But we had none of these and had to adapt.

As things turned out, our ice yacht became a grossly inferior replica of that of 'Dick' and 'Dorothea', as shown in Chapter 24 of *Winter Holiday*.

"It's Moving!" from 'Winter Holiday'

What we lacked was the substantial mast 'step' which, in the book, was made by 'Mr Dixon' and 'Silas'.

Too late, we realised that even this depended on a constant following wind. What would have been far easier to make and a firmer support for the mast, was a plank 'bowsprit' to which we could secure a forestay to counteract the after-pull of the shrouds.

In the barn attached to where we stayed, we found what would serve both as a mast and yard, an old dust sheet and assorted bits of rope and string. We never achieved a forestay and holding the mast up firmly remained a tiresome task for Juliet. What we required was a strong following wind.

Early next morning, after huge amounts of Mother's porridge cooked the night before, we set off at first light. Everything was already lashed down on the sledge but still awkward as we pulled down to the eastern side of Esthwaite Water to Waterside Cottage and onto the ice. Unusually during that still winter, there was a gentle breeze wind and now a tinkling in the frozen trees, just what we had been whistling for since daybreak.

Once the mast was up, stepped on a nail from below, Juliet was obliged to keep up a gentle forward pressure to brace it against the shrouds. I hooked on the yard which hoisted our square sail and Juliet held on to the loose foot. I towed the sledge further out and, with wetted finger, positioned her before occasional wafts of northerly breeze. At this point we were able to sit, Juliet with her back against the mast as we named our ship *The Fram* and waited patiently for each puff of wind. These filled the sail but nothing seemed quite strong enough to unstick us from the ice and start the slide, still less the roaring momentum, so memorably described in the book.

Fram-like she refused to stir except when encouraged by our frequent shoves. There we stayed, feeling rather foolish but it did not seem to matter as the sun rose higher, foretelling of another perfect day.

*   *   *

During that previous summer and autumn, Juliet and I had dragged in huge stocks of the fallen timber which lay everywhere in those unspoilt woods above the house. Apart from a toothless panel saw in the barn we trimmed with an axe. Heaps of rotten trunk we managed to break up by levering it between two adjoining trees and stacked it to leeward outside the barn to dry.

Healthier trunks were a problem but I remember a series of quite large dried-out ones, being supported on a chair in the slate-floored kitchen and gradually being fed, day and night, into the fiercely glowing fire. This was long before central heating yet the pipes became unfrozen and we retired with hot water bottles and large stones heated in the oven. While the bedroom wash bowls remained frozen, we slept in comfort during those still and bitter nights.

Besides a wall-defying ghost in the kitchen, which we never saw, David Crook's precious presence remained in initials in a kitchen cupboard.

The house possessed some delightful features – and an imposing radio-gramophone. In Colthouse, even the vital broadcast receptions were spasmodic and it was my job to hold the aerial, or was it the earth wire, in the hope of hearing Uncle Mac reading delightful bits of *Winter Holiday* introduced with The Skater's Waltz – or those heart-stopping speeches which presaged further events in the war.

Our main winter enjoyment was with dearest aunts and happy stories around the sitting room fire. Subject to heavy snow, the library van made its circular tour via Wray and quickly learnt to stop at the back door. From this we carried books up to our chins as Juliet got through one a day and I needed a week or two.

With Mother, Juliet and the teacher-frequent company of Hilda and Marjorie our mutually adored maiden aunts, we played games and often read round in a circle. They concentrated on books we could all enjoy, invariably this included the *Swallows and Amazons* series. Except for awful spelling, I'm sure my joy for reading and so much else was helped by this.

Juliet and I (alternately) shared a pair of handed-down skiing breeches. These were redolent of rugged out-door activity and became the object of rare covetousness. I confess to some exasperation when finding Juliet on one bright morning "reading in the breeches!"

Whatever I managed to read, my thought and activity was inspired by Ransome counterparts and their convincingly *possible* actions in the books. They were also a main example in times of stress. Failing to find similarly orientated friends continued to fill me with dismay.

The time came, aged eleven, when I searched in vain for any signs of romance between 'John' and 'Nancy'. Then, perish the thought, any "sly biological urge".

On a rather different plane, it did not occur to me for thirty years, perhaps because Ransome characters are clearly above all that sort of thing, that there is a complete denial of other bodily needs, the sort of thing which might, just occasionally, warrant camp latrines or ship's 'heads'.

Scanning the authentic-looking plans of *Teasel, Goblin, Wild Cat or Sea*

Bear today, one can only marvel at such total abstinence. How ironic when, years later, I read of the sad reality in poor Mr Ransome's case!

Nevertheless, it was the sense of realism, purpose and adventure, the very way of thinking which nurtured our dreams and seemed to make even the commonplace absorbing to this day. Also, while triumph in adversity is hardly an original theme, we found sustained inspiration in one book after another.

Indeed, it was the common sense and fortitude of 'Captain John' in *We didn't Mean to go to Sea* which I tried so hard to emulate when, late the following summer, we were obliged to return to Huddersfield and its satanic mills, for Mother to take charge of our family business as Woollen Merchants in Huddersfield.

This was the start of many darkest days but, as if to soften the blow in 1941, we all holidayed at a small hotel at Skelwith Bridge with Father on leave. For this I had made special plans and, on arrival, made careful note of all four 'Ransome' addresses listed in the local telephone directory. I also asked for three packed meals to be left on the hall table and went to bed unusually early, to work out the best route – to track down Arthur Ransome.

Chapter 2

Travelling Hopefully

It was still dark when the clockwork alarm began its noisy vibrating clang. The sky seemed clear and the water very cold in the washstand. On the dressing table lay the carefully studied Bartholomew map, a clean handkerchief, 2/6 (12.5p) for emergencies, my scout knife and compass. I felt my way quietly downstairs and, sure enough, on the hall stand lay three packets of sandwiches, marked 'Master Berry', a banana and apple too.

Outside, a heavy dew lay everywhere and it was good to find my cycling cape tied firmly over the saddle. My bicycle had travelled with us up to Windermere in the guard's van, and I was soon pushing it up the long Oxen Fell road as the sun rose and the first birds began to sing. The machine was the most valued thing I had and, being a dead weight, was especially blessed with a three-speed Sturmey-Archer gear. Unfortunately, it had suffered a collision under the previous ownership of my cousin Stephen and proceeded in a crabwise manner which took practice to control.

I laughed, remembering the previous evening. Father had asked if he might borrow it to visit the Skelwith Bridge Hotel before dinner. We saw him off down the steep hill, but he must not have taken my warnings seri-

Setting Off

ously and we heard later how he had run into a ditch at the first corner and had left my cycle there till his return.

This route to Coniston has normally seemed interminable but now there was a wound-up spring inside. The ups and downs, bits of moorland, forest and at last the wayside pool of Yew Tree Tarn and Coniston village, all appeared in earlier succession than allowed for. This made a welcome chance to seek out the way up to the copper mines as described in Ransome's *Pigeon Post* and I vowed to explore it much further another day.

It was still far too early to call on anyone so I cycled easterly, over the little bridge crossing Yewdale Beck towards the head of Coniston Water, with Hawkshead just over the hill. Here, I gazed spellbound down the gleaming reaches of the lake and got a strange feeling of familiarity. That farm with boathouses on the eastern shore could almost have been 'Holly Howe' in the books. Fanciful of course, everyone knew from the give-away inner book flaps of Swallows and Amazons, that Windermere was where it all began.

Back in the village, I sat on the churchyard wall for a welcome rest and a sandwich. One by one, the shops opposite began to open with a cheerful clamour and it seemed proper to proceed slowly towards Torver. This was a relaxing bit through woodland with occasional glimpses of railway line. After two miles was a minor road off to the left and, conveniently, a friendly native who seemed to know who I was looking for, pointed me towards Blawith. Sure enough, a mile further on was an unmistakable kink in the road between two buildings as he described. This was my first Ransome abode, neatly listed in the geographical sequence I had decided the night before.

It was a pleasant cottage on the kink's east side called, rather grandly, 'Emlin Hall', just as listed in the telephone book. Here, my steed was planted gently against the garden wall and I rehearsed sincere apologies as no warning of approach had been made, and knocked very gently on the door.

Most fortunately, this was opened by a tall and very gracious white haired lady who I now think was Miss Lucy Ransome, a half aunt of AR. She seemed able to understand my stammerings and was kind enough to ask me in. Over most welcome tea and cakes, she described how "Arthur, divided geographically from my sister and I, by little more than the width of Coniston Water", [actually, one and a half miles as the crow flies] was, to her clear regret, "not a good communicator". Gosh!

Once fully aware of my mission, Miss Ransome mentioned that the second Ransome on my list was Arthur's younger sister Cecily, but that she was "a bit poorly and really not fit to receive visitors". I promised I would not intrude and left, with most grateful thanks for her kindness.

I continued southwards and just north of the main village of Blawith, managed to locate Cecily's home, named 'Bank House', just as Miss Lucy had described. Mindful of her wishes, I was determined to maintain a very low profile while taking everything in. I passed the house in both directions and even managed to pretend I was looking at other things, a government agent could not have been more discreet.

Once round the corner, I added another tick to my list and realised that half my expedition had been fulfilled. Feeling more confident I proceeded on a reciprocal course until turning east for Nibthwaite and immediately, on my left and close up to the road, found Mill House the ascribed home of Mr Oswald Ransome.

Everything had gone so smoothly and apart from learning a little about the real quarry, my presence here did seem rather unnecessary – but then I saw, leaning up against the front of the house, addressed to 'Mr Ransome', something quite unexpected and confusing. There lay a substantial kedge anchor of the *We Didn't Mean to go to Sea* type. I could hardly believe my eyes!

The anchor had clearly been in service and its stock was made fast in the stowed position. Apart from being bound for transit, it was almost as it might have lain folded up and useless on the sea bed, with the *Goblin* dragging her cable towards the sea. I knelt and ran my hands over it reverently. This was beyond all imaginings. Then I saw and examined minutely, the small metal wedge on its little chain. In the book, it describes how "A little iron fid drops into a slot in the stock to keep it in place".

By this time I was in a different world. Was it, I wondered, the unshipping of this rather bent, tiny and insignificant-looking piece of metal, as described so graphically in the book, which had caused the anchor's untimely folding on that fateful occasion, and the truly epic drama that followed in consequence?

All boggling was cut short by the emergence of a most affable and unassuming gentleman who proved to be Mr Oswald Ransome himself. He was a rather confusing relation of AR and not unlike a newspaper photograph I had of him.

He confirmed that "Arthur lives up the eastern shore, in a large bungalow called 'The Heald', about level with Fir Island". He went on to say, "I haven't seen him for ages and whatever am I to do with his anchor?" This, though clearly meant for Arthur, had understandably been delivered, far more conveniently, to Oswald. It was addressed on the luggage label, rather vaguely, as was the custom in those less exacting days:

To Mr Ransome,
Coniston,
Lancashire.

There are missed opportunities in all our lives and this was certainly to be one of mine. Admittedly, the 'Fisherman anchor' was a large and heavy object, as 'Captain John' himself had found ... almost as much as they could manage ... when desperately trying to stop *Goblin* drifting out into the North Sea in thick fog ...

But I had become a contemporary of 'John Walker', and very proud of my strength. What on earth was I thinking of? If only I had offered to lash it to my crossbar and deliver it to the correct Mr Ransome by hand, I would have had the perfect introduction. Even if I had had to walk the further four miles to this, the one vital address on my list. I would have done so with a feeling of privilege, but there was too much going on in my head, I didn't think to offer and the missed opportunity haunted me for years!

It was in this unthinking and saddle-sore state that I took my leave and, at Nibthwaite, followed the narrow minor road going north up the East side of Coniston Water. This twists and turns and has fields, mainly interspersed with woods, ups, downs, and tantalising glimpses of the lake but hardly a house in sight. Was that an island I had seen so close to the shore? On this occasion there seemed no time to make sure and no end to the corners and hypnotic undulations. On and on they went as, with aching limbs, I very nearly cycled past my objective.

But here it was, almost on its own and discreetly named 'The Heald'. It was set back and raised above this remote access, with plenty of surrounding woodland, and more between it and sparkling views across the lake. Surprisingly, it appeared a double-fronted comparatively modern bungalow, seeming much too large for one person but he would certainly have a separate study with lots of books in it. [NB. 'The Heald' remains privately owned by different occupants from long ago. I respectfully ask readers not to intrude.]

The setting was beautiful but. being miles from anywhere, with all the wartime restrictions in1941, I wondered if he had enough to eat ... There was no sign of transport, little petrol anyway and any shops were miles away by road.

The Heald

I hesitated. After so many rehearsals I should have been ready but still needed time to think. After his friendly card, he would clearly be pleased to meet me at last, would welcome my surprise visit, especially in this quiet place with nothing much to do at tea time. There was so much to discuss and I had a long list of carefully prepared questions mostly disguised as statements. The last thing I wanted him to say was "Now then, secrets are secrets ..." There were other things I wanted to tell him and some to thank him for.

Contemplation went on and I was reminded of what my parents had said the evening before. They had spoken as if they knew something I did not about the writers of books and wished to spare me unnecessary disappointment. There had even been some reference to a Mr Stevenson for whom, it seemed, "To travel hopefully was the enjoyable bit". I had thought little of it at the time and felt I knew far more about Mr Ransome than they did. Certainly, everything rested on the next few minutes: the very focus of a way of life I had celebrated for so long – including the ideal characters with whom I most closely wished to associate. It was an ideal world in which I most ardently wished to live forever!

All seemed to hang in the balance as I paused by the gate, unconscious of all weariness and wanting to appear my best. Aware only of what at last was to be the moment of truth.

More time was taken in parking on the grassy bank and looking at the remote Beatrix Potter-type chimneys, the 1920s slate frontage, its covered veranda and the two welcoming bay windows.

My heart was pounding and I remembered another quotation, recently learnt at school – something about "one's affairs and there being a tide to catch ..."

Then, all at once came the answer to all doubts and hesitation. Silly not to have thought of it before:

What would 'John Walker' do here?

Of course there was only one answer and it was teatime too. There was so much to discuss and I would almost certainly be invited in. I clutched his precious reply card, this was to be my passport – and must have been posted from this very place the previous year. I pushed open the large wooden gate, walked resolutely up the long curved path and boldly rang the bell.

Long moments passed and I began to wonder if he was out and this was to be a wasted journey. I looked across the tops of trees and there to the north west appeared to be Coniston Old Man. What must have been Mr Ransome's thoughts as he woke to see that each morning?

All at once there was the shuffle of slippered feet, the sound of much unlocking (why? I wondered) and suddenly the door opened and all preconceptions evaporated. Here was not Mr Ransome. Instead, it was a huge and dark-haired lady housekeeper. She wore a green flowered gardening overall and stood towering and perspiring far above me looking down. Strangely, she seemed to know exactly why I had called without my saying a single word – and spoke with some weariness and in a foreign manner I had never heard before. The entire 'conversation', of which I remember every word, went exactly as follows:

> "I'm afraid Mr Ransome is not at home and seldom receives visitors. I am so sorry I cannot help you – and please will you be sure to shut the gate!"

All carefully rehearsed gambits withered as I stood looking up, even the anchor waiting for Mr Ransome at Nibthwaite and the precious proffered card from Mr Ransome himself, seemed unrecognised as the door began to close. I found myself thanking her politely and turned awkwardly to go.

Suddenly, everything seemed to have gone rather misty as I staggered awkwardly down the steps and long drive, just knowing I was being watched. All of a sudden I was overtaken by a desperate tiredness and inability to think what to do next except to get out of sight – and shut the gate.

Half a mile up the road, still absent-mindedly walking and pushing the cycle, I gradually became conscious again, particularly of light headed hunger and remaining sandwiches in the saddlebag. Here, the bicycle and I collapsed onto a bank overlooking the lake – to eat the remains of breakfast, lunch and tea.

For minutes I sat on my cycling cape, ruminating about the long cycle back. Then, quite without warning, I fell over, sound asleep in the long grass.

Asleep in the grass

The sun was low over the hills when I woke. I was damp, stiff and cold but surprisingly refreshed as I started pedalling back. All thought seemed to have become scrambled and I wondered uselessly how things could have been managed better.

I conferred again with 'John Walker' and he was kind enough to point out that "an advance has been made, at last you know where 'Captain Flint' lives". Gosh, yes! "How many Ransome followers living far away had achieved even this"?

Plan 1 had been executed and clearly no advantage could be gained by a second assault in the near future. Deep disguise did cross my mind but any detection would be counter-productive. An interval and careful planning was essential before the next foray. A greater challenge had been identified and with it increased knowledge and determination. And I had all the time in the world!

Almost in relief, I began to think of the rest of our holiday, the chance to discover 'Wild Cat Island' and many other places in the books. Besides all that, there was so much I wanted to do with the family . . and there was that rather nice-looking girl in the hotel ...

In some surprise, it occurred to me for the first time that Mr Ransome, and certainly his housekeeper, were almost certainly mortal too. For half my life I had been almost worshipping another human being. Someone who, just possibly, may even have frailties like the rest of us. What a fool I had been!

It was a pivotal moment and, in the same vein, I realised that in another year I would be a 'teenager' – and, according to Mother "may have different interests". A component of childhood had just fallen away. All at once, the *alter ego* of 'John Walker' had become a young man.

* * *

As the miraculous pubescent dictates of human nature approached, I developed all the disruptive priorities in what were perceived as a most un-Ransome-like interest in girls.

For some obscure reason it was decided that I needed my first pair of long trousers and, as all our male clothing was supplied by Berry Brother's stock of high quality but unassailable remnants, a most unsuitable navy chalk stripe was made up by our devoted local tailor. In these I stood with new-found pride in front of the electric fire in the dining room. Frost was on the ground and I had never experienced such soft warmth to the lower limbs. There was an unexpected smell however and, by the time I had discovered its source, I was almost on fire and the calves of each trouser leg had become molten brown and brittle. They simply dropped off as I moved away and I was returned to shorts.

* * *

After the delights of Lakeland, my fifth school was a Grammar School six miles from home. What turned me off from the start was the gloom of pervading sycamore trees, the permanently empty tennis courts and, "to preserve the parquet floors", a nauseating whiff of gym-shoe bacteria which became a life-long aversion.

The second master said it all:

Active verbs: "My nose smells and my feet run."

Passive Verbs: "Your nose runs and your feet smell."

Then there was the co-educational factor which meant I could never concentrate. Besides which, not being able to spell or assimilate some academic bits condemned me to the 'Crafts' grade which, with Art and Sport was all I wanted anyway.

Worst of all was an apparent lack of Ransome-like adventure. This may have been because of our teenage thoughts but I felt like an alien, never learnt anything and found myself ever-spiralling down in confidence and self-esteem.

It was only my few close friends who made life seem worthwhile. By coincidence, one of these lived next door. Brian was younger but, destined to become an international Dr of Science and Professor of Computing, was several forms above in every way. He encouraged as best he could but it was his acquisition of a large lump of carbide that allowed my first employment, albeit in those gentler days, as 'a distributor'.

I had always associated carbide with antique bicycle lamps but it proved to have far more illuminating properties. The day came when almost everyone possessed a minute halfpenny consignment and on a designated morning, at the stroke of ten o'clock, we each dropped it into our ink well.

I was in a lecture theatre at the time and will never forget the geography master's expression as the milky blue liquid foamed and billowed out all over the place. The fumes were potentially lethal in a confined space and we joined the mass exodus of the whole school and subsequently queued for three days to speak with the head master.

Shortly before we left there was an Open Day and Brian and I, hoping to improve our behavioural image, rigged up a miniature cable car across the science lab. This soon became a centre of packed attention, until a parent stepped on some inadequate insulation, blew abundant fuses and received quite a shock. I'm so thankful that the sueing culture did not arrive until years later.

Another misfit who became a life-long friend was Stuart. He had been a flourishing chorister until his voice broke and it was his habitual reference to happier days in a cathedral city that earned him the nick name of 'Lichfield'.

The 'War Effort' was still all the rage in those days and the unlikely five pounds I raised by making balsa wood fighter planes all went into the Spitfire Fund.

Our most 'War Effort' holiday was potato-Lifting for seven weeks in Moulton Chapel near Spalding. On arrival, we were each issued with a large sack in which we pushed straw for our bedding on the cold village school tiles. Early each morning, we cycled to the potato field "in which we served". This stretched to every horizon and portions were divided along a seemingly endless furrow into equal cricket pitch lengths. Each of these was worked by either two boys or one local woman. The aim was to collect potatoes into large wicker baskets before another circuit of the remorseless horse-driven spinner had thrown a harvest of potatoes far and wide. Stuart and I foraged with frenetic haste, initially trying to catch the spuds as they arced off the spinner yet we were invariably last in picking up and caused an embarrassing halt on occasions. During the brief lunch-time sandwich break, we collapsed exhausted and slept where we fell. I have had lumbago ever since!

The following year was a complete contrast as we cleared a forest for pit props near Appleby. This was before 'bushmen' and chain saws so a triangular chunk was sliced out of each larch or spruce near the ground with a large, razor-sharp axe, calculated to fell its eighty-foot length into orderly rows. Some fell across a nearby road but thankfully there was not traffic. Our sixth formers became adept and took unnecessary pride in leaving stumps which looked as if they had been adzed like a Thompson table top.

From the bole upwards, our job was to shave off all the branches cleanly with a billhook. In getting the hang of things, Stuart almost severed his left thumb. We then pitch-forked all branches and surrounding scrub into huge fires which left the one-time forest looking like a desert. For this we received our meagre board and stood in line for our ten shillings (50p) each week – but we had enjoyed it and felt we had done some good.

On one Sunday, we cycled for eighty-three miles round The Lake District via Kirkstone Pass and rowed on Grasmere until being called in with some annoyance after I had organised the four of us to take an oar each as in Oxford v. Cambridge to increase speed. It rather spoilt our day and I vowed once more to quell all foolish propensities.

After scraping through School Certificate, it was an immense relief when Stuart and I received our first gainful employment from Father who hired us to re-paint our window frames for 9d (4p) an hour. I have never been keen on heights and at first it took twenty minutes to get up to the gutter. I thought of it as climbing a mast and, with practice, we were each hanging out all over the place.

To celebrate financial independence, school certificates and the end of hostilities, we set off for France in Stuart's Ford 8.

Second only to young ladies, our main interest was in fast cars and after Mulberry Harbour and touring Brittany, we headed straight for Le Mans. Unfortunately, there was no motor racing scheduled but, remarkably, we found access to the circuit and I was able to time Stuart as he ran across from the starting grid in the approved manner and jumped in for a 'Le Mans start'. It was almost as in the books we read so avidly that we raced along between the pits and grandstand, reaching over 40 mph as we passed under the Dunlop Bridge. We hadn't seen another soul until, while expertly power-sliding through the famous S-bends, we met a charming French family having a picnic halfway across the road. I shall always recall their belated awareness as we slid by with inches to spare. Later, we ran into a sand bank and completed the circuit in what must have been a record time. We set up camp in the pine forest within. It was here that we had our only ever serious disagreement as Stuart, finding our bottle of red wine 'too dry', was found to have laced it with sugar.

We each had £20 when we set off from home and nearly half of this was left when, after 2,000 miles, we reached Paris. There, our chosen *pension* was found to lie the other side of a series of one-way streets and, as these were all pointing in the wrong direction, we felt obliged to travel the last mile in reverse gear. Fortunately, we were treated with notable kindness in those immediate post-war days and no one seemed to mind. That evening, we made a detailed study of the *Place Pigalle* and lost most of remaining funds, but thankfully not much of our innocence (Stuart being destined to become a Canon in the C of E) in a night club while trying to quench the unslakeable thirst of our escorts with expensive 'champagne'.

*   *   *

Once home, the awful question of careers was raised and, as an academic dwarf, my own instincts were for something creative. What I really had in mind was the 'restoration of property' but this was hugely outweighed by what I was told were 'practicalities' – which, after hundreds of years meant Textiles and, for me, a working life of gloom.

It all began courtesy of an uncle-in-law, by going "through the mill" in his historic five- storey complex. I started logically at the initial process in one of the well-named 'Teasing Sheds', mixing black wool with white to make grey. Our 'Fearnought' machine was also well-named as it would have devoured an ox. The operator was just out of gaol and had a habit of balancing a ladder on his chin. He considered himself rather tough and though we got on well enough, he thought quite wrongly, that I was in league with the management and we had one or two set-tos. This was just before more guarded machinery came in and during one bout while the Fearnought was still running, we slipped on the greasy floor and very nearly got grabbed by the spikes of the feed rollers. I had visions of us being fed through the machine and 'teased' to shreds into quite unsaleable pink raw material. At the time, I would hardly have cared!

The average size for humans was much smaller in those days and I liked to think my modest height was acceptable. I never remember being bullied and being taught to box at prep school was quite the most helpful thing I ever learnt.

Just after the war, it was unthinkable for a man to admit fear, but times have changed and it is not unknown for grown men to speak of 'fear' today. On a different plain, I council our daughters and granddaughters, "If ever you feel under threat, appear cheerful and *never show fear*".

Next, after 'carding' and the deafening 60mph shuttles in the Weaving

Shed, I was under the guidance of an elderly but skilful general handyman named Albert. He was near retirement and wafer thin, but contrary to all apparent logic, could push a heavy barrow heaped with boiler ash up a wavy plank. Full of modest wisdom and natural honesty, he was highly regarded by everyone.

As sons of the directors were demobilised, they ended up, willy-nilly, at the mill. One of them decided the flag pole needed a halyard. This splintery thing was high on top of the windy lift shaft tower but, after a scramble, he was successful and liked by all.

Hoping to emulate, and determined to throw off my fear of heights, I asked Albert to hoist me up the open lift shaft to the top floor of the carding mill as if I was a bale. He was very reluctant but stood at the controls on the top floor as I thought a little prayer and grabbed the slippery cable hook on the ground floor, to be so-slowly hauled up, floor after floor. By the fifth, I was holding on desperately but Albert stopped the hoist motor at just the right point. There I swung back and forth over the dark empty space, the tension was awful and I was seriously tempted to let go but just managed to swing far enough and vault between the threshold wall without tripping and the ceiling, landing almost sedately beside Albert, whose relief was tinged with considerable disapproval. Just then, despite still being a spiritual pygmy, I had the extraordinary feeling that I had been "looked after from above".

Weeks later, Albert collapsed at work and I carried him home. Sadly, he had to lose both legs and while visiting, I met his son-in-law who was just back from the decommissioning of the German Battleship *Scharnhorst*. This had meant stripping out all 'weaponry' and one item was the Commanding Officer's ceremonial sword. He was allowed to take this home but, concerned for his children's safety, gave it to me.

*   *   *

Except for such highlights, more of the darkest days were to follow and I began to feel progressively useless.

In contrast, my twin sister Juliet, chose her own career and started life in farming and later, social work, pottery, painting and writing. For years I thought her disproportionate share of talent was something to do with pre-natal osmosis.

It is strange to believe that in those days we addressed our parents as "Daddy" and "Mummy" – but Juliet's first letters from Reading University informed me that, henceforth, we were to call them "Father and Mother". She was right of course but I couldn't help feeling that some expression of our childhood love for them was lost forever.

Similarly, much earlier, while absent-mindedly seeing Father off on the station platform, to do his bit in 1939, I was reminded that "grown men do not kiss goodbye".

Times were still changing when, years later, we had Elizabeth and Kate, to find we had become the far more homely "Dad and Mum".

Back on my seventh birthday, I had been given a rudimentary box of woodwork tools and practised unwontedly on woodwork about the house. Carpentry, sometimes using the same hammer and smoothing plane, has been a main interest ever since.

But what have natural aptitudes to do with 'careers'? I think we are *all* given relative strengths and weaknesses as part of God's logical and varying purpose. Like animals, we have been adapting and evolving for thousands of years, to fulfil the diverse needs of humanity. I believe there are ideal careers for each one of us if we can find our *true* vocation, preferably early on, and have the self will, even selfishness if necessary, to *go for it* in spite of parental disappointments. To fail in this is to fail in life.

I speak with excruciating hindsight. Evenings were spent at the technical college but during precious weekends I returned to "artful bodging" and, while in scientific mode, built a basic 'crystal set' radio as well. This was open-plan with, amazingly, only three working parts. Sheer simplicity was its attraction and I feel we are missing this appeal today.

However, in my first attempt to create an aerial, I threw a lead weight tied to fine string right over the house. I had quite forgotten that Mother was having her much needed weekend rest, far worse, that her bedroom sash windows lay one outside the other in the wide-open position. Typically, the string hinged on the far gutter in just the wrong position and swung the ball of lead like a pendulum, with a huge 'explosion' through both large sheets of glass. It speaks volumes for Mother that, covered in splinters, she never added to my exceptional misery.

Thoroughly contrite and full of apprehension, I later climbed through an attic window and up the slippery roof to the ridge. Once there, I noticed how tall were the chimney stacks and tried to think of them as of the many masts I was destined to climb. To dangle a wire between one set of chimney pots and the next was another test of fragile nerves.

The high spread of wire could not have been better as an aerial and my bed springs served as an earth. After much prodding of the magical crystal and sliding a metal contact over the tuning coil, came the sudden enchantment of Radio Luxembourg. We lived in sight of the transmission masts on a far-away hill. This was where Stuart worked and I liked to think he was responsible for the perfect quality and surprising volume through my single earphone. Resting this between my ear and the pillow habitually lulled me to sleep and, using no electricity was never switched off. The sheer basics and "something for nothing appeal" gave years of wonder and delight.

*   *   *

At last Father was at home and while concern and love for family was paramount, it was golf which really took over again. Mother remained our main guidance and strength and we shared her family relations and friends from far and near. She was loved by everyone but sadly never fully recovered from having to stand for long hours at the absurdly tall office desks and being in charge of us at home, our air raid wardens and local refugees

"First Attempt" self portrait

throughout the war. At some point I caught a flea and, until DDT arrived ten years late, was frequently bitten quite raw by their attention.

All our aunts were very special but in different ways. Auntie Katherine was one of Mother's five older sisters, a wonderful person, who had given up her talented career in art to marry a then-impoverished but highly regarded tobacco farmer, Donald Black, in Rhodesia. Back in pre-war days, she took a year off in Huddersfield with their four tennis-oriented children who were to attend the same primary school as we did. At morning assembly, the head mistress announced, rather naively, that "the Blacks from Africa" were about to arrive in the next few days. At this there was general elation – until the Blacks turned up and were found to be white like the rest of us.

Years later, the day came when I found access to Auntie Katherine's arched trunk in the attic. This contained her enchanting water colours and piles of bewildering life studies – my first introduction to the adult female form unsanitised by *Lilliput*. As Auntie was far away, I ventured to borrow her brushes and oils and have succumbed to her influences ever since. Fortunately, I found some 'hardboard' used for black-out but unfortunately, thinking it looked like canvas, painted on the rough side. Without any priming, I managed my first painting, a self-portrait in oil.

As another escape from grim reality, I slowly devoured the whole of Conan Doyle, Buchan, W.W. Jacobs, Forester and Nevil Shute *et al.* Dornford Yates and his pre-war adventures fighting gangsters with 'Berry' in the Pyrenees, was especially part of it, yet I cringe today at his snobbery. My most enduring influence as a youngster was Ransome and he remains a rejuvenator to this day.

Meanwhile, that dreadful term "non-essential personnel" fitted me perfectly and just after my eighteenth birthday, bolstered by Father's respected service, I naturally chose the Navy and was accepted for my two years of compulsory post-war conscription.

It was with some relief that I spent 21st August 1946 travelling by train to HMS *Royal Arthur* at Corsham, in Wiltshire – as I was due to appear in court that day. This was for parking outside the theatre, as seemed only natural after a performance in those days. With me was a brother of James Mason (to whom Mother, as a friend of the family, had taught Latin before his departure for boarding school). He was just demobbed and "livid" by being summoned too. It seemed to us that "all gratitude for War Service" had evaporated by 1946.

I had been excused from attending court in the circumstances but, to complicate matters, it was the same mill-owning and long-suffering uncle-in-law who was the magistrate serving on the bench that day. I heard later how, being a relation, he had stood down when my case came up. But, as if this was not enough, the next offender happened to share Uncle's 'unique' family surname. It was thought by all that he had stood down for the wrong defendant and for a time there was chaos in court.

It sounded to have been a very fitting end to the era.

Chapter 3

Lost and Found

HMS *Royal Arthur* was a shore establishment surrounded by beautiful countryside near Calne in Wiltshire, we explored everywhere and gorged ourselves on free fallen apples. Here we were kitted out with uniform, a hammock and single blanket which was to be our practical (albeit unchanged) bedding for the next two years.

The Ordinary Seamen's 28 shillings (£1.40) weekly pay was most welcome. This does not sound much today but it was my first wage and, being fully maintained with food, accommodation and tobacco, it represented about 48 pints of beer, more than even we could get through and, in consequence, the start of my savings of £100.

Among the wardroom staff was a likeable Lieutenant Philip Mountbatten who had an MG sports car and seemed to be off most weekends. According to our Petty Officer in a conversational aside, he was "busy courting", but nothing more was said.

While there, each of us was scrutinised and given a narrow choice of branch in which we might serve. I blame Arthur Ransome entirely for choosing to train as a Visual Signalman – too late to realise that basic spelling was traditional too.

As one reason for this choice, I wrote that 'Farther', with whom I had so often corresponded, "served the Navy in both world wars, etc". For the next fifteen minutes in consequence, I was obliged to express a keen interest in 'Phonetic English', of which I knew nothing, and only narrowly missed being reduced to 'Catering' and the wearing of 'fore & aft rig'. So began a whole new series of attempted cover-ups and dyslexic-enhanced embarrassments.

After Disciplinary Training in Scotland and the vast Portsmouth Barracks where we were obliged, unless on 'cooks to the galley' routine to 'double' across the parade ground,

Our real Branch Training started ashore at HMS *Scotia* near Warrington and we were dismayed by the curriculum. This covered both Naval and International Code flags, with the nightmare combination of eighty-three different meanings, according to with what and how ("superior" or "inferior") displayed. As if this was not enough, the phonetic alphabet had to be changed once more – to allow our American Allies to understand something of what we were talking about. Then there were 'Fleet Manoeuvres' which were great fun. Each of us represented a ship in convoy on the parade ground, changing course in 'line ahead' or 'turning together to port or starboard' in response to shouted flag signals.

Morse, by light or buzzer, was transmitted at bewildering speed and, of course there was Semaphore, which reminded me so comfortingly of The Books. This we practised from all angles and even at meal times, using our fingers as in sign language across the mess – as I would have so-liked to describe to Mr Ransome. In addition, Touch Typing was part of the curriculum and has been a boon ever since. Given today's demands, I think we should all learn this at school.

I was never quite old enough to draw my 'tot' of rum and, with some of us being rather vulnerable, I'm glad this 'uplifting' age-old tradition is no longer a perk. The monthly allocation of cigarettes and large cylindrical tins of tobacco, topped up by duty free, was far more than we could get through initially and, almost certainly the start of my asthma. Smuggling pipe tobacco home to Father past guards on the gangway (later, floating it down the Gare Loch) or hurling it high over barbed-wire fences became the bit I really enjoyed. We developed techniques which were worthy of prisoners of war and Father was appreciative as ever I can remember.

The best thing about Signal School was being taught by Chief Yeoman Hirst, DSM, BEM, one of the finest men I ever knew. I learnt much later how, from 1931, he had served in *Galatea, Defender, Nelson, King George V* and *Agincourt*. By strange coincidence, his home was in Huddersfield and he was to become an esteemed friend of the family. Years later, *en passant*, he told how, while on the bridge of HMS *Nelson*, he saw someone, obviously smoking, ascending in the dark from below. As was the form in those days, he shouted "put that light out" but it turned out to be Winston Churchill – and he didn't!

There were some scenes in action that he could never forget, HMS *Hood* going down with 1,415 men and only 3 survivors. Also, while on the bridge of *KG5* while on close Arctic Convoy, travelling at 20 knots in a fog. It seems that up ahead, the destroyer *Punjabi* had sighted a mine and was seconds too slow in correcting her course from 90 degrees to starboard. She was sliced in half by *KG5* and he could always picture the forard half sliding down to starboard and the after half to port – and the tragic attempts to jump across.

* * *

After twelve drastic months in training school, Ransome would have approved far less, in those post-war days of reduced defence expenditure, of my subsequent "sea time". This was while permanently moored and united with power lines ashore to the now famous Faslane Jetty in the Gare Loch.

We had four German Marine ex-prisoners aboard who were responsible for cleaning and lugging huge amounts of slops suspended on an oar. I think they were homeless and seemed friendly enough but aloof and confined aboard.

There were no clothes-washing facilities that I ever found and we just washed our white fronts, undies and socks while having a bath. I had no smoothing-iron so I slapped them onto a ship's boiler and was once commended for being "smart". I wore clean socks every other day and, unmarked, these did occasionally vanish until 'Granny Berry' so-kindly knitted me some with bright green toes.

We slept in hammocks tightly slung each night above the mess table. The supporting 'irons' were about eight feet (2.45m) above the gangway and we used these for pull-ups and to compete, swinging the overlapping five feet (1.50 metres) from one to another – which was rather dicey above the bare steel deck.

There was a small occasional evening cinema and on Sundays we either slept over or were shipped to some other vessel in the Gare Loch for the regular fifteen-minute service. I regret to say we found this rather taxing except for the social events which followed. We needed these breaks as, falling asleep while on duty was not the done thing. It once happened to me and I count myself fortunate only to have had a bottle of ink poured over my head.

I was the only 'Visual' conscript aboard and the relief for someone serving nine months in another establishment. Ours was 'Headquarters' ship, our Commanding Officer in charge of 'Reserve Fleet Clyde'. His nominal function was the control of Northern Shipping and some of this was done through me, using radio telephone and teleprinter. He was extraordinarily remote however and I only actually met him twice!

About once a month, a minor duty was the hoisting of flag A at the yardarm to signal 'Water Boat Alongside' when our tanks were running dry. The natural form was to fly this at the Port side yardarm as, with our bows facing north, the tanks in use were on that seaward side. However, with *Rampura*, another large Canadian-built Maintenance and Repair ship alongside, it was difficult to see from eleven miles away, still less to whom the signal belonged.

On one bright morning, I experimented and found it was far more visible hoisted on the Starboard side, secure in the knowledge that no water boat could possibly squeeze between us and the jetty. More considered thoughts were cut short by an urgent call from the Admiralty on the teleprinter and I hurried below.

All was as usual until the forenoon watch when the water tanker, kindly obliged us by extending her hoses to fill unused tanks to Starboard. Gradually a list began to develop in that direction, become more and more apparent, and the whole ship's company less than exalted by having to walk along slippery sloping decks and through oddly angled water-tight doors for the next few weeks as we furiously wasted water and gradually regained equilibrium.

Meanwhile, even runs ashore were scant relief from excess ribaldry as, typically, one mischievous landlord in Helensburgh asked us "why HMS *Mull of Galloway* is leaning to one side".

* * *

The second time I met the Commanding Officer was shortly after obliging our ship's telephonist who had reported an urgent need to leave his post. He assured me that my official presence was just a formality as, before 0600, no traffic was expected and his frenzied introduction to the intricacies of running the Northern Reserve Fleet Telephone Exchange did seem academic – until he turned the corner and the whole switchboard sprang to life.

My only real experience of operating a busy telephone exchange was from watching the very efficient ones on American films and, in desperately trying to calm things down with similar aplomb, the Admiralty who wanted our Commanding Officer, was accidentally put through to the Sewage Works at Dunbarton – and all hell broke loose!

I shall always remember being ordered to:

> Curb all initiative, on no account try to improve anything and, above all, never, never, offer to help anyone in need.

* * *

After two years of post-war discipline, I was slightly surprised by civilian life. Finding myself too breathless for running about, golf became the thing. It was one of my older and responsible cousins, Stephen, who became a close friend and most patient mentor. Gordon was another contemporary with whom I also shared fast cars, country pubs, girls on pedestals, golf and happy Lakeland exploits.

In those days, typical off-duty clothing was a tattersall shirt, cravat, sports coat, narrow cavalry twill trousers and suede Western-Desert-type 'brothel creepers'. Girlfriends were an elite rare treat. Apart from having other ideas, with little in common and being so expensive to run, they often failed to get into the excessively boisterous spirit of country pubs.

Most of my friends, whether they liked it or not, were similarly wedded to woollen textiles going back for generations. Indeed, local genetics were exemplified by Mother's, albeit over the top, 'Moore Family' as recorded by our Uncle William, the public Records Office and historian John Lister. Back in the 1500s and 1600s, the nearby hamlet of Outlane is where the family lived – (suggesting we have moved/advanced two miles in over 500 years). Mr Lister identifies the clothiers engaged in and attending the market as follows:

> It is really a black list of the "Names of those who make woollen cloth with the woof called 'flock'". The King had appointed a commission, composed of Sir Marmaduke Constable, Sir John Nevyll of Liversedge and John Pullayn, to make an enquiry about the deceitful cloth-making of Yorkshire [sic], and this list, as the result, was handed to Cromwell, Henry's ruthless minister. Thomas Cromwell was in the habit of jotting down such terrible "remembrances" as "Item, to know the kings's pleasure touching Master [Richard] More" [of Owtlayn]; and "Item, when Master Fisher shall go to his execution, and the other."

Whether "the other" was 'Richard More' is not recorded, but the offences in 1533 seem trivial enough, as most of the clothiers had only one or even half a deceitful cloth in their possession – and to "thrifty northerners" including sweepings in the weft does seem natural.

Three centuries later, Mother's family lost everything when Dobsons's Bank went broke in 1825. But native talent and character prevailed; Mother's grandfather became a carpenter, cabinet-maker and, finally, a master wood-carver. We still use one of his dressing tables.

Father's family did much the same. Godfrey Berry's 'Wells Mills' Northgate, is affectionately remembered for spinning a yarn so fine that, to show it off, he unreeled a pound of it from Huddersfield to somewhere past Leeds 17½ miles away.

But, in "going bond for a friend, he failed in business", and, with his wife, finished up in charge of the local post office in Moldgreen.

*   *   *

As an only son with no viable aptitudes, I most-wanted to do something "creative" but was naturally chained to the family business from birth. Initial training started in 1948 with cloth designing in Leeds – where I had no idea that Ransome himself had spent early life close by, nor that in principle, I was sharing his earlier thoughts as, from Saturday lunch time, Huddersfield friends and I would race for The Lakes and arrive back breathless and shaking at our office desks on Monday morning.

While we tramped the fells and patronised local amenities, for me the charm of Ransomesque behaviour and his unique way of seeing things endured. Sadly, it seemed impossible to share this with my otherwise civilised friends, still less promulgate 'children's literature' over several beers in mixed company at night.

At Berry Bros., it was the company of our chief cashier who made life bearable. Like Father, Jackson Smith had been First Lieutenant in an armed trawler. For him, most of the war was spent on the Murmansk convoy. Churchill referred to this as "the worst journey in the world" as they braved U-boats, dive-bombers and appalling Arctic conditions to deliver military aid to the Soviet Union. Quietly modest, he was among the finest men I ever knew!

Mr Smith never spoke of what had gone before and what possessed him to spend the rest of his working life commuting from his ancestral home in Keighley remains a mystery. So, fortunately, I was able to crew for him in his yacht *Rilla*, along with his wife Clare and son Peter, when not away at school. This was initially exploring off the East coast and irks me to think how we may have seen Ransome's *Nancy Blackett* without actually recognising her in Scarborough harbour. Mostly, we were berthed in the Bridlington I knew so well. We were pulled there like a magnet at weekends.

Rilla was designed by Bellingham and built in the best tradition by Cooper of Conyer in 1936. Rigged as a Bermudan cutter of six tonnes, 28.5ft long and a mere 22 ft water line, she had a canoe stern and was a most beautiful sight. Below, she had a Stuart Turner two-cylinder, two-stroke motor. This had a two-plate 'sailing clutch' which, when disconnected under sail, allowed the questionable advantage of the propeller spinning free. We decided that a fixed propeller, like a helicopter with a fixed rotor, would offer less resistance while sailing and we asked the yard to bolt the clutch plates together. They botched this by not drilling and threading far enough, so the union was incomplete. All seemed well until a sunny afternoon off Flamborough Head when we were in a dwindling easterly and tide, trying unsuccessfully to beat into the wind and getting nearer and nearer to the cliffs.

In his leisurely way, Mr Smith started the engine only to find it was not turning the propeller. Meanwhile, the towering cliffs became more over-hanging and intimate than I had ever seen – with Mrs Smith preparing to fend them off with a boat hook. It was the unflappable calmness of Jackson and Clare that really amazed me. In panic, I rushed below and pulled out a bunk board, tied a loop of twine round it and took it up on deck. With the skipper's permission, I lay face down on the starboard side deck, just aft of the stays and started paddling for all I was worth. By some miracle we got enough steerage way and missed the cliffs by inches. Once established, I continued to paddle for the next four miles. Entering Bridlington harbour in full view by this means was a lasting embarrassment and we had words with the yard.

* * *

Trying to sell suitings to a dwindling number of country tailors for 32 years was not my idea of fulfilment, but evenings allowed freedom, good food and beer tasting in friendly country pubs all over England. One favourite coun-try hotel was down a narrow lane sloping to a navigable river. The propri-etors were a charming and devoted couple and I felt privileged to become a friend over the years, sipping beer down by the water and bird life, talking of times gone by.

It sounds improbable but Gerald had been, for limited periods only, a millionaire three times over before I knew him as a contented pensioner. Among other things, he was an accomplished racing motor cyclist before the war and behind the little bar in the sitting room was a photograph of him being 'push-started' by George Formby.

He had been "a bit of a stunt rider" too and well remembered in Birming-ham for roaring round the top of new gasometers.

When war was declared, Gerald dropped everything, joined up and was put on an officer's training course. By chance it was decided that they should all learn to ride a motor cycle. The sergeant in charge was very strict and, having completed the exacting circuit himself without falling off, became furious with Gerald for "not paying attention" and ordered him to attempt it too. At this, Gerald feigned complete embarrassment and confu-sion. He mounted the motorbike back to front, sitting astride the petrol tank and grasping the controls behind. All derisory laughter ceased however, as he slapped her in gear, revved up and let in the clutch. He raced round the circuit including all obstacles on the way, to amazed acclaim.

Their early lives had been fairly wild at home and abroad. Then, from being dedicated to the pursuit of enjoyment, they became Christian believers and concentrated on helping others.

All went well for decades until Gerald, who had never managed to become entirely teetotal, found a whisky bottle in the kitchen and took a surreptitious swig. Tragically, this contained not whisky but detergent and one can only imagine what he suffered during his last two years. Sally suffered even more as she could never forgive her "irresponsibility" in making the accident possible. I just know they are now in heaven!

*   *   *

Another diversion was being drawn to past associations, notably by my old scoutmaster and his family, not to mention their very presentable French *au pair*. With her I was allowed, on a very tight rein, to visit old haunts and sail his well-remembered gunter-rigged open 14-foot dinghy on Windermere. This was for picnic teas on the island of Ramp Holme and other perceived Ransome haunts. I made similar voyages with Dr Macan's son. Tommy was years younger but did not hesitate to remonstrate when I attempted to bury a 'non-indigenous' banana skin.

I'm thankful that neither of them were aboard on another occasion however as, after the usual, liquid lunch, I had set off alone from the shelter of Ferry House basin. Under full sail, there was barely enough wind, until rounding the ferry landing. Conditions then were perfect until three miles further south we were roaring along before the wind – but with the dinghy's bows rather lower in the water than seemed natural. It became a classic case for luffing up and shortening sail, a late reminder of Ransome strictures *"Your father was quite right to have strong views about Windermere. It is much more tricky sailing there than at sea"*, as ruffled water appeared right across the lake from wind funnelling down some valley to the east.

I was already sitting out and as far aft as possible and slacking off more sheet but enjoying things far too much to let go sheet and luff up entirely. Indeed, I was even hoping she might plane – but an unexpectedly strong squall struck as we reached the ruffled bit and *Navicular* simply sailed under and sank out of sight.

*   *   *

All I had been able to grab before she disappeared was a treasured copy of *Motor Sport*. Life jackets were seldom worn in those days but, fortunately, my zipped-up anorak trapped just enough air under the chin to keep it above water. This was as well, for in spite of being a good swimmer, I had far too many things holding me down.

As things quietened down, I was reminded of the traditional maxim, *"Always stay with the ship. Do not attempt to swim to shore. (It's further than you think.)"* Being in the middle of the lake, this seemed common sense but, with the 'ship' being out of sight, I could not for the life of me recall the alternative procedure.

To make matters worse, it was a weekday and, after a good look round from water level, I found there was nothing, absolutely nothing else in sight.

Nevertheless, I shouted "HELP" a couple of times in the traditional manner but this was just a formality. I also said a sincere little prayer, another formality I regret to say in those days, as I smoked the rest of my cigarette, scanned bits of magazine and, feeling rather a 'Duffer', wondered what to do next.

Only gradually did I become aware of what I had done and feel utterly mortified by such irresponsibility in a borrowed boat. I thanked heaven when, after ten minutes, I noticed something sticking up many yards away and this turned out to be the top few feet of a gaff. The dear old thing had decided she had just enough positive buoyancy for a last look around. I was beginning to feel the same!

I was slowly losing buoyancy and becoming aware that the slightest movement would lose more of the precious air trapped under my chin. This meant keeping rigidly still and with small waves breaking over my head, becoming aware that I was colder than ever I can remember. The pain became excruciating until, all too slowly, a welcome numbness was taking over. The question of how to get the boat, and indeed myself ashore, was one of those abstract conundrums one dimly ponders before sleep – and sleep was all I really cared about.

*   *   *

I woke to the impression that I was being attacked and found myself upside down, spewing into scuppers and being pummelled and slapped. As the scene began to clear, I discovered that I was lying on the deck of a motor cruiser, the guest of four young Liverpudlians – who assured me they were only trying to get me "back in working order".

It transpired that, from miles down the lake, they happened to have spotted the held-up magazine which seemed to be waving and were curious to see what it was. By the time they got alongside the magazine had vanished and, so very nearly, had I.

As soon as I could think and speak, I asked them to look for the dinghy. By good fortune, just the tip of her gaff was still visible, some thirty yards to windward, in the trough of each passing wave.

With much commotion, they hastily drew alongside and, just in time, made fast to her. But it took ages to raise her a bit at a time. Then, ages more to reach her bows and grab the painter.

The trouble then, was to explain how, while she was still submerged, anything but the gentlest tow would pull her bows out.

This exigency did not register at first and I had to slip the painter twice before all revving of the engine ceased and we were able to proceed with the engine just ticking over, and finally beach her at Grubbins Point.

The problem then was how to re-float. Not only was her own metal bailer twenty fathoms down but she was worryingly misshapen by unaccustomed internal pressure and that from the beach. Also, with gunwales barely above

Passing away time

water, as fast as we swept water out with hands and crockery, it was replaced via the open-topped centre board case. Clearly the rate of bailing had to exceed this inward flow, until the case too was above water.

Most fortunately, those excellent lads were kind enough to sacrifice their drinking water and allow me to swish their milk-churn water container through masses of water till the centre board case was clear. More leisurely bailing could then follow with all the receptacles we could muster. I could not have managed at all without their generous help and, so mercifully, the thought of any salvage demands never appeared to have entered their heads.

By evening she was dry and it only remained for me to thank them very sincerely, row back and report shamefully by telephone to the Macans – who typically evinced far more concern for me than their precious *Navicula*.

I really owe my Liverpudlian friends, and certainly the Almighty, for the over fifty years I have enjoyed since. Strangely, as I write, it occurs to me that the actual instrument of deliverance was a long-submerged copy of *Motor Sport*.

*   *   *

In those days, it took nearly three hours in a firm's car to cover the direct, 90-mile route from Huddersfield to Windermere. Then came the motorway and we discovered it takes well under two hours to cover the hundred and twenty miles – and Lakeland has been under far greater pressure ever since.

It is strange to recall how, in the early fifties, I used to stay at remote farms and cottages for Bed and Breakfast at ten shillings (50p) a night – and now read that, in his youth, Ransome could stay for a week for this same nominal cost.

The summer holidays of 1958 followed my 30th birthday and mounting viability problems at work. Commensurate with vanishing cash flow was the understandable wanderings of a rather 'talented' girl friend. Country pubs and relaxed friendship was what I usually craved for – but against all apparent logic, I found my old and half-forgotten quest welling up, "to discover the truth behind the 'Twelve Books'".

It was a huge help to have use of a car, but next morning over breakfast at a nearby farm, I was really reminded that all remaining scent had gone cold. Worse still, all 'Ransomes' had vanished from the local telephone directory but "nothing worthwhile is easy", and I decided to start where I had left off in 1941.

It was quite a thrill to motor over cycle tracks of 17 years previously. 'The Heald' was much as I remembered but I circumspectly called at 'Heald Brow' nearby instead. Over early morning coffee and biscuits with a kind Mr and Mrs Kilner, I tried to lend some dignity to my childish purposes by explaining my 'Research Project' to locate the author and notional 'Walker family' in 'The books'.

As feared, Arthur Ransome had flown without trace even before the Kilners arrived and, according to a local authority "was of a remote disposition". Anyway, apart from a vague feeling that associates had recently returned from abroad and were lurking further up the lake, they knew nothing.

Much further on, there was mention of a family named Rawdon Smith, who lived at the splendid-looking 'Tent Lodge' near the head of the lake. There was also a Mr Holt of the shipping line who had retired to a bungalow in the village. Still further on, I was told of a house named 'Lanehead' whose occupants had recently reappeared. They too were thought to be contenders but had a name which sounded quite unlikely to be the quintessential 'Walker family' I had in mind.

But 'Lanehead' was on the way to 'Tent Lodge' and calling, even reluctantly and without an appointment, seemed the methodical thing to do – with nothing to fear except making another nuisance of myself – and gaining foreknowledge of a more probable quarry close by.

It was mid-morning when I found the rather rambling mansion on the left of the road, just north of the entrance to 'Bank Ground Farm' which lay halfway down towards the lake. Lanehead itself was painted a yellowy ochre and possessed a substantial stable block. This almost adjoined the house which sprawled further along, close to the road and there was nowhere to park except a small track on the opposite side.

Exploring on foot, I found a perfect 1920s 'dromedary'-type lady's bicycle resting contentedly within the large open doors of the barn. It was covered in dust and the large wheels had smooth flat tyres. It seemed uncannily like those heavy-laden machines, usually going uphill, in *Pigeon Post*. How strange!

I walked back to the only likely looking entrance to the house at the north gable end. I was still in two minds about whether it was worth the extra stop. But somehow, I felt drawn to the short garden path which led, in those days, to a glazed green porch. Once more I was feeling like a door-to-door salesman and I clutched my war-time credential card from Mr Ransome just in case. Beside the door was a dear old brass bell pull and with growing misgivings I pulled this vigorously and heard a far away bell clanging wearily in response. I rather hoped there would be no reply and I could proceed with a clear conscience.

I was just turning to go when I heard footsteps from far down an echoing passage and moments later the door was flung wide, as a rather elderly gentleman stood there smiling. I started my repeated spiel about the 'Research Project' when he cut me short with "Come in, come in my dear fellow" – almost as if I was expected and long overdue!

The very long hall down which we passed was almost in darkness but then, through a door, just as in some storybook, we passed into a different world. Here was a very large room, crossed by strong rays of sunlight, a relaxed wonderland so redolent of past times, of scholarship, art and faded gentility. I have never experienced quite the same vibes.

To the west a large bay window gazed across the lawn, where four huge pines divided glimpses of the lake and Coniston Old Man rising into a distant blue. We were in the far end of the house where, in the gable wall, another window faced south above the marble fireplace (where did the smoke go I wondered) and an unexpected summer fire smouldered in the quaint Victorian grate beside a crashed-out sofa.

The walls were a dark faded bottle green and books rose almost to the ceiling. Between the books were pictures, pictures everywhere – and what exceptional works they were! A very recognisable Burne-Jones hung high on the north wall and there were exquisite turn-of-the-century oils, portraits and landscapes as fine as ever I had seen in the Royal Academy. What really sang on that complementary background were small much later oils, simply framed and of bright Eastern landscapes.

A peeling Latin script hung at intervals around the ceiling rose and a surprisingly fine and valuable Turkish carpet was laid vulnerably straight on to the worn and knotty floor. In spite of several out-of-place pieces of fumed oak Art Nouveau, it was the nearest thing to heaven I had ever envisaged.

My host, as I only discovered later, was the retired surgeon Dr Ernest Altounyan, aged 68. He was dressed in an old sports coat with baggy grey flannels and had a distracted way of running fingers, one strangely twisted, through springy iron grey hair. Full of youthful charm, he exuded an aura of boundless energy and kindness. He spoke in that perfect English of a bygone era and in the rather high braying tones one associates with the more donnish aristocracy. Yet there was no hint of side – still less of a distinguished past.

We sat facing each other by the fire and he asked to see the Ransome postcard properly and chuckled a surprising amount as he read it through. Feeling rather foolish, I started to tell him more about my 'Research Initiative' and though thoroughly enjoying myself, mentioned that I planned to call at Tent Lodge before lunch time.

He seemed unmoved by this and, after more chuckling, said something about the sun being "over the yardarm" and going to the door called out "Titty, we have a visitor, let's have some wine and pistachio nuts".

I could not believe my ears! This was a name Juliet and I had only read about and heard in our dreams. How could I have heard such a unique name, of a favourite 'fictional' character from the 'fictional' books which had enriched our childhood and would always remain ... ?

Minutes later, a raven-haired lady came in with a tray and greeted me with such quiet modesty, in the softest and most beautiful voice I had ever heard.

Time stood still!

Chapter 4

Beginnings

Going down to the lakeshore with Dr Altounyan the following morning was protracted bliss. Out through the south-angled bay window we went, open almost as always in those days, with a much-worn sill leading to a faint impression across the lawn. I felt hair standing on end at this point and wondered how many very special characters had passed this way before.

A short path between hugely overgrown rhododendrons brought us to a little iron gate and down an open meadow which I was told belonged to the Bank Ground Farm below. A winding stream wandered across this and as we jumped it he called "watch out for cow-pats" as we ran down to the wall. Here was some primitive entrance and a path running between high walls, with a sheep slit leading into the field below. Beside it, in those days, stood a tall and dilapidated tannery.

We were now in an open field running gradually, then rather steeply down to the lake. I had never been in this place before yet something seemed familiar. A little further and my heart pounded. Above to the left, a scene etched forever from a favourite childhood image quite caught my breath.

There, unmistakably, with its oddly recognisable square corner window, a rare give-away feature [now slightly altered] was 'Holly Howe' – the farm where 'the Walkers' were staying at the very beginning of *Swallows and Amazons*. It was exactly as so illustrated, for me by Clifford Webb, in the book's Chapter I.

The only bit missing was the "boy Roger tacking up the field" to where his mother was patiently holding the vital (and now much-quoted) telegram:

```
BETTER DROWNED THAN DUFFERS IF NOT DUFFERS WONT
DROWN.
```

This was from 'Commander Walker' in Malta, and was translated by Mrs Walker and certainly by most crew members as "yes" to the children's holiday plans and so much more.

It suddenly occurred to me that it was 'Commander Walker' with whom I was walking down the field – someone who, I was beginning to realise, might quite well have sent such a telegram in real life. I was still to learn how much in keeping it was with his character and culture while a surgeon with his wife in far away Aleppo. This allowed their four elder children, left behind in England under the nominal charge of a resident housekeeper, to sail, in real life, alone in two small boats here on the lake. Later, I was told that the telegram really was of Ransome's creation – but what an insight into Dr Altounyan's Middle Eastern way of thought, so remote from the over-protective culture we now espouse.

Down the familiar field I started to run and then came the steeper bit with its foot along the lake shore and the so-recognisable 'Holly Howe' boathouse, This was the first of three and instantly recognisable from the frontispiece of *Swallows and Amazons*. However, it was the middle boathouse, belonging to Lanehead, which was subsequently used by the family for generations.

Down the narrow passage between the first and second, I found the selfsame jetty, in fact, shared by these two boathouses. This had been the start of so many dreams yet, amazingly, we were unable to walk out on it. The jetty had now become rubble disappearing into the water. This was an appalling

'Holly Howe', from 'Swallows and Amazons', drawn by Clifford Webb

shock, the only negative experience I had for days!

But there were other things. Turning, I looked into the Lanehead boathouse with its narrow slate landing along two sides and the back to its green entrance door – and there, gently rocking, lay a drab but indelibly recognisable *'Amazon'* – or *Mavis* as she was called by the Altounyans. It was just like coming home!

Gazing down with rivetted attention at *Swallow*'s erstwhile companion and sharer of so much joyful adventure, it was hard to imagine how this humble old boat had been the vehicle of such love and rapt attention – but there *Amazon* was and I was lost in sublime recollections of all the images she had created.

Dr Altounyan looked on with patient amusement. At last, we wandered back up to the house, and over tea I met his wife, Dora, for the first time.

Though troubled with infirmity, she was in so many other ways like my own mother – the most gracious and courageous lady one could imagine. I was later to discover her quiet thoughtfulness and considered observations, about Art and Life or just life in general. It all seemed especially relevant and encouraging to my own rudderless state which must have been apparent. Many years later, it was to be largely through her aesthetic guidance and insistence that I should follow my true vocation.

She it was who had painted the Syrian oils which hung in such profusion in the Lanehead drawing room. Though we spoke, at first in mainly general terms, I just sat enthralled. Born in 1886, she was the daughter of W.G. Collingwood, the distinguished painter and Ruskin's confidant and companion. Lanehead had been her main western abode since the age of five. The whole ambience was one of scholarship, travel and the inherited driving factor shared at least with her younger sister Barbara and daughter Titty – art.

She had spent much time painting landscapes in Aleppo when Dr Ernest's practice was at the Altounyan Hospital there. I learned much later that among their visiting friends was T.E. Lawrence, who met Ernest in 1911 and became a friend of the family. He possessed two paintings by Dora, now on permanent display at Clouds Hill. Agatha Christie sat to Dora in 1936, so did Freya Stark who refers to the Altounyans in her books. Not the

least of her sitters was Arthur Ransome, resulting in delightfully free watercolour sketches when he had more hair, and a formal oil which hung in the next room.

Dr Altounyan explained how he was "half Armenian with a Scottish/Irish mother from Armagh". "Something of a mongrel," he insisted. Among many other things, he was schooled at Rugby with Ransome. He was devotedly loyal to both East and West – but found them difficult to reconcile in an increasingly unsettled political climate.

Gradually, I learned how the Altounyans lost their delightful village home at Soulokolook, and a good deal of land, when the area surround-

Arthur Ransome, pre-1914 water colour studies by Dora

ing Alexandretta was ceded to the Turks in 1939. Even graver circumstances followed when the Vichy French took power and they fled to Jerusalem, but were able to return soon afterwards when the British occupied Aleppo in 1941.

From 1941 to '56 they witnessed the expulsion of the French, the birth of an Arab-nation state, numerous *coups*, the West's mishandling of Jewish-Palestine affairs and the subsequent disbarring of Syrian political leaders from the West, culminating in the Near East crisis of the Tripartite attack on Suez. Syrian support of Egypt did not reach military proportions but positive action included the expulsion of non-Arabs. It was a tragic story, seeming so unnecessary and far too much to take in.

The Altounyans, victims of so much international politics, had returned permanently to the Lakes in 1958. Their crippling losses of land, property and hard-earned wealth, not to mention their own vital services to a devoted and poverty stricken community in Aleppo were never spoken of to me in such terms. There were regrets but never a wisp of self pity from anyone!

Indeed, there were the beginnings of calm acceptance by the time I arrived. They were all so financially poor yet a privilege to know in any circumstance. It was Titty and her husband Melkon with whom I often stayed and had meals. Melkon's family were refugees from the mountains where the Altounyans used to spend their summer holidays overlooking the Bay of Alexandretta. As youngsters, Melkon and Titty, about eight years his senior, fell in love at first sight and it was the more-established Titty who asked Melkon to escort her round the walls of Aleppo – which took them seven days!

But for wretched politics, I think Titty and Melkon might, so happily, have remained in Syria, to live a simple life surrounded by his family vineyards and orchards, allowing her to paint, as was her true vocation. Instead, they escaped to the UK, Melkon to train with Perkins Diesel factory in Peterborough and later become a diesel authority in Windermere – just in time for me to join them, almost as if it had been planned. I well remember my introductions to the whiff of diesel on those happy evenings round the Lanehead kitchen table.

In her quiet way, it was Titty who kept the household going, even eventually with three children and undomesticated parents in that large old house. I could only marvel at how she managed, Melkon too was being subjected to considerable strain as heavy lifting is inseparable from commercial diesel engines. His back problems gradually became more severe, resulting in premature retirement, with added strain and a seemingly impossible burden on resources.

During my early visits, Melkon had a motor bike to get to his work in Windermere, but the rest of the family had no road transport of their own. They either had to walk the two miles round the head of the lake to Coniston village, or take the more direct route by boat. Clearly, *Mavis* was the preferred option and it was usually Dr Ernest and/or Titty who, by sail or oars, collected provisions and communicated generally with the village. Ernest thoroughly enjoyed the pilotage bit and it is certainly shorter as the crow flies.

Most of the moderate socialising was at Lanehead itself and, about this time, Dr Helen Darbishire, once principal of Somerville, whose brother, a doctor of science, lived across the lake, visited Lanehead with about twenty very forthright female students. Their interest was in Wordsworth and his association with Ruskin. I only wish I had taken notes of what Dora said of the two of them as we all sat on the drawing-room floor. Most of us then went on to Brantwood where Dr Darbishire, who was nearly eighty, gave her own spirited talk and answered questions as she had done for generations.

As Mother was a First War Somervillian and one of Dr D's huge number of friends and admirers, I ventured to renew our acquaintance. Later, she comments in a letter to Mother, "I had not realised that John had literary connections". Gosh. Nor had I!

*   *   *

Visits to Lanehead were always a delight but *Mavis/Amazon*, source of so many dreams, remained imprisoned in the boathouse and this clearly sad-

dened Dr Ernest too. It seemed that "urban Teddy Boys" had found access via the Tent Lodge footpath, and amusement in demolishing the 'sacred' jetty. They had levered the top large sheets of surface slate over into the water followed by the much smaller and easier underlying walls of slate. It is hard to imagine the motive of such desecration as the Altounyan family were so open to everyone, as was access to the jetty and boathouse interior in those days.

Such an avalanche would have restricted passage to and from the boathouse in any circumstances, in the dry summer of 1958, problems were exacerbated by a low water level, there was no way out.

I could not get this out of my mind, but gradually saw

Dora's self-portrait, from earlier days *(by courtesy of the family)* a way in which to repay some of Lanehead's abundant kindness – and indeed, a small 'thank you' for the years of pleasure which had stemmed from this very place.

That evening, I asked Dr Ernest if he would allow me to rebuild the jetty and, in some disguised disbelief, he trustingly said "Yes"!

*   *   *

The following morning was bright and warm again. After an early breakfast with Melkon and Titty, I fairly romped down to the boathouse. I was clad only in rolled-up shorts, shirt and sailing pumps but even the water turned out to be agreeably warm and the lake bed easy to walk on with its soft bed of leaves. But I trod warily as I approached the debris and the shallow water soon became opaque with mud, the piles of sharp and slippery slate could not be seen.

Surprisingly, I had found hardly any tools in the house so, odd lumps of slate would have to act as a hammer and a washed-up plank nearby seemed destined to be a crowbar and leveller. I soon found that the order of reconstruction was to reverse that of destruction. The trouble was that most of what remained of the original jetty was under water and became out of sight as I walked about.

Gradually, I separated the irregular loaf-to-cushion-sized lumps of slate which lay among the debris. From what remained of these I could see the largest were to form the outer courses and had to be built in first, each resting on three points, sometimes wedged with smaller stones and bound with cross pieces to the inner core of rubble. Moving gently and feeling about, these were placed at equal intervals, bridging those below and continuing the original outer perimeter.

I spent much time searching and, with hardly any of the original platform on which to lay out stock, selection had to be done under water and there were frequent and sometimes drastic re-builds.

Dr Ernest appeared each day to 'admire' the remarkably slow progress and call me in for tea. I was thoroughly out of practice and would suddenly find myself exhausted as we trudged up the field. Then there would be a daily count of bruised and lacerated fingers, ankles and particularly tendons, cut and bleeding from contact with the sharp and invisible slate. Dr Ernest plastered me up.

At last there was a complete outline showing, nice and evenly just above water level. A professional would probably have managed the whole thing in a couple of days and I would dearly like to see how it was done. As an amateur, it took me seven days, an absurd amount of time, but I was determined to get it right. Also, it was sheer therapy and I had time to learn as I went along. This must seem a laboured account, yet the element of very special creativity was food for the soul, the sun beat down, I was staying at Lanehead and having another happiest time of my life.

All went surprisingly well, with exactly the right amount of rubble to fill the interior. At last, the considerable large top slabs of paving became accessible. These were irregular, an average three feet 'square' in area but only about three inches thick and could be reared up temporarily against the now substantial wall of the jetty.

They were distinctly worn on one side, a clear indicator of what had to remain uppermost – and a history of all that had past. I thought particularly of 1928 and the start of *Swallows and Amazons.*

I began to realise the top surface was a jigsaw and some edges had been chiselled to conform to the outer edge. Starting from the two still in place by the boat house, I gradually worked towards the outer limit until, with huge relief, I found that only three remained and matched the curved outer perimeter exactly, the last one fitting like a horizontal keystone. I can still picture almost every top slab in the jetty.

Remarkably, as I tramped about, nothing seemed left on the leafy lake bed and, in a nervous moment of truth I levelled with the straight edge of plank for the last time. Yes, the whole surface was now in a gently declining slope towards the lake, as I could only hope was the original. The job was finished and at last I was able to walk about on it and jump up and down without feeling movement ...

All at once, I became conscious of someone standing beside me. It turned out to be the very live and grown up 'ship's boy' Roger, who was up with his family for the weekend. It was our first meeting and developed into what he called a "launching ceremony".

'They Set Sail', frontispiece of 'Swallows and Amazons'. Clifford Webb's drawing, showing the original jetty.

Roger was full of kind appreciation for the 'new' jetty. He inspected every bit and gave considered approval of its construction in detail – although gently pointing out that the far end had a stone with sharp point protruding towards the lake. I found he was right but I had no chisel to trim it off and we agreed that repositioning it would have entailed an impractical amount of rebuilding. For a time, the thought of *Amazon* injuring herself on this was a worry.

I was not responsible for the subsequent libations with a concrete mix but this quickly made the jetty 'urban Teddy-Boy-proof' and at least as good as the original in this respect. It delighted me 40 years later to see it robust as ever and little changed from what can be seen from the frontispiece of *Swallows and Amazons.* The pointed stone is still there but it no longer matters. Beyond it, a very substantial and raised wooden jetty has been added to its length.

Several days of holiday remained and with these we celebrated the release of *Mavis/Amazon* with a number of voyages. It was now so easy to float her out of the boathouse and alongside the jetty, where we climbed aboard, stepped the mast and set sail. Almost invariably, our course was set for 'Wild Cat Island'.

Peel Island, as it is known by natives, lies well to the south as the crow flies but, against a typical SW wind funnelling up the lake, we must have trebled the four mile direct distance, through the water. Every bit of it was a tonic with vistas never seen before and each equally long tack bringing us close to glorious scenery. After Fir Island so close in shore, Peel Island itself appeared, like a tuft of moss near the eastern shore and unforgettable memories from the books.

I told Dr Ernest of a very different experience on Windermere when I had been invited by someone in a pub to take a ride in his new speedboat. In this we travelled everywhere at thirty miles an hour and the first three minutes were filled with the thrill of sensational speed and acrobatics. Then I became aware of the trauma and general upset we were causing to multitudes of living creatures, above and under water and even in surrounding valleys. Also, our forays were so purposeless, the scenery unrecognised and of no account, the lake itself suddenly diminished in size to a disappointing blur, viewed through the splashed and bouncing screen as we crouched inactive except for violent shivering.

The speedboat's market value and running costs must have been incomparably greater than the written-down value of dear old *Mavis* and we discussed this over a lavish hotel lunch. It was assumed that I should like to do exactly the same thing in the afternoon but I was so repelled that I found I had a previous engagement. Instead, I walked in fields and woodland along the banks south of Bowness and was filled with delight.

On a rather different scale, Dr Ernest was later given a free helicopter flight, swooping low over Coniston Water and its surrounding hills. He found it a thrilling experience, yet, judging by his singing and waving of arms on the island, he enjoyed our simple voyages in *Mavis* almost as much.

He always insisted I took the helm and on my first voyage, we sailed down the west side of the island and placed ourselves well to the south and in line with the entrance to the 'Secret Harbour'. This proved almost as depicted by Ransome as we turned into line and maintained minimal steerage-way under shortened sail before the southerly breeze – instead of sculling with a single oar over the transom in the so-sensible manner of 'Captain John'. I was allowed, with Ernest's running instruction, to negotiate the narrow harbour entrance and its submerged rocks. Holding a well-tried bearing, we slid between the long, high and sloping walls of the inner harbour with utmost ease – just as I had imagined it a thousand times. The inshore appearance and 'leading marks' as described in the books were bound to have changed in the intervening thirty years, yet the general scene remains breath-takingly evocative.

With centre-plate raised, rudder still shipped and our weight slightly aft, there was an oddly familiar 'scrunch' as her bow ran up the beach beside that same large stone which appears in AR's illustrations. This was in dappled sunlight, but one could imagine how necessary leading lights would have been on that special night of adventure described in *S&A*.

It was the safest natural

'The Hidden Harbour' in 'Swallows and Amazons' – drawing by Clifford Webb

haven one could imagine but the skipper carefully made the painter fast to a tree stump, one of the 'leading marks?' I wondered, before we walked up the winding path past the little cliff and out into the sheltered clearing just as I knew it would be, even to the burnt patch of a fire and trees from which the tents had been slung. From there we explored the northern 'look-out' with its view up the lake but with no definable 'lighthouse tree'. The whole island was smaller and narrower than I expected but perfect, right down to a land-ing place on its eastern shore.

I heard how the Vikings had made their first sortie from the sea up the River Crake and had used the island as a base from which to make their expeditions about a thousand years ago – so hauntingly described in W.G. Collingwood's *Thorstein of the Mere*. Mr Collingwood and his son, Dora's brother Robin, had also excavated and discovered evidence here of a small Roman settlement. So much had happened in this small area and, once more, there was a tangible feeling of ancient history. Yet even this seemed recent and less spectacular than those glaciers which gradually started Lakeland so spectacularly and lovingly tens of hundred thousand years ago.

Roger even spent his honeymoon in this perfect place, though it is hardly as sacrosanct today! It appears remarkably near the eastern shore and Ernest told how Ransome habitually camped on the island – and how Ursula, Dora's youngest sister, had cycled from Lanehead with the proofs of his book on Edgar Allen Poe. With these, carefully tied to her head, she swam across to the island to join Ransome who, amazingly, corrected the 160 pages with her help, allowing her to take them back for posting off in the same way. It must have been quite a scene at the time, yet how much simpler. Today, I envy their proof-reading skills, still more their simple way of life!

The wind has a habit of dropping at tea time and I regret that on such voyages we were invariably late for supper – but one gathered that, for Ernest, still not acclimatised to managing without domestic staff, this was normal, especially while in the grip of one of his frequent and enveloping enthusiasms. How Titty managed, later as a mother, virtually on her own in the small mansion without staff, frequent open-house infusions of family and stray visitors, I can't imagine.

I clearly remember one four-mile row back from the island, wondering how the children managed this heavy boat when the wind dropped after tea. More often we ghosted back before quite undetectable breaths of air. I think we both enjoyed the sliding along in effortless silence, close past the beautiful changing scenery, as the most rewarding part of all.

On one return voyage, we discussed his poetry and I asked what was meant by 'rhythm' in verse. He responded briefly with an example and may have used the term Anapaestic Tetrameter – and spotted my bewilderment. At this he stood up in the boat and repeated, in a voice which must have been heard in Torver, *"The **Assyrian** came **down** like the **wolf** on the **fold**"*.

Ernest's use of this particular example still seems a quite extraordinary coincidence. I told him how exactly the same bit of Byron had been delivered by my boarding school form master in 1939 – while leaping from desk top to desk top across the class room, waving his gown like the wings of a bird and terrifying some youngsters with his Assyrian behaviour. I'm still

not sure if I can detect rhythm in poetry reliably; but I do remember being quite grateful there were no other boats in sight or sound of us, on that quiet and lovely evening.

Reminded of his own school days at Rugby, Ernest told me how Ransome, Frank Perkins and he had hired a yacht on the Broads in their summer holidays. It all sounded excessively jolly – with

Dr Ernest in *Mavis/Amazon* off Peel Island/Wild Cat Island

Ernest showing Arthur, though now hard to believe, why it was necessary to tack "this way and that" into the wind.

All went well until the day they approached Yarmouth and a sign which read 'NO HIRED CRAFT MAY PROCEED BEYOND THIS POINT'. To their enquiring minds on such a glorious day, this seemed a clear invitation to see why. All-too-soon it became overtly apparent. As if by magic, they were accelerating considerably faster than they had thought possible – and the water itself was moving with them. They were in fact on a rapidly falling tide with no hope of making progress against it – being driven ever faster down through the Yarmouth they had hoped to explore at leisure – and on out to sea.

Once there, they reasoned, the tide would take them back with almost equal force at tea time. In the meantime, "it was just a matter of patience". But being out at sea was a different matter, the pleasant breeze had become a strong south-easterly and it was a case of beating into it for several hours just to keep station. It soon became clear that yachts, designed for river work can be considerably over-canvassed, too light and shallow-drafted for the North Sea. They spent the afternoon unreefed and flagrantly hard over, the lee rail under and frantically spilling wind.

Ernest had occasion to go below and, sitting to leeward in the darkness of the cabin, remembered looking up at a section of the thin clinker planking through which the sun behind was glowing alarmingly "like a china cup".

I never heard the end of his story but clearly they all survived. I waited in vain to hear Ernest repeat the title of AR's famous book, *"We Didn't Mean to go to Sea"*. He didn't – but I still think this early experience may have been one of those at the back of Arthur's mind when he wrote it.

* * *

Ernest had a deaf ear and a very bent little finger. As time went by, I respectfully asked what had caused this. He described how, while picking up the wounded, a German shell had landed close by, causing the injury and leaving him with bits of internal shrapnel.

On another voyage, Ernest told me just a little of his long and fascinating life at home and abroad – though it was not from him that I later learned of his extraordinary and distinguished career. One topic was his friendship with and mutual high regard for T.E. Lawrence, for whom he professed serious doubts about alleged proclivities. I think the association started with his surgical treatment of Lawrence at the Altounyan hospital in Aleppo – and he commented, "Lawrence was later destined to become the greatest single influence in my life". After Lawrence's death he wrote the poem *Ornament of Honour*, "as a memorial embodying what I believe to be our common philosophy of life".

Thanks largely to the Lanehead magic, I found the self-doubts which had so long assailed me were swiftly evaporating. Dr Ernest's letter of 2-7-58 was a timely encouragement; and his tendency for licence and exaggeration, manifest in the very first line:

Lanehead
Coniston
Tel Coniston 293 Lancs

2.7.58

My Dear Berry,

What an excellent and wise young friend you are proving! And how ungratefully lax I seem to have been in answering your excellent letters but the reason is purely physical. I am absorbed in a desperate attempt to save the Amazon from a very watery grave.

When I got your detailed letter about glue tar varnish and fibre-glass I was already committed to fibre-glass in spite of the clinkers and was working every day, often without lunch, from morning until I returned completely exhausted as after an all-day session in the operating theatre.

First I blow-lamped every square mm of the outside, then scraped down to the rough board and blow-lamped again. Then Mr & Mrs Thwaites and self with a stop watch and frantic weighings and calculations proceeded to mix polyester resin, a catalyst and an accelerator, a lb. at a time, and, armed with paint brushes, our hands smeared with barrier cream and finally protected with rubber gloves and with a last minute glance at an imported thermometer, we proceeded to get the one pound mixture on to the hull and went on doing this hour after hour.

The whole confounded mixture set like steel in 30 minutes and stung like a wasp if it got on the exposed skin. Also, while setting dripped in fantastic rubber-like stalactites which rapidly became finger piercing spikes of wire. So much for the first coat. In between each mixing – all highly inflammable and stinking the brushes had to be immersed in a solvent (also highly inflammable) or they too set like stone.

Next, the cutting and tacking with copper tacks, strake by strake of the fibre-glass open net rolls and the attempt to get these rolls to stick on the wood and tuck into the clinker ledges. And, of course, I have not yet mentioned that the boat had to be turned over after securing the netting with four coats of resin accelerator catalyst and filler to the gunwale. You will not be surprised to hear that I retired to bed before my grandson if allowed to do so!

Well I write because tomorrow the last coat goes on and we hope to put her in the water for the weekend when Frank Perkins of Peterborough comes to sail in her and my son Roger to jeer as he told me not to do it like your excellent self.

As if all this was not enough, the grocer's van arrived from Peterborough as a birthday present, Frank P. and Sir Frank Nixon, having clubbed together in London over a drink, to give it to me. And then of course, one insurance company after another refused to insure me as I was over 60!!

It appears that the poor dear insurance companies are setting up a government of their own and trying to stop the over 60s from driving at all. An excellent idea but I am the wrong chap to begin on especially as I had only just passed my driving test. Let me know about this if you can. I telephoned to Perkins Ltd. who insure cars by the hundred and he persuaded his insurance Co. to give me third party risk cover so I can at least drive to the village and am waiting to get cover for my passenger.

The pier is splendid and will shortly display the Cambridge Cruising Club Burgee as I find I am still a member. It will also display a notice "Lanehead Landing – all dinghy sailors welcome". I am in fact enjoying myself except that I have not got a job and don't know if they can go on sending me money from Syria. But who says that poetry doesn't pay? The Lawrence Trust have just sent me a cheque in appreciation of my Ornament of Honour!

I do hope you will come again soon, though we still can't put you up as the whole house revolves round Titty and she is expecting! My wife, however, actually made, single handed, some tea cakes yesterday but I am not allowed to wash up as I do it too badly. ...

My next job, always supposing that the Amazon does not peel off and sink, is to finish framing my wife's pictures and then invite people to come and see them.

Please regard this place as your very second class home.

Yours ever, EA

Dear Ernest was a natural storyteller and a twice-told and somewhat apocryphal party piece, stoutly denied by the parties portrayed, went something like:

Future son-in law: Please may I have your daughter's hand in marriage Sir?

Dr Altounyan: Well now, that rather depends ... Point is ... Can you sail a boat?

Future son-in law: Matter-o-fact sir, I'm Commodore of the Royal ___ Sailing Club

Dr Altounyan: But my dear chap, of course you may!'

* * *

With the exception of Titty's confinements, the family were surprisingly tolerant of my frequent visits, and I don't think it was just to get rid of me that, over breakfast one morning, I was told that Ernest had "invited" me to go for tea at 4 o'clock with the famous inventor and scientist Mr George Constantinesco – and so for me, over the next five years, quite another fascinating story ran in parallel and remains etched on the brain.

An earlier Ernest, oil painting by Dora

The Constantinescos lived at Oxen House, just across from Peel Island. It is thought by some to be 'Beckfoot' in the books. Such conjecture is entertaining but seldom profitable as the Lakeland sites described by Ransome, though genuine in spirit, are thoroughly "stirred about", deliberately to protect the environment from the rest of us. Amusingly, he told how he came to confuse his own fictional geography with fact to such an extent that he almost got lost on occasions.

Anyway, that afternoon, the sun shone and the SW wind brought me tacking the four miles to Oxen House in just nice time for tea. I beached *Amazon* on the promontory as instructed and walked through the garden to be welcomed by Mrs Eva Constantinesco, a dear and understanding lady, so perfect for sharing an exceptional lifestyle with an accomplished musician, mathematician and extraordinary scientist.

I later found he was the coiner and developer of 'Sonics' (a new science using impulses through liquids, solids and gases to transmit power) and the instigator of 'Feron' (a new type of reinforced concrete).

His 'Fire Control Gear', which gave us superiority in air gunnery from 1917 during WWI was a notable application of 'Sonics' and it was only natural that he became the valued confidant of such frequent visitors as Segrave, Bentley and the Campbells *et al.*

Over home-made scones and fits of laughter, I was told how Ernest had previously "invited" two ladies to have tea with them at Oxen House. Just feet from their boathouse was a vestigial bit of field wall sticking out of the lake. To this he conveniently came alongside and "landed" them both. They must indeed have been too shocked to protest and were found some time later, still balancing there.

It seemed that the 'Duffer' syndrome really did live on!

Landed

Chapter 5

Revelations

O n one weekend visit, quite out of the blue after breakfast one morning, Dr Ernest surprisingly announced that he and I were to have morning coffee with the Ransomes at Hill Top Cottage, Ernest having "invited" us of course. I astonished myself by feeling strangely calm, indeed almost regretful, as everything was so perfect just as it was. Nonetheless, this had to be the orderly culmination of so many early aspirations. There was another factor, an extraordinary feeling that I was being *programmed* and this was *meant to be*.

Lanehead to Hill Top is 7.5 miles (12km) as the crow flies but not as we travelled that morning along narrow circuitous lanes. Dr Ernest had been there with Dora a number of times and was certain he knew the way but there is a huge choice of route towards the latter end. I had left my compass behind and I cannot blame Ernest as navigator for trying most of them. This did wonders for local knowledge, revealing a pastiche of woodland, small fields, hills, valleys with rocky outcrop and streams worthy of Dornford Yates, not to mention the charcoal burners of Ransome's day. It was quite by chance that we did find Hill Top Cottage, on one of the steep down-hill bits and I parked facing the bank with a large stone under a wheel, which seemed to be left there on purpose.

Hill Top Cottage

All nonchalance had departed and adrenaline was pumping away just as it should. I had no idea what to do with it except to remember every detail and keep my head down as we walked up a roughish drive and knocked on the door. What really surprised me was that Dr Ernest looked so ill at ease!

We must have been late and both Dr and Mrs Ransome appeared on the doorstep. First impressions were of their sheer size, his old age and how finely shaped were his very large hands. Her hands were the largest I had ever seen on a woman, eminently practical and strong but rounded like the rest of her. She looked scarcely less fierce than on our first meeting, over half a lifetime earlier, at The Heald – which I decided not to mention.

They greeted us politely and led the way through the cottage to a sunlit terrace at the back with coffee cups and biscuits all laid out. Dear Ernest was in full spate by this time, "Ernest at his most Ernest" as AR later remarked. Meanwhile, I was feeling completely blank and foolish as I looked about.

After asking kindly after Dora, they seemed to show a comparative coolness towards Ernest and I found this strange and distressing. After all those years, from school days at Rugby, his regard for Ransome was only to be expected, but this did not seem to be returned by either. They sat in frequent silence and looked almost 'native' at times.

Instinctively, I was determined not to behave like a fan, a description I have always detested, and I was getting the impression that such people were no longer in demand at Hill Top anyway. This was confirmed, in one of their warmer moments, by a description of alleged "fans" [they can't have been] once found wandering, uninvited, round their garden.

Years later I discovered that the uninvited wanderings had taken place nine years before, at their previous and most prestigious home ever, 'Lowick Hall', as Arthur's diary records:

> 9-10-49: Large well dressed girl in the garden with 2 others when told she really ought not to be in someone else's garden shouted that I was a blackguard and a parasite !!!! I suppose Nye Bevan & Mr Shinwell's teaching.

I sat mostly in embarrassed silence, merely answering when convention demanded and gazed at the scenery. The garden was a fairly large and pleasant basin with a field rising behind with some delightful outcrop poking out in places, several trees and only the occasional bird and sheep to disturb the peace. It was certainly a haven but what really struck one about this once much-cultivated nest was the number of weeds. They were everywhere.

Conversation became more and more spaced out and it was clearly time to go when, quite suddenly, I became determined not to let our visit, and so many happy and long-established associations, go sour without some effort. As we prepared to leave, I spoke up and said how much I liked the peace and beauty of their surroundings. There was a pause as, with a sense of nothing to lose, I tactfully professed to "have the same slight problem with weeds at home" – and suggested I had found the answer.

At this, everything stopped, Mrs Ransome's eyes lit up and I seemed to be noticed, even examined rather closely up and down, for the first time. We all sat down again and had another coffee while discussing the acknowledged weed problem. Then, as we left, I was invited in a whispered aside, to "pop in" on my way home.

I think there must have been more discussion among the ARs when we were gone, all very subject to the gravitational pull of declining health and relative confinement. Thirty three years later, while going through the Ransome's diaries at the Brotherton Library in Leeds, for quite another period, I could not resist asking for the diaries for 1958 to see if there was any comment. There was! Mrs Ransome's diary often goes for weeks without a single entry but, for this she had found the need to express herself, rather on the spur of a moment it seems:

(Sunday) 17th August 1958: Ernest with Berry in tow – most unwelcome visitors.

Ransome's entry for the same day is longer than average for a single subject and, for once, entirely legible, almost as if he wished to make a point:

Ernest Altounyan brought a Mr Berry (who had called at Lanehead? Why?) with an answer I had written to a fan letter of 20 years ago. Ernest had put him up at Lanehead for 3 days and as usual had more or less given him to suppose that he (Ernest) made my books!! What a man! But in the end I shall be driven to explain that all I had done was to change the names in an already half finished book, solely to give the little Armenians the fun of pretending.

Of course this really was a sad and grotesque travesty, completely at variance with the Altounyans and his original dedication of *Swallows and Amazons* – with which I had grown up:

TO
THE SIX FOR WHOM IT WAS WRITTEN
IN EXCHANGE FOR
A PAIR OF SLIPPERS

Things had come to a head just four months before my visit as, for the 1958 edition onwards, his renewed dedication reads as follows:

AUTHOR'S NOTE

I have often been asked how I came to write *Swallows and Amazons*. The answer is that it had its beginning long, long ago when, as children, my brother, my sisters and I spent most of our holidays on a farm at the south end of Coniston. We played in or on the lake or on the hills above it, finding friends in the farmers and shepherds and charcoal-burners whose smoke rose from the coppice woods along the shore. We adored the place. Coming to it, we used to run down to the lake, dip our hands in and wish, as if we had just seen the new moon. Going away from it, we were half drowned in tears. While away from it, as children and as grown-ups, we dreamt about it. No matter where I was, wandering about the world, I used at night to look for the North Star and, in my mind's eye, could see the beloved skyline of great hills beneath it. *Swallows and Amazons* grew out of those old memories. I could not help writing it. It almost wrote itself.

A.R.

Haverthwaite May 19th, 1958

Not unreasonably, Titty thought it was a sad move and that 'Uncle Arthur' was no longer interested in them as grown ups. If so, what an extraordinary reversal? His affection was unquestionable when they were children and is carried through convincingly with each character as we read the books, but then what?

I have always thought AR's use of real names lent credence and character to the stories, but time has shown it to be ill-advised from some points of view. Titty told me that he liked them as children up to the age their characters had been portrayed in the stories. Trouble came when they began to grow noticeably beyond this and think for themselves.

While the books and AR became recognised world-wide, there seems scope for general acknowledgement – as he does in dedicating *Pigeon Post* to Oscar Gnosspelius, for what must have been considerable scientific assistance. But the sustained help he may have got from Dora and Barbara Altounyans is hard to detect.

Another factor must have been poor Arthur's declining health; as he grew more dependent and the powerful influence of Evgenia became overwhelming. In consequence, other close relationships suffered, notably with Ernest and Titty. It seemed so sad and unnecessary yet I believe that an enduring affection remained.

I knew none of this in detail at the time and Mrs Ransome's invitation to "Pop in on your way home", though miles out of my way in those days, I thought suggested a more relaxed chat over a few drinks. And I needed the chance to explain how little I knew about gardening!

*   *   *

I was greeted pleasantly enough on this second visit to Hill Top but they seemed more preoccupied and tense than I expected. As we sat down to coffee and biscuits I experienced most unfavourable vibes. There was something blatantly inquisitorial about how I came to know and visit Lanehead. Determinedly, I kept it casual and told them very little except for my long-established love for the Lake District and boats. Instinctively, my regard for the books and their 'fictitious' characters were never mentioned, still less my research and drawn-out wanderings. There were clearly no points or appreciation to be gained, from branding me as a *fan*.

All at once and quite out of context, I was told that "Ernest was using" me as an excuse for his visit – but why, I should have asked, did he need an excuse? Then it was seriously stated, something to the effect that "Ernest is trying to make out that he made my books!"

I found myself being asked to believe that the children in the books, in spite of so many happy times together, of which I learned far more later in the context of family exchanges, and the happy and grateful letters from the Altounyans in Aleppo to Ransome at the time of publication. Were these to do with first names only? I was also expected to believe that Ernest was in some way trying to take the credit for the whole inspiration and, in some extraordinary way, its execution! I knew instinctively this sounded untrue and said so

Years later, in 1976, I read in *The Autobiography of Arthur Ransome* the following:

> I had for some time been growing intimate with a family of imaginary children. I had even sketched out the story of two boats in which my four (five including the baby) were to meet another two, Nancy and Peggy, who had sprung to life one day when, sailing on Coniston, I had seen two girls playing on the lake-shore. For once I had without difficulty shaped the tale into scenes and even found the Chapter-headings. The whole book was clear in my head. I had only to write it, but dreaded the discovery that after all these years of writing discursively I was unable to write narrative. I well remember the pleasure I had in the first Chapter, and the fear that it would also be my last. I could think of nothing else and grudged every moment that had to be given to other activities.

I know how he felt, but without knowledge of the above, I told them I felt unqualified to comment. However, as the irascible theme progressed, I felt compelled to intervene. Even as a very recent acquaintance and outsider, I knew that at least some of what was being said was preposterously paranoid. In retrospect, I think Arthur was pulled hither and thither by some of his thoughts.

The conversation became so unreal that, for several minutes I must have become disoriented – feeling that I knew much more about the books and their characters than they did, forgetting completely that I was speaking to the author.

I went on to say that 'Dr Altounyan' obviously revelled in his family and his keen interest in life was unquestionable, why not? He was by nature an infectious enthusiast who delighted in every aspect of Lakeland. What possible offence could that be too?

Then I told the Ransomes, very deliberately and in all honesty and seriousness, that I could not remember Dr Ernest or any member of the family referring to their fictitious counterparts in the books. The subject just never arose in a family which had more than enough interests and real character of its own.

I related how I had not even seen a copy of any of the Twelve Books in their house and, as a self-confessed "bit of an enthusiast" myself, I might have expected some references to the part they might have played. It just did not occur. Any references to "Uncle Arthur" had been in considerable affection but in quite a different way, quite remote from the books themselves.

In reply to more remarks, I stated, so unnecessarily, that the Altounyan children had "never asked to have fame thrust upon them". If, in early years, some had experienced enjoyment in sharing what only later became the author's romantic property, was this a crime? There was no reply to this!

The Ransomes, particularly Arthur, had not finished. Astonishingly, the name 'Titty' itself was then raised and I was dumbfounded and appalled when Mrs Ransome chipped in and called it "ridiculous" – "so why, *quite without permission, was it used*, I asked?" No reply to this either!

Of course, in reality, this was an affectionate nickname, from *Jacob's Old English Fairy Tales, Titty Mouse and Tatty Mouse*, which however ill-advised was, as the Ransomes knew very well, used only by family and close friends. I did happen to know that, at school, after publication, this distinctive and unmistakable label had become a positive burden to one of such a very sensitive and retiring disposition.

While her official name was Mavis, close school friends and readers of the books, came to know her as 'Titty' and embarrassment was inevitably caused, not to mention the few who chose to give it a physical interpretation. More to the point, she had acute misgivings about her namesake in the books, feeling so untruthfully, that she was inferior and not so clever. This was typical of Titty. Yet, as Ernest mentioned to me on two occasions, she had one of the finest brains in the family!

Much of this was churning round my mind and I had been speechless with growing anger – all the long-held thoughts of reverence tending to evaporate. The references to Titty were the last straw and I may have run on a bit – and suddenly found myself banging furiously with my fist on the table.

Abruptly, Dr Ransome rose to his feet and announced that unless I calmed down, he would "have to ask me to leave".

This really was unbelievable; not only was I a closet "fan", but my visit, at some inconvenience at the end of a long day, had been intended to discuss their vacancy for an *honorary* gardener. I should not get home till the small hours and had to be at my desk by 9am.

I told them that I could not accept what had been said, and if there was any further mention, particularly of Dr Altounyan, I should feel obliged to leave anyway.

* * *

Even ten seconds can seem an awfully long time. We sat there, all three of us visibly trembling in red-faced anger. Was this to be the culmination of a life-long deferential awe, the extinction of another gullible 'fan', a well-earned lesson in human fallibility?

We remained on this knife edge for what seemed an age. Then strangely, it was Dr Ransome who finally spoke up. He stipulated that "Ernest will not be mentioned again". Phew!

It was a very near thing. I concurred. We all had another coffee and got down to the subject of gardening.

We must also have discussed cats and the robust nature of Father's flame gun, for I was soon to receive the following letter from Mrs Ransome. This is in noticeable contrast to her diary entry of eight days before (which remains unchanged).

25th August 1958:

Dear Mr Berry,

It was kind of you to try to find a home for our Bulbo, thank you very much.

I wonder if I may take your offer of help in the garden seriously? Because I would accept a few hours of help from an intelligent gardener armed with a flame thrower as a gift from the gods.

I understand you spend most weekends in the district – but I feel it would be imposing upon you to suggest that you spend one Sunday during September (the 21st or the 28th for preference) hard labouring in our garden.

Yours sincerely

Evgenia Ransome

Concerning cats, Mrs Ransome's diary entry earlier in the year reveals the endearing side to her nature and is to do with birth of the same 'Bulbo':

7th May '58: Sally looks very slim – must have had her kittens, I wonder where? She invited me to walk with her as [if] she wanted to show me; She led me all the way to S. farm, where she got into such a thicket of brambles – I gave up.

8th May: Sally keeps inviting me to walk with her but she seems to disappear under the holly trees up on our ground.

9th May: Found Sally's lair under the roots of the holly tree with one kitten undersized even for a three days old. I wonder if she produced more but only one survived?

Clearly both the Ransomes, sharing no offspring of their own, had a loving affection for animals. Arthur writes in his diary:

19th Sept: In the afternoon we delivered poor Bulbo to his permanent home, which we do hope will be a happy one. He is the most characterful and engaging of kittens, but horribly inclined to climbing [up the curtains].

From Mrs Ransome, 1st September 1958:

Dear Mr Berry,

Thank you very much for your letter and the promise to come to deal with our weeds on Sept 21st. I have begun to pray for a specially dry weekend for your visit.

Will you be coming by train or by car? If by train – we shall fetch you from and return you to your lodgings; just let us have the address.

You must also let me know what fuel your flame gun uses and what is the consumption so we could lay in the necessary quantity.

And, please, do not insult me by suggesting bringing your own sandwiches – you will take pot-luck with us naturally.

I had a man cut the rough grass yesterday and have burnt most of it already – but millions of seeds were scattered and I am much looking forward to burning them all with your help.

Yours sincerely,

Evgenia Ransome

Meanwhile, I found myself eager to learn the rudiments of weed control and Father kindly gave me the fundamentals in a nutshell.

Yet another letter was received, dated the 18th September:

Just a line to confirm that we are expecting you on Sunday the 21st about 10am.

I hope the weather will continue fine and dry but even if it does not – come just the same and have lunch with us.

Chapter 6

Cultivating

As far as one can tell at 5am, it promised to be fine and warm on Sunday 21st September 1958. So far, Mrs Ransome's prayers had been answered!

My gardening clothes were not fit to be seen, certainly not for lunch with the Ransomes. Instead, I donned what had been thoughtfully laid out, my everyday sports jacket, flannels, shirt and tie, just hoping they would survive. Cornflakes were crammed down and I collected the thick-cut sandwiches from the fridge which Mother had prepared with her blessing.

The front passenger seat had been removed the night before and Father's flame-gun, though a tight fit, was finally inserted and travelled beside me, free to dribble residual fuel on newspapers, with extra cans in the boot.

The journey from Huddersfield towards Lakeland has always lifted the spirits with every mile and, to fully enjoy it I allowed heaps of time. This was fortunate as the objective was fractionally south of both Bartholomew and Baddeley maps and it seemed ages before striking familiar territory. This was in the lane above Hill Top Cottage, just in time for the sandwiches as blue smoke began to curl from their chimney. A simple matter then to coast down and report for duty on the dot of 10 o'clock as planned.

They were clearly impressed and I was greeted most affably. Dr Ransome insisted on coming down to the car, and seemed interested in my Morris Minor, which he said was "just right" for me. I assumed this was because it was small and green, but later, found he was considering one for himself, a very different proposition!

I later heard how he tried sitting in the driving seat of his close friend Colonel Busk's Morris 1000 and found it "a pretty tight fit". The problem then, was to get his feet on the pedals, and worse still, to close the door. The Colonel had had to push this shut from outside!

But I still think we could have managed and it is a pity I never thought of offering to take the Ransomes on excursions. Visiting certain sites, particularly those in the books could have been so much fun!

Gradually, I became aware for the first time, of Arthur's perceptive and amusing style of conversation, and the thoroughly interesting gift of description we find so infectious in the books. That his speech was delivered in the precise, almost pedantic tones of a pre-war news broadcaster was another, fondly remembered trait.

It was a welcome change to see him beaming with good humour, quite a tease in several respects. Indeed, he had already made a number of very searching, playful and surprisingly personal remarks by the time we had got the flame-gun on to the terrace.

I found it quite unnerving that he did not miss a thing. For example, he said my brogue shoes were "far too good for gardening" (they were). Then, with my mind on other things, I filled the flame-gun's tank with paraffin while leaning over it, smoking a cigarette. Of this he said nothing, though his manner suggested it was very bad form (it was).

The sun blazed down, just as so often implied in the books and all was ready by the time Mrs Ransome came round the house to meet the much-anticipated flame-gun for the first time.

I should explain that this apparatus was about five feet long and could be carried or trundled on wheels as required. Where it differed from similar machines of the period was in the size of its soft brass fuel jet which, from frequent pokings-out, had become grossly oversized.

As the pre-heating meths burnt low I asked them to stand well clear, hoping fervently that it would behave itself. I carefully pumped the tank up to prescribed pressure and unscrewed the release valve. Nothing happened and I had awful visions of having to call the whole thing off. I gave it two more resistant pumps. The FG gave a loud cough and a gob of ignited fuel shot thirty feet across the garden, hitting the far bank which burst into flame. Gradually, it settled down – to its usual roar, like that of a demented jet engine.

I think we were all shocked. I began to apologise but they could not have heard – and I need not have worried as I could see how impressed they were, even more so when the whole cylindrical end and lowered hood became white with heat.

The main target area was the vegetable garden, the banked-up bound-aries where growth was deep and the dandelion-infested drive. Everywhere was snuff dry and with each pass a two-foot swathe of weeds and seeds, the supposed object of my visit, crackled and burst into flame. Our only concern was for wild life; with this in mind I started in the middle and worked outwards, giving scope for escape.

After two hours, large areas of the garden were a black and smouldering ruin. Having been left on my own and, hopefully out of sight, I was increas-ingly concerned by possible reactions. Again I need not have worried, Mrs Ransome was delighted when she called me in for lunch.

*   *   *

It was pleasantly cooler in the house and I remember passing shoelessly to a dining table under a front window. There, to the far side of the front door hung a whole assortment of Arthur's outdoor raiment, all very "Sherlock Holmes", alternating with bagged fishing rods for every occasion.

The slate floor was largely bare and rendered remarkable acoustic as the Ransomes walked about. There was no electricity at Hill Top until five years later so all lighting depended on their characterful oil lamps. The table to which we sat, they on one side, I on the other, was of substantial scrubbed wood without any unnecessary cloth or mats. The whole effect was of monastic simplicity, a foil for the intriguing smell as really massive helpings of curried beef and boiled rice were borne proudly forth, ready served, by Mrs Ransome, her promised "Pot Luck" lunch, a new experience and favourite ever since, especially when washed down with copious (rather too copious) drafts of cider.

A fine cheese board followed and then we all sat back replete, for coffee and a smoke, for Ransome a pipe, Evgenia a small cigar and cigarettes for me. Long contented silences followed and I was beginning to feel very much at home. I only wish I had *kept quiet*, or even succumbed to drowsiness and laid my head on the table in the manner of 'Jim Brading' after his single-handed passage at the start of *We Didn't Mean To Go To Sea*. Instead, I asked Dr Ransome what he thought of "the China question", and so began a long tirade.

I had come to find my host rather predictable in some respects, and certainly he was wholly behind Mainland China of those days with all its hopes for new-found democracy and the expansive well-served freedom this promised. Mrs Ransome, who normally seemed in charge of things, made no contribution and he went on to say that the United States were quite wrong in their presence and support for the "Old Guard in Formosa" [now Taiwan] which had a record of repression that was "simply not understood by the West".

Clearly, he could remember and imagine what was happening from experiences on the ground – and recollections of his *Missee Lee* leapt forth. It seemed that while he had become somewhat disenchanted with Russian Communism ('Socialism' was the only name for it I ever heard him use), his regard for the "down-trodden Mainland Chinese" and what they might achieve, was touchingly intact.

He did seem to go a bit far and, not being a fellow traveller as far as our NATO Allies were concerned, I felt it was only civilised to declare my own affinity. As I ventured to lend them some support, Mrs Ransome looked on in enigmatic silence.

I may, in turn, have run on a bit, and this seemed to amuse him in an agitated sort of way. His voice, already rather higher in pitch than expected, became more and more so as he appeared, *quite laughingly*, to protest, "Mr Berry, Mr Berry!"

He never offered to discuss an issue or counter my disagreement. I think there must have been some obscure danger signals at this stage but they were quite unrecognised by me, except that Mrs Ransome's somnolent posture did seem to have become rather frozen.

To accept dissent from the censorious 'Genia', as I later discovered, must have been a daily necessity. But, from a presumptuous young pup, wittering on about a China he had never visited, was quite another – and certainly not the unquestioning compliance he had come to expect from a "fan".

After such an active life, AR was by then, subject to increasing physical and mental confinement. The effect was heightened, in consequence, by his naturally dominant wife. I think a reservoir of frustration had built up and needed an outlet.

I can see it all so clearly now as, at some point, I must have gone too far. There was a short pause before he rose, leaned across the table, grabbed the lapels of my sports jacket and hoisted me clean out of my seat. I remember how large he appeared at eye level, being well over six feet and seventeen stone.

Again, no attempt at reasoned argument, just another "Mr Berry! Mr Berry!" rather higher and more intense this time, accompanied by a pistoning back and forth before I was released – and slowly subsided.

It was a surprisingly robust performance and, though less than terrifying, a novel participation to be "mauled about" by a seventy-four year old. What must he have been like in his prime!

A rather shaky start

I was just so thankful that none of my friends were there to see, as I would never have heard the last of it.

I had made no attempt to resist and my concern was wholly for Arthur – as I'm certain was Evgenia's too. Then, as though nothing whatever had happened, we all had another coffee, I thanked Mrs Ransome for the excellent lunch and excused myself to go gardening.

*   *   *

I had come to regard Dr Ransome as a rather left of centre sympathiser but in spite of Mrs Ransome and his previous Bolshevik proximity, *never ever* as a revolutionary collaborator. Regard for his own country, its people and certainly the British Navy is overtly apparent from the books and, as Titty told me early on, his younger brother had served with the British Army in France, later to be killed in the trenches of WWI, what more proof is needed! Quite apart from Dr Ernest's supportive accounts ... I knew instinctively that Ransome was a very loyal British subject.

What confused opinions was his undoubted regard for Russia and its people. Forty-four years later, an article in *The Observer* on 21st July 2002 was a revelation:

> While far from a traitor, fellow protagonists and world-wide admirers never knew of his far more radical affiliations – as a spy in Russia for MI6, a British secret agent, code numbered S76.

> Strangely, I believe his regard for Russia and its people was equally unquestionable. It was the Bolshevik aspects he deplored and he did all he could to put things right by conveying what must have been vital intelligence. A life of adventure was grist to AR's mill – but whether his beloved Evgenia ever knew what some of it was about, we may never know.

* * *

In later years, as my visits grew in frequency, Arthur was finding replies to his devoted book readers rather a trial. Every so often, a parcel of their letters would be forwarded by Capes and the most oft-repeated question, concerning character and places, was "are they real". To answer each of these in detail, however evasively, had become a problem and with his latent kindness, somewhat stereotyped answers had become the norm.

I like to think they often found my presence a welcome change but when I got round to the 'Constantinescos', they could not hear enough!

I told them about the compressibility of liquids (unrecognised by some in those days) yet the fundamental attribute of 'Sonics'. Hence liquid spring suspensions and silent cannons. Also rock drills and ship propulsion without propeller shafts to name but a few – to his certainty that U K would never prosper till it adopted decimals and so on.

They and the Ransomes had never met but their mutual admiration was very apparent and I found myself swapping yarns between. While the ARs were closely familiar with Oxen House across from Peel Island, any imagined similarities with 'Beckfoot' in the books were never mentioned. It was the GCs themselves who interested them.

They knew little of George Constantinesco's remarkable life from birth in Craiova in 1881 and, for example, becoming an accomplished pianist, outstanding mathematician, radical builder of reinforced concrete bridges, buildings, and early tarred roads – all before he left Roumania aged 29.

As they partly knew, George was best known during WWI onwards as the man who invented the wave transmission (sonic) synchronising gear (C.C.

Card from Eva and George Constantinesco showing Oxen House's boathouse beyond Peel Island

Gear) for fighter aircraft firing machine guns forward *between* the revolving propeller blades.

The Germans used conventional mechanics and it must have been entertaining at times to hear of them shooting off their own propeller blades. Inevitably, they eventually captured one of our fighters, but could not understand how the firing mechanism worked.

Mercifully, after absurd periods of delay (because 'compressibility of liquids' was implied) the C.C. gear was finally adopted as standard equipment on British and American aircraft in WWI and gave our fighter pilots crushing air superiority up to the end of it. The gear continued in service up to the beginning of WWII, when it was superseded by guns in the wings etc.

Churchill once described George Constantinesco as "a wizard who in earlier days would have been burnt at the stake". What more can one say?

*   *   *

The newer boathouse, back from the lake, was a different world. Beside it in the long grass, like that in daily use in Eva's sitting room, was a prototype stove made from 'Feron' reinforced concrete, with its binding matrix of steel wires.

As I remember, this boathouse was very long, originally built to house an experimental high-speed watercraft. Along each plastered wall was a substantial work surface on which lay the most fascinating mechanics I had ever seen – so modestly referred to by GC as the 'museum' yet home to a number of his 133 spectacular inventions. Some of these may still be seen in

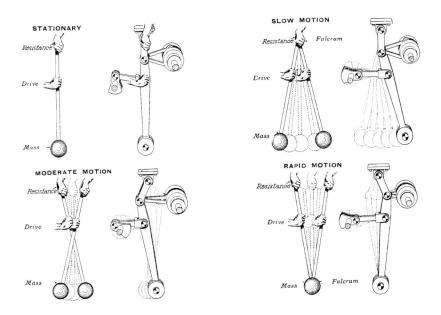

The Constantinesco Torque Converter

the external Science Museum at Wroughton near Swindon and some in Romania.

One exhibited a very small Automatic Torque Converter driven by the motor of an old domestic fan. The converter had a smooth lifting pulley poking out in front and Mr Constantinesco switched on the motor and asked me to grasp the pulley to represent a load. This slowed it down and he prompted me to grip harder but the auto torque transmission still insisted on turning the pulley, albeit at a reduced speed. I did manage to stop it but only with considerable friction, while the humble fan motor ran on seemingly unperturbed. This illustrated outstanding efficiency from such a small but ingenious device of few moving parts and theoretically 90% efficient (in suitable conditions)!

The sonic converter permits fully automatic conversion of torque without gears or clutches, simply by changing the frequency of input effort

I told the ARs how earlier life had not been without challenges for George and Eva Constantinesco. One example was how they tested the Passenger Railcar with his Torque Converter in Romania, aware of two other national enterprises vying for the same contract. For this they were obliged to run on the same lines as the local 'express', sandwiched between its journeys on a rather tight schedule. All went well till travelling uphill in a long dark tunnel they started to loose traction.

With Eva at the controls, George jumped out and discovered that the tracks had been smeared with grease – courtesy of the competition, it seemed. There was no time to lose, he took off his jacket and wiped the

Constantinesco's automatic car being led by Sandra, with string attached to the accelerator.

driving wheels as best he could with hot water while Eva was just able to find enough grip to get them clear – with minutes to spare!

Nonplussed by all this, the ARs asked if the GCs had any children and I told how his only son, Ian (by his first wife, Sandra) remembered the Torque Converter's early days. His father's idea was to produce a £100 car capable of 100mpg.

> As a promotional ploy, my father would allow me, aged eight, to drive his prototype 2-seater on the open road from Weybridge to Putney Bridge – to the astonishment of passers by. This was to show that it was so easy to drive that even a child could handle it.

Worthy of the *Better Drowned Than Duffers* syndrome, as the ARs had to agree.

I told them how I had "invited" the director and financial adviser of the internationally famous tractor-making firm near Huddersfield to visit the Constantinescos and see "how different things could be". This was partly to explore the latest advances in 'Diesel Sonics' and, of course, his 'Continuously Variable Transmission'. Alas, things proved too simple and different for conventional experts to fully comprehend!

Subsequently, a follow-up team of three well-known top engineers were despatched to examine more closely – but thought, quite wrongly, that "shock waves" and "ratchets" were involved. Everything was stopped and poor Mr Constantinesco was involved in much unproductive correspondence. Full of despair, I called at the factory hoping to locate the problem, only to be told emphatically by the MD that anything approaching "90% efficiency" was impossible and they could not afford to ignore the opinion of their highly paid experts!

* * *

It transpired that initially, the top brass had set off from Huddersfield in the firm's Aston Martin. This had just returned from distinguishing itself at Le Mans. Unfortunately, the pampered machine was not used to ordinary progress on narrow winding roads and threw a slight tantrum as they reached Torver. This obliged the visitors to complete the journey "on hot and dusty foot", arriving at Oxen House rather late. Meanwhile, the car managed to cool down and, while they were having lunch was delivered by the milkman, causing howls of amusement all round, subsequently for the Ransomes too.

* * *

Aged nearly 80, there were just five remaining projects which GC wished to promote. In desperation, I brought Father up to meet the Altounyans and, more to the point, Mr C at Oxen House. But there was nothing we could do.

After 45 years, I'm so fortunate to be back in touch with Mr Ian Constantinesco – and gratified to be told by Ian that:

> Advances arising from the work of George Constantinesco continue to be made. Although his mechanical Torque Converter did not reach commercial fruition during his lifetime, it has never been forgotten and it set the scene for the development of clutchless and gearless transmissions in common use today.

> Continuously Variable Transmissions with electronic control are now available (I have one in my own car).

> GC pointed out way back in 1926 that the ideal transmissions of the future would probably use the best features of hydraulic, mechanical and electrical transmissions combined. His prophesy is now on the way to being fulfilled

* * *

On 13-2-60, dear Dr Ernest wrote to me in his self-deprecating way:

> "... I am so pleased your father approved of me ... I certainly look forward ... to our future swapping of yarns.

> We are still dithering in financial uncertainty, but the end of this month should be decisive. My house is sold and we are waiting to see if they can send us the cash from Syria [it never came]. Meantime, we continue to live on [prescribed] drugs and a little Grocer's Burgundy.

On 6-4-60, Ernest wrote:

> ... Please do what you can in any way you think is suitable for Constantinesco. I have just written in my final appeal to Hailsham and told him that we shall be losing him to Romania unless something happens definitely about a job for him this summer and I can certainly do no more ...

Unlike life for poor Ernest and Dora, for me it had never been better. At a Christmas cocktail party in 1959 I had met Judy and life became complete.

* * *

But some unease between Hill Top and Lanehead remained. My happy and relaxed associations with the Altounyans continued and every visit was delightfully rewarding. I liked to feel I had done something to heal the Ransome-imposed divisions but still found myself with a foot in either camp, never mentioning the goings on at one establishment with the other.

I came to realise that Dr Ernest was unhappy with my visits to the Ransomes and in spite of all their happy old times together, he experienced a most undeserved sense of exclusion. I feared that he even had temporary doubts about my own loyalty. Of course, this never wavered – though I could hardly tell him so – or that my devotion to the family will last for ever.

Far more relevant and serious, after lifetimes of service, the Altounyan family had finally fallen victim to international politics. Their desolation was hardly apparent outside the family, yet with their expulsion from Syria, all they had ever worked for there was taken away.

Arthur's pact of silence between us concerning 'Ernest' did remain intact. But, decades later I found his diary entry for that very first day of "Cultivating" – and I do wish Ernest could have seen it too:

AR 21ˢᵗ Sept 1958: Mr Berry brought his flame thrower. He is devoted to Ernest Altounyan & to Constantinesco.

Chapter 7

Amazon and The Houseboat

It was back in the summer of 1928 that Ernest and Dora, themselves keen sailors, decided that their children, then aged from 11 down to 6, should be taught to sail. They settled in at Bank Ground Farm but, while the rest of the family were unpacking, Ernest (and some say Arthur too) shot off by taxi to Walney Island near Barrow-in-Furness and found two fairly new and heavy 13- to 14-foot fishing boats, built for the shallow waters of Morecambe Bay. They cost £15 each, and were delivered at dusk on a large lorry to the lakeside in Coniston. It was an impulse for which the family (as far as *Mavis* was concerned) were to be grateful for three or four generations to come.

The boats were simply rigged in much the same way but *Swallow*, having more beam and a substantial full-length keel instead of a centre plate, was much roomier. *Mavis* of course means Song Thrush and is also what 'Titty' was christened. *Mavis* was noticeably narrower in the beam than *Swallow*, had an extra thwart and an iron centre plate which was difficult for the children to raise and lower.

Ransome, being a close family friend and amiable eccentric, was delighted to join Ernest in the sailing lessons. Once the children could swim they were allowed to go out on their own and it was one of the happiest times of their lives. When the family were returning to Aleppo, Ernest asked Ransome to "Write me something to make me smell the wind and water again". He could hardly have anticipated that their very way of life had become the inspiration for *Swallows and Amazons*, published two years later.

Each boat had different virtues under sail and oars. But *Swallow* grew to be the children's favourite and it speaks volumes for their character and affection for 'Uncle Arthur' that they chose her for him to sail on Windermere. He did this until 1935 and what became of her then remains a sad mystery.

Roger Wardale's book *Nancy Blackett: Under Sail with Arthur Ransome*, includes his authentic drawings of both *Swallow* and *Mavis/Amazon*. He has kindly allowed me to reproduce them here.

Of course, boat design has been going on for thousands of years, but there have been considerable changes in design, construction, execution and ease of use even since the 1920s. After about sixty years of frequent daily use, *Mavis* was certainly showing her age. Richard Pierce, the designer of *Beachnut* boats, wrote to me about *Mavis*. Here is part of what he said:

My one and only experience of sailing *Mavis* was unforgettable, she was

 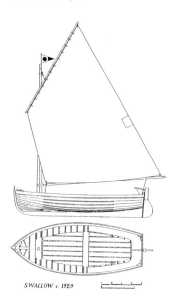

AMAZON *c. 1929*   SWALLOW *c. 1929*

Amazon and *Swallow*

unique in my experience. Most boats have a few quirks and flaws; *Mavis* in my opinion is without saving grace!

A basic requirement of a lug-sail dinghy is full forward sections so that as the hull heels the righting moment increases. *Mavis* is so slim bowed her stability does not increase as she heels, and indeed is progressively diminished ...

NB The form of *Mavis* is typical of small rowing boats built for the surf-free waters of Morecambe Bay, where the fine bows would not resist progress too much in a short chop. The fine forward sections are most unusual and inappropriate for a small sailing boat. Larger Morecambe Bay sailing craft do use this fine bowed form, but of course boat design does not scale up or down well, and anyway the Morecambe Bay boats set their mast further astern than *Mavis*. Another consideration is that coastal winds are always steadier than lake breezes.

I'm reminded of Ransome's own description of her behaviour, contrasting to that of *Swallow*, in 'The Race' Chapter of *Swallowdale*:

A black patch of wind-combed water was sweeping down the lake marking the track of a squall coming down from the mountains.

"They'll be getting it first," said Susan.

"*Amazon* won't like it," said John. "She's not as stiff as *Swallow*. Besides, all together, we must weigh more than them. Look, she's feeling it already".

They saw the little, white-sailed *Amazon*, far out in the middle of the lake, heel suddenly as the squall struck her. They saw her luff and come up into the wind with her sail shaking for a moment. It filled a moment later, but again she heeled over and again she came up into wind.

"They've got all they want," said John.

In *reasonable* conditions, she could be sailed in comfort for hours and seldom can such pleasure have been given, to so many, for so long (for so little). Even so, from the Lanehead/Bank Ground jetty to Peel Island and back, it is 7 miles (11km) – in a straight line, immeasurably further under sail. Alternatively, it could be quite a hard row home and, for those children, a long and exhausting day!

Safety was another aspect. They were taught not to stand up when afloat and, before sailing alone, each had to jump into the middle of the lake fully clothed without drowning.

There were no newfangled buoyancy bags fitted or life-jackets in general use at the time – and clearly there could have been no guarantee against a capsize. The consequences of one, out on the lake, could have been tragic (as indeed it was to prove for others in 1942). One can only respect the validity of Richard Pierce's discernment, and wonder how those young Altounyans survived! That year, Taqui was 11, Susie 9, Titty 8, and Roger 6. Brigit was only 2 and had to be enlisted later.

In the early days, the question of who sailed with whom, and in which vessel is something I should have settled years ago. I like to think of the crew at least, changing over, while the official skippers were Taqui and Susie and I suspect they jumped ship from one to the other too.

In Taqui's home-made-pastel-decorated Easter greeting card to us in 1996 she remarks:

> Though 'Swallow' had our hearts, 'Mavis' belonged jointly to Titty & me and we loved every plank of her – and still do. It must be the gay weather making me sentimental.

In fairness, Ernest, like Arthur, was obviously aware of the boat's limitations, and the children were never allowed to sail her if there was even a hint of "broken water".

Curiously, sixty years later, one of the skippers entrusted to take members of The Arthur Ransome Society for brief sails aboard *Amazon* was Jim Andrews. At the time, Jim knew nothing of Ernest's restriction on the children's use of the boat. After trials, however, he rapidly concluded from his own knowledge and experience of dinghies in general, that because of her tendency to bury her bow in strong winds, she should not be sailed in more than Force 3 – a 'moderate' breeze, when fresh-water waves begin to curl and break.

Taqui, as a brisk and agile over-eighty-year-old, was staying with Jim and Judy Andrews at their home on the banks of Windermere, when this particular *Mavis*/*Amazon* safety-decree came up in conversation. Taqui immediately burst out laughing, explained their own childhood rules as laid down by her father, and said she and Roger "used to have the *fiercest* arguments" as to what exactly constituted "broken water". One can just imagine!

From whatever angle we judge today, it says something very special about the character of those children in real life, not to mention the confidence of their parents later when they were far away in Aleppo, with only the non-seafaring Armenian cook in nominal charge at Lanehead. Yet the young Altounyans who, in real life, never had tents themselves, except in Syria, occasionally, after the wind dropped at tea time, ate their sparse provisions and, quite spontaneously, slept under sail and stars – alone on Peel Island. Worthy indeed of their role in the books!

I'm told that children of such propensities today, given today's accepted standards of discipline, reliability and moral awareness, would be put on the 'At-Risk Register'.

* * *

Unhampered by extensive knowledge and experience, I had found *Mavis/Amazon*, always brown-sailed in my day but white-sailed previously, a delight from every aspect of my devotional bias. Though far from "yachty," she had an air of being well-tried, well-loved and user-friendly – a true compliment to the Ransome spirit and antithesis of the modern lightweight dinghy.

Ernest usually stood by to allow me the pleasure of preparing the boat. With his occasional recommendations, we would be away in minutes. From lying dormant in the boathouse, *Mavis* would be brought alongside the jetty or paddled a few strokes clear in the little bay. Hanging rudder to transom could have been tricky, as it involved aligning first the upper and then the lower gudgeons while, unusually, threading a long metal pin down through them in turn. In consequence, one tended to leave the rudder shipped unless there was any risk of grounding. Similarly, the tiny tiller was permanently united to the rudder head. But it was no surprise that lowering or raising the heavy centre-plate had been a challenge to those young children.

It took only moments to step her short pole mast through the forward thwart and slot it into the keel. In our day, the fit of the mast through the thwart had become worn and loose, causing the mast to wobble about a bit until she was under sail, more testament to the years of pleasure she had already given! The halyard always lay rove through the masthead sheave and from it hung a hooked metal 'traveller' encircling the mast. On this the yard's strop was hung and hauled chock-a-block. The fall of the halyard would then be led under the mast thwart and made fast to the after thwart with a slippery hitch. This allowed the helmsman to lower sail immediately in an emergency (and I only wish I had used this method in *Navicula* for my ill-judged sail on Windermere). The jaws of the boom were then shipped round the mast and down-hauled to take the diagonal crease out of the sail; just as in Chapter I of *Swallows and Amazons*.

Her inherent simplicity was therapeutic and the pleasure she had given seemed to shine through. Dear Dr Ernest invariably gave me the helm, and in due course, her general use.

When we were able to sail home in the evening, the final triumph was to lower mast and sail while still under way, and with practice, coast gently into her berth in the darkening boathouse.

* * *

As with many other things, I was not in the habit of discussing my Ransome associations with anyone. Yet, shortly after our first meeting, quite out-of-the-blue, Judy told me how "the twelve Ransome books" had been a main inspiration from childhood, affinities shared by her elder sister Christine. They used to assess contemporaries, certainly in one respect, by whether they were 'Ransome fans' or not.

Except for making sure that I qualified, I kept mum and Judy went on to describe, with an unprecedented show of pride, how her sister Christine's maths teacher at Badminton, had once taught a "Roger Altounyan at Abbotshome". He was thought to have a strangely similar background to the "fictitious Walker family" and this strengthened convictions that the Twelve Books had some substance in real life.

The following Easter, we visited The Lakes and called, rather casually, on "some friends of mine". This was at Lanehead and she was amazed to find that they already appeared to know quite a lot about her. As always, Ernest and Dora were delightfully kind and hospitable – and gave us wine and pistachio nuts at 10 o'clock in the morning. Titty had quietly looked forward to meeting Judy and turned up later – inadvertently rendering Judy speechless when introduced – but she, Asadour and Rahel were "so cheerful and friendly".

By this time, Judy was agog and wondering if any more fictional awareness could possibly materialise. She became silently absorbed as, by kind invitation, we stepped out of the sitting room window, crossed the lawn and through the little iron gate, which Ruskin and Ransome must also have used, and ran down the field. What really amazed was finding 'Holly Howe' before racing down the steeper field both of us had imagined from childhood. We arrived at the boathouse quite breathless and walked through onto the jetty. She had not been informed of its restoration and it was hugely encouraging that she found it hauntingly familiar. Then, turning, she saw '*Amazon*', lying there with such modest composure and suddenly felt she was one of the 'Swallows'.

The following day after an early breakfast, I collected Judy from her B&B in Torver. The lake was calm as a mirror but, as the sun rose higher, promising ripples appeared. Soon after reaching Lanehead, Titty was loading us up with provisions thought necessary for the island. Some of this included lard and a frying pan which we never used but seemed an echo of earlier days. All this and our 'sea-faring' tops were carried down to the jetty. From there we foraged along the shore to find the heaps of washed up driftwood which I was reminded we should need on the much-foraged island.

Another long-imagined moment had arrived as we pulled *Amazon* out into the sunshine where Judy, visually transfixed, held her steady while I raised the mast. With all dunnage safely stowed up forrard, we shoved off, pulled clear of the little bay and hoisted sail.

The wind was pleasantly light and southerly, yet there was the familiar rippling noise under her forefoot and our progress left a visible wake. We proceeded in a series of broad tacks from one side to close in on the other down the lake. It was almost as if Judy knew her way but the views of hills and unspoilt shoreline were more beautiful than even I imagined. As usual, we were the only vessel or humans in sight and, all too soon, the diminutive Fir Island was spotted on the port beam and we were almost half way there.

All of a sudden, Judy managed to see far-away 'Wild Cat Island' for the first time. Here, as if wishing faster progress, she reminded me that she had been taught to sail while on holiday on the Isle of Wight and gratefully took over.

In our haste and delight, we stayed under sail and, from well south of the island turned towards the 'Secret Harbour' under loosed canvas and wafted on with bare steerage way but on the exact course under my instructions, as Ernest had shown. Gliding in, safely clear of the submerged rocks, we were soon within those high rock walls. Once more it was a breathless experience for us both as we slid on and on and gently up the beach. Just as so many times before in our imagination, we stepped ashore and made fast.

Judy could not believe her eyes, yet it was she who led the way up the winding path, past the small cliff to the little grassy clearing with its burnt patch in the middle and trees all around. Here we dumped everything and looked about. As Titty had warned us, there was hardly any combustible wood. It seemed that successive generations and many Ransome-inspired children had also acted out their dreams and the island had a pristine, cared-for look. We had been prepared to forage for any litter but not so much as a sweet paper could be found.

Judy and *Mavis*/*Amazon* in the secret harbour 'Wild Cat Island'

The National Trust now owns the island and asks us not to light fires but, a safe well-used fireplace remains, and we gathered leaves for dry tinder (instead of newspaper as did the 'Ds' initially for the 'observatory' in *Winter Holiday*) then thicker twigs arranged in the proper pyramidal 'Susan' manner we had leant from the books. A small fire was soon well alight and I hurried back to our stack of fuel in the harbour. Fearing the worst, I tried to cut forked sticks to support the kettle with my scout knife and, as usual, they split hopelessly every time we attempted to hammer them with a stone into the rock-hard ground. None of this seemed to matter as we relaxed where the 'Walkers', or rather their real-life counterparts, had set up camp thirty years before and for the rest of their lives.

Our fire was without any surrounding stones but it gradually became beautifully red in the middle. It was on Titty's barbecue spits that Judy threaded our bacon and sausages, turning them to cook surprisingly well, becoming 'smoked' in the very best way. The telescope on the rug was later given to a very appreciative Asadour.

Real exploring started after lunch, from the 'Secret Harbour' and the rocks to the south. We explored minutely up the west side with its views across Coniston Water to Oxen House and sheer drops into the lake, stood on the miniature cliff of the northern headland with its spectacular views up the lake – "but where is the Lighthouse Tree?" she asked. Then, amidst the thickly wooded island and mainland trees, we gazed across the diamond-clear shallows to the close-bound mainland, which we vowed to explore another time. It was only this and the rather smaller, narrower

Cook Judy on 'Wild Cat Island'

Recumbent skipper *(photo by Judy)* at the helm of *Amazon*.
Note the slight runs from Ernest's fibre-glass sheathing, the
quick-release halyard knot and tiny home-made tiller.

than-imagined, overall size which seemed unexpected. Yet the whole ambience was of delight.

Time rushed by and after several coffees, the fire was put out with water and all was tidied up. We were expected at Lanehead for tea and, after a history of late meals, we were determined to be on time. We tore ourselves away, to coast back up the lake in perfect peace. Everything was coming together in a way I could never have anticipated.

It was all part of a "happiest day of our lives" as we wafted silently back up the lake.

In spite of inherent shortcomings, *Amazon* was always a joy to sail. Under canvas, her simple unstayed rig seemed naturally balanced and she possessed pleasantly-light weather-helm. Her original tiller may have been replaced more than once and was polished to a gleaming reddish brown by years of handling. It was astonishingly short, with only about a foot protruding from the rudder head. It had lots of knobbles like a tree branch, which indeed it was. Sadly, it was to be discarded thirty years later during restoration and is now replaced with something more conventional-looking, albeit a shortened axe handle!

Both *Swallow* and *Amazon* had a rounded notch in their transoms, such as that which 'Captain John' used for single-oar sculling into the secret harbour. Strangely, with *Amazon*, there was also a puzzling rather rough notch to one side of this and I'm so pleased to see this has survived restoration – as Taqui told us it was cut out by Oscar Gnosspelius "to accommodate an outboard motor!" Sacrilege, one might think today, but a happy reminder of family friendship and his very different transfiguration from the 'Squashy Hat' of *Pigeon Post*.

There were to be many other voyages and setting off was always an uncanny reminder of her sister ship as described in *Swallows and Amazons*, 'The Voyage to the Island':

> The *Swallow* slipped slowly out towards the mouth of the bay. She made at first no noise and hardly any wake, Then, as she came clear of the northerly side of the bay she found a little more wind, and the cheerful lapping noise began under her forefoot, while her wake lengthened out and bubbled astern of her.

Thinking of this passage often lulled me to sleep as a child, followed by sublime dreams of shared existence with 'the Swallows'. I never thought to experience that – still less with Judy, or to know and share that sound with the 'Walkers' in real life. Yet there we were, and as we cleared the little bay and caught the first puff of wind, "the cheerful lapping noise began under her forefoot" and *Amazon* was soon cleaving though water, more like an ocean liner than bouncing from wave-top to wave-top in the frenetic modern manner. She seemed to encapsulate the essence of a more profound and kindly age.

Besides the centre plate, she had, like *Swallow*, the benefit of a long, though shallower keel and this gave her a directional stability which was most agreeable. It always reminded me of the arthritic car I had which held its course so beautifully on a motorway. Even in a slight chop, it was possible to keep *Amazon* in line with a point on shore and allow no excuses for unseemly waggles in the wake.

With no foresail to slack off, coming about required momentum, yet the old boat invariably managed to carry enough way. She had always been heavy, but after Ernest's sheathing ministrations, she came through the wind like a tea-clipper, in a wide and dignified curve.

In most weather, we sat comfortably inboard and any strain from the sheet could be taken by a downward-facing pin protruding from under each transom knee. It was the simplest matter to release this when tacking or in an emergency – merely by slacking off the sheet, causing it to drop off the pin.

*   *   *

Later, as a married couple, our first Lakeland stay together was at Lanehead in the best bedroom. Propped up in the doorway was an accomplished oil of a very nude lady. The figure stood in a naturally relaxed state but we never got round to ask who the artist was, still less the lovely and rather familiar-looking model. Downstairs, we had found Titty trying to light the kitchen range without kindling, as this had run out.

After breakfast, with a Ransome-type purpose, Judy and I ran down to the boathouse, left *Amazon's* mast, sail and yard on the jetty and rowed along the waterline foraging for driftwood and soon shipped a huge cargo. Being a completely open boat, she had plenty of stowage space for our purpose. Each day and far less easily, we took up all we could carry for fire lighting at Lanehead and this lasted for months.

Unfortunately, Judy was busy radiographing at the Middlesex Hospital when, typically in those days, it was a large number of family who gathered at Lanehead in 1960 and once more the indispensable pilgrimage to Peel Island got under way.

In control as usual, Ernest's role was to pack huge numbers into the back of the Fordson 'delivery van', but somehow I was detailed off, with Taqui's two boys Roger and Nicky, to take the water route in *Amazon* [always *Mavis* to them] and do the ferrying when we got to the island.

Naturally, we didn't complain but, anxious to be on time, we ran down to the boathouse, only to find *Mavis/Amazon* full of leaves. We took everything out, even removing the bottom boards to clear the bilge. Among familiar items, we found a couple of broom sticks, their ends joined by the four corners of a large tablecloth. None of us could remember using a table cloth, even a clean one, on the island. We put this ashore and paddled clear of the bay, raising sail in the sunshine.

As I remember, we beat down the lake against a rising SW wind until, inexplicably, we found ourselves funnelling *before* the wind between the island and eastern shore. Fortunately, the plate was raised to clear any rocks but we still waggled embarrassingly down wind, at risk of a gybe, before lowering sail and rowing ashore.

Even in such moderate circumstances it was a reminder of the young-sters aboard and I continue to marvel how, typically in the early days, Taqui and Roger in *Swallow* and Susie and Titty in *Mavis*, managed not to be 'duf-fers' and stay alive. How different from the 'Nanny-State' culture we now espouse, and sadly, find so necessary today!

By now, the polyester-sheathed bow of *Mavis* seemed especially vulner-able to the shore-lined rocks and I remember standing knee-deep, holding her, as two over-loaded ferry trips of laughing family used my back as a bridge.

Ernest had decided he wanted a swim, the only one of us to do so, and he and Dora stayed ashore. His health, though never his spirit, was now dwin-dling and, for the first time in my experience, he appeared slightly miffed. It seemed that he had looked forward to our leisurely return before the wind – and had just discovered that *I* had left his 'square-sail' back in the boat-house.

It saddens me still that he went home in the Fordson van and, though we continued with cherished correspondence, this was the last I saw of him.

*   *   *

Dora wrote on 12-11-61:

> My dear John,
>
> I must tell you that I don't think we shall be able to come [to stay] in the near future. E is not well. He had a slight stroke ... though is <u>very much better</u> [typical of Dora] ... hope we shall meet before long'.

Two further letters spoke of discomfort and hospital.

Then, Dora, 14-3-62:

> 'You will be sorry to hear Ernest died yesterday afternoon ... '

Dr Ernest's death, aged 72 on 13th March 1962 was my first conscious bereavement and I had feelings hardly experienced before.

It was only after that I learnt of his achievements. During the First World War he was injured by irremovable shrapnel while picking up the wounded. Explosions caused deafness in one ear and was the cause of his bent little finger. He was later awarded the Military Cross in France for gallantry in action. His close friendship with T.E. Lawrence started in earlier days when Lawrence was doing archaeological work on the ruins of Carcemish on the Euphrates and used to come to the Altounyan Hospital for medical attention. After Lawrence's death, Ernest wrote the poem *Ornament of Honour*, "as a memorial embodying what I believe to be our common philosophy of life" and his appreciation of Lawrence in *T.E. Lawrence by his Friends* is said to be the most revealing in that book.

Lieutenant-General Sir John Glubb had Ernest with him for the Iraq campaign and described him as "one of the pillars of my life". He wrote in *The Times*:

> Dr Altounyan was neither a secret service agent nor a politician. He acted to some extent as a connecting link between the British Army and the Syrian leaders in the Second War and he was in the confidence of the Commander-in-Chief. It was his hope to see Syria independent and a friend of Britain and he never concealed his hopes ...

> Ultimately he met with disaster owing to his loyalty to Britain, a sentiment which all his life he never attempted to conceal. I do not remember ever having met a more public-spirited or more courageous man.

At St Andrew's Parish Church in Coniston the taped Armenian lullaby, chosen by Roger, suggested such colour and surprising lack of melancholy, yet was lovingly appropriate.

All family and friends were afterwards assembled for a reception at Lanehead. Then Roger, his cousin Tadeus, Melkon and I walked down to the lake and rowed *Mavis* across to the far shore.

A passing fisherman seemed puzzled and asked if it had not been Dr Altounyan's funeral earlier that day. Roger said "Yes, but this is what he would have wished".

* * *

After being sailed by three generations of the family as *Mavis*, she is now officially re-named *Amazon*. This was done, while she was still undergoing restoration. At the inaugural meeting of The Arthur Ransome Society (TARS) in 1990 – by the youngest 'Walker', Brigit. As she mentioned at the time, 'Bridget' [Ransome's spelling] the 'Ship's Baby', was now 'Ship's Grand-mother!'

Ernest, towards the end, in *Amazon*

Ernest's lovingly applied

glass-fibre sheathing had all to be removed, and gradually all the rotten timbers were replaced. Finally the hull was repainted in white, with a dark-green top strake, just as when Arthur had known and sailed her long ago. She was even given a replica white cotton sail, copied from an old photograph of her sailing on Coniston Water.

The financial cost of all this, largely donated by enthusiasts, hardly relates to her nearly-new purchase in 1928. It was even more than building a replica in 1990. Such is the regard in which the family and books are still held!

Though still belonging to Roger's family, *Amazon* is on permanent loan to the Windermere Steamboat Museum. From there, for a fortnight each summer between 1991 and 1994 she was sailed gently on Windermere. This was while in charge of experienced members of the society and it provided young TARS enthusiasts with a memorable experience.

Unfortunately, the annual soaking and swelling of her ancient hull, to make her "seaworthy", caused serious problems. Instead, she now reposes indoors in a facsimile of the 'Secret Harbour' which I was asked to paint, around the infinitely prized, static exhibit at the museum. It seems especially fitting, as years earlier she had been "borrowed" and left precariously by the River Crake bridge – and Roger had placed a notice on her, in the Nibthwaite boathouse, which read: *This is an old boat in Peaceful Retirement.*

S.Y. "ESPERANCE"
'CAPTAIN FLINT'S HOUSEBOAT'

The Manchester Guardian of 21-01-60 celebrated "Ninety-one years of the Esperance". An article by George Pattinson described how the steam yacht was originally brought from Barrow-in-Furness to the lake in one piece. The double railway track had to be taken up under all bridges and a temporary single-track laid through the centre, to allow her passage underneath. Such was the prestige of fame in those days.

Her owner, Mr H.W. Schneider, steel magnate at the Barrow-in-Furness foundries, went on board each morning from his house in Bowness, now *The Belsfield Hotel*, preceded by his butler with breakfast. This he took in the forward saloon on passage to the railhead at Lakeside. Afternoon tea was enjoyed on the trip home.

Though she became 'the Houseboat' in the books, I don't think AR ever claimed to have boarded her, until the making of the first *Swallows and Amazons* film. In the book illustrations of *Winter Holiday* and *The Picts and the Martyrs*, her main cabin appears far more beamy and accommodating than in real life.

Esperance lay for years on the bed of the lake after someone blew a hole in her side – but was salvaged by Mr T.C. Pattinson. She is now maintained and housed in the loving care of Windermere Steamboat Museum, with *Amazon* nearby.

Chapter 8

Hurlingham Court

Until electricity came to Hill Top Cottage in November 1963, it was unimaginably cold during winter months. With no mains gas, the Ransomes had the choice of either huddling round a paraffin heater or escaping to London.

Typically, exodus occurred in mid October, to the fourth and fifth floors at the top of 40 Hurlingham Court, London SW6, directly overlooking the river alongside Putney Bridge.

By then I was a junior officer in the RNVR and "conveniently", as Evgenia kindly put it, I often spent a week, while on family business, at The RNVR Club [now The Naval Club] in Hill Street.

Arthur, quite without my knowledge, had been there more than once as a guest of a Commander Edward Seago. He recorded in his diary, "as usual I could not remember who he was" and later, that he was a "very good painter" whose work they visited in Suffolk.

Back in November 1958, Evgenia had written from Hurlingham Court, thanking me for the loan of *Shetland Bus*, a book about smuggling patriots out of enemy territory. "My husband read it and thought it good – but I don't think I shall read it as it is too much of a war book and I hate reading about wars".

The following day she wrote: "We shall be here on Monday ... , so do come at 7pm and take pot luck with us at supper ..."

Evgenia's diary for 1st December 1958 states: "John Berry to supper. Arthur fell down on leaving Cape's office ..." This is the second mention of such a fall, which was down the stone steps, when leaving his publishers, then at 30 Bedford Square. One cannot help wondering why. The consequences on this occasion were to become severe, starting a series of misfortunes from which he never fully recovered.

Arriving via Putney Bridge underground, I found their substantial block of flats close-by, and a lift at the back took me to the fourth floor. I naturally knew nothing of Ransome's accident earlier in the day and noticed no signs of injury as he opened the door.

Unfortunately, I was full of cold and when about to shake hands, sneezed explosively over both of us instead. The effect on Arthur was palpable. He had a way of repeating himself when I aggravated him and positively wailed "she'll catch it, she'll catch it", clearly wishing that I would turn tail, and seemingly unassuaged by my firm assurances that it was a late attack of hay fever.

These were still early times and it did appear to be one of Arthur's less good days and I was reminded of our potentially delicate relationship. If I had any perceived value at this stage, it was as honoury gardener to Evgenia and I had no intention of turning tail.

Reluctantly, he took my bowler hat, coat and umbrella, then began a running commentary about the several dark family oil portraits which hung in the gloom of their tiny square hall. Ahead of us was a door marked 'Staff only' and from this Evgenia thankfully erupted and everything changed as she dispensed cordially affectionate greetings. She had even remembered my appreciation of the lunch at Hill Top and soon we were all seated round another enormous and excellent meat curry with steaming boiled rice.

Just before we all tucked in, she produced a huge bottle of cider and passed this to Arthur to open. He addressed himself to this manfully and got quite red in the face as he wrestled with the screw top from every angle. It refused to budge. At last, in clear shame-faced embarrassment, he passed the bottle to me with a distinct gesture of challenge – and the obvious hope that I too would signally fail. All this was in front of his Genia and after a life-time of fortitude, it clearly mattered in an almost childlike way. Anyway, I grasped the stopper and, with a tactful show of considerable effort, prized it loose and said, quite illogically, untruthfully and obsequiously, "but you had already loosened it, Sir!"

This was just one of those instinctive off-the-cuff good-upbringing comments, yet it proved a turning point in my relationship with Arthur. It went down astonishingly well, indeed, his whole manner became changed and relaxed. He chuckled and replied, "I had wondered if you would be honest enough to admit it!"

Gosh! Some people would have given me a wink at this stage and, although Evgenia's eye was firmly upon us, I know he was being perfectly serious and could wilfully believe it was he who loosened the stopper.

For all his manly virtues, on this and previous occasions I had developed several firm impressions about Dr Ransome. Obviously, he had well-proven gifts of creative imagination. More than that, I believe he had developed remarkable powers of self-deception and mode of thought, a faculty of artis-tic licence that could turn one thing into quite another as circumstances decreed. Also, even at nearly seventy-five, he possessed an almost child-like predictability, once you knew the signs. In some respects, I believe he had never quite grown up and so, thankfully, when circum-stances demanded, could still contemplate through the eyes of a characterful child.

All this must sound improbable and far-fetched, but I really did find him relaxed, jovial and friendly towards me from this point on.

He did not seem at all domesticated and was clearly exonerated from table-clearing and washing-up. I offered my services in the galley but these were resolutely refused and he and I retired to the sitting room. Here were large fish behind glass, pictures of Arthur fishing, an ancient parson and countless images of cats both on the wall and in pottery, brass and wood.

Over his pipe and my cigarettes, I was shown the contents of a substantial bookcase. This was one of many but seemed confined entirely to his works. Besides the books we know so well lay the corrupted foreign translations – and it was on these we concentrated.

I cannot be certain but got the impression that, not only did *Winter Holiday* precede *Swallows and Amazons* in the Czech translations but they had omitted the signalling code in *WH* which of course is so much a part of it. He clearly found this trait distressing and it is hard to credit the apparent lack of co-ordination which made it possible.

Any true Ransomite would have been saddened by what I saw and some illustrations, to our privileged eyes, seemed woefully out of character. It is in our nature to lean over backwards to placate foreign cultures but much of what I saw was full of spurious drama, poorly drawn by someone who had never sailed a boat or even read the books. I seem to remember double-ended yachts, not dinghies, sailing arbitrarily with the same close-hauled sheets but in different directions. I just knew they would be served by equally indifferent text.

I was so overcome that I do not remember Dr Ransome's explanation for his own illustrations not being thought transferable – in *any* language, why not?

In puzzling contrast, research has since shown up some exceptionally fine drawings which Ransome found unsuitable for the first illustrated books, from 1931.

In passing, I told him how I was first captivated by *Swallows and Amazons* with its superb illustrations by Clifford Webb – and how I still held these in reverence as a sublime and inseparable part of the book. I wish I had left it at that but went on to say that I thought it must have been "a brave decision" to take on the illustrations himself.

This did not go down at all well and, for a moment, I wondered what was going to happen – but things had changed, I was now being regarded as a rather irritable friend. He went on to emphasise that *faithful portrayal of character and subject, not pretty pictures, is what book illustration is all about* – something I have always tried to remember. Certainly his own works fulfil these qualities abundantly and have been equally treasured.

I do believe Arthur got some very relevant help from Dora, her sister Barbara and perhaps a Mr Hugh Lofting. Really good drawing can be detected in places and now in some obviously professional preparatory sketches published in Wardale's *Ransome the Artist*. Dora never admitted to taking part to me and I cannot remember any specific acknowledgement of outside help with drawing, except for the vague and part-humorous 'Captain Nancy Blackett' in *Peter Duck* who is supposed to have written "Everybody wanted to help with every picture, even passing natives who saw what we were doing." – written by Arthur while staying with the Altounyans in Aleppo.

There was a plain and restful air about the Ransome's flat. Its rather ordinary furnishings were still of the thirties and had the lived-in and scholarly, but ordered, ambience of Hill Top, with no concessions whatever to 'effect'. All was very much in keeping with AR's few illustrated 'interiors'. Only a pair of twirly oak-stained candlesticks with chrome capitals seemed out of place, a legacy from Russia no doubt.

It was especially kind and rewarding for me to be shown his study. Like other work-places I have known, this was especially redolent of character, soul and endeavour. It was very similar, in its simple ambience, to the photograph of his workroom in the barn at Low Ludderburn.

Amazingly, here was the same antiquated black Remington Portable, and I wondered how many miles of paper had passed beneath its much-dimpled platen. Years ago, it was just right for a foreign correspondent but, as I had gently hinted before, quite unequal to a fine office machine which is what he really needed. It was the 'words to a page' factor which put him off changing, yet this could so easily have been addressed. Years later, we are able to read his first inspired attempt at *S&A*, entitled *The Swallows and the Amazons* and wonder how much even his practised gift for composition could have been aided by a computer.

My mind was spinning to absorb everything. It would have been inexcusable to even glance at the papers on his plain, rug-covered worktable. Even so, from afar, I could not help noticing a 'Ransome and Rapier' share certificate, a comforting hint of old family connections still presumably intact, and of possible support in times of need, though I had not then read of the Ipswich Family connections and could hardly ask him.

The formal mechanics of 'English Composition and Grammar' have always escaped me and I have had to rely on what sounds correct. I certainly knew nothing of the respect held in German Universities before the war for Arthur's archetypal use of the English language. Still feeling slightly squiffy, I was on the point of mentioning his occasional use of "bad grammar", but have since been assured this is natural colloquialism, as would be used in normal conversation by the 'Walker' children – and indeed, the Prince of Wales. Most fortunately, the moment passed and AR remained a friend from that day forth.

*   *   *

My memories of the Ransomes at home in London are limited. A more rounded picture is made possible with the earlier experiences and better memories of others – in both cases, very different from mine.

Fair Exchange

Among earlier visitors to Hurlingham Court in the 1950s was Tania Rose, daughter of Morgan Philips Price – Russian Correspondent for *'The*

Guardian' from 1914/18 and a close Ransome associate in those days. It was thanks to Brigit for suggesting that we "confer".

Tania told me that her late husband was William, better known as 'Bill Rose' the screenwriter. Bill's agent was also a close friend of his – who by chance got into conversation with Ransome in the Saville Club – and it emerged that AR knew Tania as a child when visiting the Price family in the 1920s. Anyway, the next thing was an invitation for the Roses to dine with the Ransomes.

On their way to Hurlingham Court, they noticed that Bill's film *Genevieve* was showing at the local cinema and in course of conversation this was mentioned over dinner. At this, Arthur and Evgenia, while not normally driven by cinema, were understandably impressed. Dinner was hurried through and the Ransomes insisted on them all going to see it – "and they did appear to enjoy it," said Tania. I'm sure this is gross understatement. I can just picture Arthur laughing uproariously throughout.

It may have been on the strength of this that the Roses were invited again, this time to sample Evgenia's home-cured smoked salmon. Apparently, the subject of discussion turned to cats. The Ransomes told how they had had two and every night after dinner, Arthur and Evgenia sat reading on opposite sides of the fireplace, each with a cat on lap. The sad day came when one cat died and they fell to wondering what would happen that evening. They need not have worried. The surviving cat sat on its usual lap – until "half time", when it climbed down and crossed over, to spend the rest of the evening curled on the other lap.

When Bill's next film, *The Ladykillers*, came out, Ransome was kind enough to send them a cutting from one of the broadsheet Sunday papers by its music critic. The article, called *Detection by Music*, was amusingly written and described how the villains in the film were pretending to be a string quartet as a cover for their crime. In real life, the gramophone record used for the film was a Boccherini *quintet* which neither Bill, Tania nor the film makers had spotted. The Roses were "touched" and, like the Ransomes, very amused.

'Rest' by Evgenia

Arthur tying a fly

The last time that Tania saw them both was in 1962, at Hill Top. By then, alas, Arthur could hardly walk but seemed as lively as ever. They must have talked about Russia because Tania was planning to go for the first time with her father. It was a tense time for the Ransomes who were currently under offer for an attempt to make a film of *Swallows and Amazons*, and seemed to regard her as an authoritative screenwriter. They talked a lot about their major concern – how to safeguard the story from adapters!

After Arthur's death, Tania visited Evgenia frequently at Aynhoe and liked to feel they became friends. I think Evgenia had mellowed by then and she remembered her talking freely. Tania also found it hard to accept previous accounts of any hostility, from Evgenia, having grown towards the Altounyan 'children', not to mention records of her super-critical attitude when reading through each of the books on completion – times when Arthur had, very wisely, contrived to be far away.

She found Evgenia's memories of Arthur "were of undivided love".

* * *

Another Hurlingham Court visitor, with experiences very different from mine, was the late Ellen C Tillinghast of Burlington USA. She told how she had corresponded with AR in the nineteen thirties, as I had, but renewed it in the late forties and received an invitation to tea, if she "ever came to England". Thus, she visited Hurlingham Court, just two years earlier than I in the winter of 1956-7. The invitation included her ten year old twins, 'Nancy and Peggy' (as in the books) as well as Elizabeth, aged nearly nine. Very sensibly, she wrote a full report to her mother on the very same evening and, thanks via Roger Wardale, here follows an abridged account.

TEA WITH THE RANSOMES

The joy of joys and wonder of wonders has happened ... we have met Arthur Ransome!!

Right by the Thames, just a step from Putney Bridge Underground Station is a large block of flats called Hurlingham Court. We walked through to the back which overlooks the river and took the lift to the 4th floor. Mrs Ransome greeted us and, in the whirl of removing coats and laying them on a chest, Mr Ransome himself appeared. He stood there happily, a large bright-eyed old man with a white moustache and white hair round a bald spot, while there was a deluge of Tillinghasts about him.

Mrs Ransome asked if any of us wanted to go upstairs, and the girls, ready for anything, said 'Oh, yes!', and dashed upstairs with her. I was left to follow Mr Ransome into the living room. There were bookcases everywhere except for the gas heater and the far wall leading to a balcony overlooking the river.

Mr Ransome looked at me through his steel-rimmed spectacles and said, 'You know, it's a mistake coming to see an author'. He implied that it would be a shock for the girls to find him 'a hundred years old'.

Mrs Ransome returned with the girls and we all went on to the balcony to see the deep red patch of sunset. Below were many moored boats in the wavering lines of light reflected from the street-lamps on the opposite bank. We were called into tea and I saw long rows of his books in English, American editions and foreign translations.

The dining room was also lined with books and photographs. In the middle, a large table was groaning under the weight of a large fruit cake, a three-tiered Madeira with creamy, rum butter-icing, assorted biscuits, piles of thin buttered bread, honey, strawberry jam and tea.

Mr Ransome said the children need not start with bread and butter – 'a dreadful custom which filled you up before you got to the more important things like cake'. So he served thick hunks of fruit cake. I had bread and honey which had been given by bee-keeping friends. Mrs Ransome said she would like to keep bees but that Mr Ransome is afraid of them.

'My wife has never been stung by a wasp!', he retorted.

> [To even things out, after reading *Racundra's Third Cruise*, we now know that Evgenia was terrified by a mouse.]

Observed more closely, he was wearing dark trousers and socks, black slippers, a grey sweater over a white shirt showing a little blue and white patterned tie and old pepper-and-salt tweed jacket. He is large with a not-too-noticeable middle or stoop. His face seems large, with no neck showing and you notice its ruddiness and bright twinkling eyes behind steel-rimmed spectacles.

We all agreed that you have to sit up at a table for proper enjoyment of a meal. The rum butter-icing prompted Mr Ransome to say that the farm people in the Lakes make it. He spoke of 'huntsmen following the hounds on foot – it is too rough in the hill country for horses – arriving at a remote farm 15 or 20 miles from home, being given a mug of hot rum with a large lump of butter rapidly disappearing in a melting swirl – the best thing in the world'.

I asked if old *Mr & Mrs Swainson* in *Swallowdale* were real, but he said, 'The one kind of question I don't answer is the 'Are they real?' ones.

Later he said that he did not mind telling me that *Wild Cat Island* is a combination of two islands, one on Coniston. The other on Windermere doesn't have a good harbour, which he appropriated from the one on Coniston. *Cormorant Island* is really there. He admitted that he took the actual geography and 'gave it a stir', but that everything really exists somewhere: *Horseshoe Cove, Swallowdale*, the passages through *Kanchenjunga* [Coniston Old Man].

I asked if he cared to say whether the idea for *Swallows and Amazons* had come to him suddenly or over a long period of time. He said he had been thinking it over ever since he was young.

All this time we were eating away and whenever the girls looked my way to see if they may have more, he urged them to take something. I said that on this day they might have all they wanted. Every now and then we quoted favourite funny bits from his books that we all liked, and eventually he exclaimed that we must know his books by heart.

Mrs Ransome pointed out a photograph of *Lottie Blossom*, the last ship they had sailed. On a cross-channel trip two years earlier from Cherbourg to Southampton they had failed to hear the last weather report. As a result they fought a fierce storm and finally arrived at Southampton worn out. A customs launch came out to their mooring and after looking at their wine and the few things they had to declare, told them to turn in and get some sleep.

When a photo of the houseboat turned up, he said it was like *Captain Flint's* and we roared with laughter at the memory of the time the rightful owner returned to find a mess in his cabin and two strangers aboard. He says that is his favourite part in all the books. In another photo [of Low Ludderburn], he pointed out the upper windows of the room in which he had done much of the writing. One window looked out at some old yew trees and the other looked out onto the fells and across to Yorkshire.

There were a number of china cats around the house and ... I asked if he preferred cats to dogs. 'Yes', he replied. 'They're more hygienic than dogs and it's so cruel to keep a dog in the city'.

Mrs Ransome produced an album of the Broads, taken on an expedition with young friends. They had sailed in a party of six boats, each identified by its Jolly Roger so that they could be recognised at a distance over the low-lying meadows. There were views of the boats tied up along the bank or tied up to a quay while people shopped ashore.

The riverside shops were most accommodating: when, at the end of your cruise, you found you still had supplies you could turn them in at any grocers, even though you had bought them miles away. Everybody was most helpful and ready to lend a hand.

I said we must be going. Of course the girls were most reluctant to leave. Peggy had just started another story and Mr Ransome said of course she must finish it. Finally we all found ourselves in the hall getting ourselves ready. I said that we would be happy to invite them over. Mr Ransome said that to be honest, his wife really preferred not going out and he would consider that they had been asked.

'Thank you very much. We've had a lovely time', *he* said in a conversational tone with a twinkle in his eye.

The children threw their arms around his middle as far as they would go and, thus encumbered, he escorted us to the lift.

*   *   *

By April 1959, the ARs remained in London as Arthur was still "too crippled for us ever to dream of going to the primitive life at Hill Top". In answer to suggested comforts, Evgenia wrote in May:

> And nothing on earth will ever induce us to have a television set in our house or flat ... And we might yet hold you to your offer of driving our car to the Lakes.

Chapter 9

The 'Swallows' (1) – Taqui, Susie & Titty

A ll good Ransome followers develop an affection for the fictional characters of the 'Swallows'. In real life they were everything that readers
might expect, but each developed into something far more.

The young Altounyans came to live in the Lakes, at first at Bank Ground
Farm (Holly Howe) above the shore of Coniston Water. Here they shared the
glorious summer of 1928 with their parents, and with Arthur Ransome,
unaware that they were being scrutinised for immortality – as indeed
Ransome himself was initially.

On their return to Syria, he must have been egged on by their written
accounts of roasting boar over open fires and risky voyages in a leaky
dinghy. Mention was also made of their tents; these were made of sheets
hung from a rope between two trees and weighed down each side with
stones instead of tent pegs. Exactly the same type of tent was used in *Swallows and Amazons – and how much more practical they would have been
than trying to drive tent pegs into that rock-hard ground on the island.*

Just as if it had been intended, *Swallows and Amazons* was begun and, by
Arthur's later account, "almost wrote itself". His beloved Lakeland country-
side provided much of the inspiration but, unquestionably, the Altounyan
'Swallows' triggered ideas.

These two chapters attempt to cover some of my own memories and
associations with 'the Swallows'.

Meanwhile, why do 'Amazons' not appear in the title of this book? The
question so often posed is "who provided the exceptional and very
real-sounding inspirations for 'Nancy' and her admiring imitator 'Peggy?'"
There have been several very able candidates in real life, but none, I think,
with such long and opportune associations as the overlapping 'Swallows'.
Of these, there is just Taqui with the robust authority and inventiveness. A
much nearer amalgam than that of 'Captain John Walker', if we are to be
honest.

Taqui, 16-5-1917 to 14-7-2001

For balance and equality of gender, Taqui, the eldest 'Swallow', is translated
into the methodical and conscientious 'John Walker' in the books, my outstanding example in early life. And, as just to confuse, it was also a real-life

John Walker of the Ferry Nab Boat Yard who looked after *Swallow* for £5 a year – and of course Ivy, nee Walker, who was Arthur's first wife.

But in real life, Taqui was a tomboy, a resourceful initiator and so much more – in fact the forceful 'Nancy Blackett'. There is no quite comparable stimulant that I can see for the 'Amazons' elsewhere (though Evgenia was an unwitting candidate). 'Peggy', the younger sister of 'Nancy' was clearly in the same mould.

Taqui remembered, when "quite young", swimming across the lake to the *Gondola* pier. This was with Georgie Rawdon Smith, elder sister of Pauline. Both were Tent Lodge neighbours, unknown by Ransome except as "redcaps on the lake shore" and somewhat "Amazonian" types themselves – Pauline still sailing, when not swimming, wind-surfing and micro-lighting, in her eightieth year.

Taqui writes of their swim: "That's 440 yards, a quarter of a mile, carefully measured by my grandfather, W.G. Collingwood, on his large scale map when we climbed the hill and burst into his study, triumphant and wet".

One letter to AR from Aleppo, before the Ransome's holiday there and the writing of *Peter Duck*, ordered, "Come out at once and see what we're really like" – typical of how 'Uncle Arthur' was addressed by Taqui; very 'Nancy'-like, right enough!

Years later with her husband Robert Stephens, the children and hordes of cousins, she was so much a part of things, that happy day in 1960, when we all invaded the island. The water was clear as glass, the bottom easily visible between the two shores. Near the island there is a prominent stone which she told me, "is known locally as 'the Pike Rock'". On this a barge carrying copper ore was once holed and sank, leaving visible remnants of greenish copper ore on the bottom to this day. She and I thought this was the inspirational 'Pike Rock', typically shifted elsewhere in AR's writing, on which the *Swallow* was holed and sank in *Swallowdale*.

In 1996, TARS started a 'Save Peel Island Campaign' and, as I was their inadequate Northern Chairman at the time, this involved months of corresponding with the National Trust and Taqui. She wrote:

> … about SPIC, I quite agree with Brigit and, reading the NT letter, I seem to understand that, like us, their main aim is that the Island should be treated with respect. <u>Luckily</u>, it <u>is</u> an island, though these days that affords less "exclusivity" than it used to long ago.

With so much character in so many fields, Taqui might have inspired a storyteller in any number of ways. Her own books *Chimes from a Wooden Bell* published by Tauris in 1990 and *In Aleppo Once* (John Murray' 1969), are close-packed with more extraordinary detail in every line than one would think possible. They must speak for themselves.

Rather typically, Taqui was fourteen when she wrote the following letter to AR. It was from Aleppo, dated 15th November 1931 and a touch informal for the period. The spelling and punctuation follow the original:

My dear Uncle Arthur,

Swallowdale is EVEN BETTER than 'S's and A's' and you needn't have been so pessimistic about it. We do such a lot in the book and so many things happen, and the G.A. though actually a great bore to the Amazons is very amusing to read about. I'm sure no Walker aunt would be such a beast as the G.A. I love that part where Titty does the wax image stunt, and when the Amazons usually much more efficient than the Swallows forgot to take off their red caps. The wreck was terrible but all's well that ends well and I am *so* glad no shriek came from the Swallows. I've been trying to dive like Capt: John ever since I read the book but like Nancy I can't possibly keep under. I don't care what you say we all think Capt. Flint is exactly like you – is you, in fact. Have you got a red and green hanky? [*Swallowdale* Ch. VI] If not buy one *at once* and don't forget it when you pack up and start for the golden sands, waving palm trees, and camels.

The Ship's Baby [Brigit] says she can make a *much* better B than the one in the ships papers, and we can all write our names without those artificial looking blots. Those head pieces upside-down don't matter much, anyway they are so bad that they couldn't look much better the right way up. The only good picture is the one of the Amazons not in Pirate rig driving with the black G.A. I do wish the best of all natives [Dora] would do the illustrations.

The race was very exciting and at one time I really thought you were going to be so impartial as to let Amazon win. The next time I'm in a sailing boat alone I'm going to try Capt. John's trick, but I think I'll wait until we haven't only one boat.

Last Sunday we went to the farm hoping to sail but to our great disgust Beetle [also AR's nickname for Dora] (or Swallow) was high out of water wearing a coat of fresh wet paint. And of course there was a lovely breeze!

The ship's baby is busy painting 'Xmas cards'. She has just shown me a robin with a red body and blue tail whose yellow legs look like bulging Xmas stockings, balancing himself in a sky of blue blots and a brown thing supposed to be the sun. She'd painted over the robins eye but assured me he'd be able to see alright when the paint was dry!!

I'm not going to write to you again until 'Swallows in Syria' [entitled *Peter Duck*] is in print, and you can't write that until you've been here so do pack up and come. There is no excuse now for staying where you are.

With love from

Capt. John

of S.D. Swallow.

Susie, 6-1-1919 to 8-2-2003

Next down among the 'Swallows' was 'Susan' – Susie Altounyan. According to Titty, she "was indeed the efficient one of the group when it came to organising the housekeeping". She also possessed just those motherly concerns required of her in fiction, making her the exemplary 'Mate Susan.' But then, as I keep discovering, she was far more.

I'm so grateful to Susie's son, Hugues Villard, for his first-hand memories which I summarize as follows:

Born in Hampstead, Susie spent most of her childhood in Aleppo and then, aged fifteen, went to boarding school in Grasmere before study in Cambridge. She was very close to Ernest's sister, her Aunt Nora, who was married to a diplomat. She spent a lot of time with the Chauvets in Brittany at their country house near Concarneau by the sea. She really loved France.

Then, my thanks also to Taqui who, in her book *In Aleppo Once* writes:

Susie and I enjoyed the social whirl together for a bit after I arrived [as a young adult in Aleppo]. It was good to have someone of my own age to talk to, but she left for France a few months after I arrived. We took her down to the boat, and she stood on deck and waved us goodbye, wearing a red and white flowered frock. Then she faded away into the distance. I

Susie, aged about 20, by Dora Altounyan

kept that picture of her in my mind for the next seven years. Susie was caught by the Germans in occupied France and spent years in an internment camp.

My Hugues summary continues:

This was at Vittel and Susie, about twenty three, spent nearly four years there. She became a lifelong friend of a young girl called Shula and they managed to read, play tennis and have tea parties while "confined". She loved classical music and later succumbed to the Beatles.

Rather contrary to how readers may think of her, in real life she was a "wild" girl according to Shula, "the tall grasshopper", with long arms and legs, big eyes and an extraordinary mobile face. She was intrepid and, typically, would go down a hill on a cycle without brakes and, somehow, cross the camp's barbed wire to pick poppies in Spring!

She was clearly active in binding the bonds of friendship within the camp and would compensate the gloom with "a literary circle or an art gallery".

She escaped properly from the camp twice with false identity papers. These were sent from her Aunt Nora "in the middle of a cake". She was captured and put into jail in Fresnes near Paris for two months, "a very difficult period physically and mentally". She was freed before Liberation in an exchange of prisoners and got back to England in a boat from Lisbon!

After the war she studied art at the Ecole du Louvre in Paris – the Impressionists, Turner and water colours ... "She could spend lots of time watching the clouds moving and changing forms" and loved flowers and gardening.

In 1946, she married her Aunt Nora's nephew, Franck Villard, in Nantes. They had three children: Lucine in 1949, Eric in 1950 and Hugues in 1951.

Taqui by Dora Altounyan

Susie, Taqui, Titty & Roger at Hawkshead in 1928

Titty as a child

Titty, adult

The Ransomes at The Heald with Dora's portrait of
Titty on the wall

Dora at Lanehead in 1928

Titty, Suzanne Rawdon-Smith and Susie,
1928

Taqui, Susie and Titty –and a Brooklands air taxi

Tragically, Lucine died from an accident in the Langdale Pikes in the Summer of 1968 and Eric died of cancer in 1997.

They all loved to travel from Nantes to Lanehead and run down to the boathouse. In the '60s they would sail to Peel Island with Ernest. As in the books, they camped, fished for perch and swam.

"Her union with her husband was a failure, but she was courageous and her philosophy was "'Live and let live'". She was devoted to her children and everyone admired her intelligence, sense of humour, fighting spirit and strength of character.

*   *   *

Though still domiciled in France, Susie holidayed at Lanehead in 1959 and I rowed with Susie and her two small boys, Eric and Hugues in *Mavis* as we closely explored all the northern character of Coniston Water, and briefly tried 'tacking' breathlessly up the field, 'Roger' fashion, to 'Holly Howe'. I was staying at Lanehead at the time and being in touch with Susie was another rewardingly happy experience.

One evening, with Melkon and Titty, we went to Tilberthwaite Ghyll. It had never occurred to me before, but they all agreed that some parts, especially the steep approach, had been an influence in *Pigeon Post.*

Instinctively, I tended not to ask questions about the books but Susie seemed refreshingly open and recounted memories she had of 'Uncle Arthur' during that inspirational summer of 1928. She confessed that there had been some competitive sailing between *Swallow* and *Mavis/Amazon* and recalled how Ernest beat Arthur in what became the way *Swallow* beat *Amazon* during 'The Race' in *Swallowdale*:

> Just as *Swallow* came over the shallows at the point, Susan and John threw all their weight over on her lee side and brought her gunwale so low that a few drops lapped across it. This, of course, lifted her keel. The wind had dropped to next to nothing, and so, on her beam ends, *Swallow* slid across the shallows and into the river.

Susie most remembered the robust form of instruction issued from the shore by their father and 'Uncle Arthur'. They were prone to shout *"Idiot!"* and *"Duffer!"* respectively for any unseamanlike behaviour.

One of Ernest's edicts was *"when in doubt, let everything go!"* and this must have been especially relevant later when they experienced occasional squalls on the lake – which she admitted could be "very frisky".

The only negative side of 'Uncle Arthur' in her view was being discouraged from trailing their fingers in the water. He branded this as "tripperish", which they thought was limiting, and very unfair to visitors.

Susie most fondly remembered Peel Island picnics and how 'Uncle Arthur' had always been such great fun: "a child at heart and one of us".

Titty, 28-5-20 to 3-7-98

Titty (christened Mavis) and Roger, were the ones Judy and I came to know best. We had fond regard for them as fictional children; as real adults they became very much more. Titty really was a deep and imaginative thinker; "a dreamer", Roger once described her, "exactly like AR's Titty", and, "perhaps a little vague at times, and inclined to use intuition rather than logic". Her younger sister Brigit, on the other hand, described her as "the liveliest and most imaginative of us". Yes, and she was certainly one of the most artistic members of her immediate generation, a gifted thread which still continues to run through one after another.

Perhaps it was that, being so imaginative as a child, Titty had a special fondness for 'Uncle Arthur'. Quite naturally, she became one of his best-loved characters. She happily remembered him being impressed by her single-handling of *Mavis* in light airs and, aged eight, escorted by Ernest in *Mavis*, by her swimming across the lake from Lanehead to the Coniston landing stage.

She told us how she stayed with the Ransomes for a while, at the age of thirteen. They, having no shared offspring – and Arthur's relations with his daughter Tabitha being irrevocably harmed by his separation from her mother Ivy – the ARs subsequently asked Ernest if they might adopt her. Not surprisingly, he refused and Dora gave them her portrait of Titty "instead". It followed them everywhere – and can be dimly seen up on the left of the Ransome's sitting room wall at 'The Heald' in photograph.

When the children became older and more able to think and act as individuals, Arthur found this confused his picture and portrayal of them, because in contrast, they age almost imperceptibly in the books. To make matters worse, they began to write to him in some discomfort from school – having been told by other children that "you are 'the Swallows'" but "not always like the 'Walker' children".

Titty boarded, along with Taqui and Susie, at Annisgarth School in Windermere. Then they progressed to the Perse School in Cambridge, where they attended as day-girls, each staying with different families. From there, Titty went on to study under Henry Moore at the Chelsea School of Art. "One of the most promising pupils of the year," according to Brigit.

Titty was the last person on earth to cultivate a Ransome Image, but while once visiting Peel Island, did admit to us "being quietly amused when hearing a small girl call out to her parents, I'm on Titty's rock!"

In 1939, her summer holiday in Aleppo turned into a long wartime stay, during which she worked for a news agency in Jerusalem and "wrote head-lines" for the *Jerusalem Post*. After the war, she returned to art at the Chelsea but, having gained her diploma, travelled again to Aleppo where in 1952 she took over the administration of the Altounyan Hospital from Brigit.

Titty and Melkon Guzelian got married in 1954 and, had politics been different, I think Titty would have loved to go back there and live a simple life with Melkon, surrounded by his family's vineyards and orchards – painting. Instead, they returned to England.

So fortunately *for me* and almost as if intended, they came "home" to Lanehead, just in time for me in1958. But resources were scant and, with a large house and elderly parents used to palatial surroundings, times became very hard indeed. Arrival of the delightful children, Asadour and Rahel, lifted everyone's spirits and Titty wrote that Rahel had been "anointed with myrrh".

But Melkon had increasing back problems and a consequent inability to work consistently as a diesel authority in Windermere. It became increasingly apparent that some other means of income was essential. They naturally refused to borrow and she and I considered the only apparent alternative – of them providing Bed & Breakfast accommodation. Though Titty was fearful of her lack of experience and the less than pristine state of Lanehead, she wrote suggesting that "*we* might start up a shop inside the house as an added attraction to lodgers and an outlet for our creative energies". This referred to our less than abundant artistic productivity but I was encouraged and flattered.

Titty, 26-10-59:

> … an eventful life is not always what one requires! I suppose I'm really one of the cabbage people, but such a lot of (to me) interesting things can happen within the horizon of a cabbage-like existence.

> All the livestock are thriving, including the ducklings, which I find much more loveable than hens. Rahel still doesn't do anything spectacular but is an adorable baby, and Asadour really does seem to gain in sense every day.

> I hope you are well and that some star or other is occupied in rising on your horizon. I don't quite know what I mean by that, but assure you they are not empty words.

How Titty could possibly have anticipated that I was to meet Judy just five weeks later at a cocktail party, remains a mystery!

Then came Ani, especially loved by the whole family, but alas, severely disabled. Lanehead, with Ernest undomesticated and Dora now handicapped by a stroke, was almost impossible to keep going, yet the rest of the family offspring, including a multiplicity of children, turned up regularly and the house was often bulging.

During family visits, Ani's feeding time was always a special occasion and I remember the sitting room being packed with enthralled youngsters. Feeling rather intrusive, I sat in embarrassed aloofness, facing outwards on the open windowsill – later to be teasingly berated by Titty for my "western decadence!"

I could never ever have repaid their hospitality; but service to others seemed to be the Altounyan family's natural role in life. Judy and I managed only once to take Ernest and Dora exploring and for an evening meal in Windermere. They both insisted on sitting on the floor in the back of my coupe and behaved uproariously, rolling from side to side as we raced round the corners up to Hawkshead Hill and down the other side on our way to Windermere. Otherwise, life at Lanehead seemed entertainment enough for everyone.

Later, with Judy, our main token of thanks and entertainment involved pubs. Typically, we took Titty and Melkon to the *Drunken Duck* above

Hawkshead and *The Sun Inn* at Coniston. There, Titty showed us round the Donald Campbell photographs with a rare show of pride. For her and Melkon it was a poignant reminder of much that had happened while gazing down from Lanehead at Campbell's activity and *Bluebird*'s boathouse across the lake. We never asked what she saw of the fatal record attempt, it was too obviously harrowing and an event she would never forget.

Titty was generally regarded as 'Mavis' locally and valued for what she *was*, few seemed aware of her vicarious fame. Indeed, as things were, the trick locally for us was *not* to shout "what's yours, Titty?" as if anyone would, across a crowded bar!

The stable block at Lanehead was gradually made into 'High Lanehead' and this allowed Titty and Melkon to let it out as a house in itself and a modest money spinner. For what it was worth, Judy and I insisted on paying for our visits and Titty wrote, in her typical fashion:

> We would consider it a great honour if you would consent to stay for a week and tell us what is wrong – All right, we'll charge you something, but it must be according to what we can manage to provide by then. So sixpence off for every spoon or waste paper basket that is missing!

Much later on 7th December 1964, Titty, writing of the death of Dora, and about how both she and Roger each thought the other had let us know in time for the funeral:

> ... a perfectly beautiful day, which was as it should have been, though I suppose too much to expect as a right, even for my mother.

*   *   *

Lanehead had been left to Titty by her parents and it was at this same sad time that she wrote: "The [Campbell] tragedy on Coniston has made us all very gloomy". Campbell was much admired, not least for his bravery, by Coniston in general. The family had known privately of George Constantinesco's misgivings. It transpired that he had written to Campbell:

> ... if the boat starts longitudinal bumps, the gyroscopic reaction is a substantial snaking which will be difficult to correct with the rudder. Your task will be to steer a gigantic spinning-top, spinning and sliding on the water! Again pardon me to insist, but really I am very uneasy knowing the tremendous risk you are taking.

But by January 1967, Titty and Melkon were depressed for a string of far more personal reasons. In spite of all that had happened in that lovely house over four generations, they at last felt obliged to put it on the market. It was on offer for months and early on, Titty asked if we could buy it for what seemed a derisory sum. Any capital and livelihood we had was tied up in Berry Bros. but the missed opportunity saddens me still. More to the point, it seemed tragic that Lanehead should be lost to the whole family forever. It was not our business, yet far-reaching consequences seemed inevitable.

For the Guzelian family, it meant the move to a small but pleasant bungalow at Haws Bank, across the lake, with a cart track down to the shore.

As if the trauma of this time had not been enough, much of Titty's lasting distress with Ransome associations stemmed acutely from this period. For, having been inveigled into giving an interview on the BBC about the books, she was in consequence severely reprimanded by 'Aunt Genia' on 3rd September 1967, a real scorcher! In response, on 2nd October, Titty, wrote a reasoned but forthright riposte, severing their acknowledged relationship

Asadour, Ani, Titty & Rahel at Haws Bank in 1968

forever. At the time, I caught not a whiff of it from either side and feel I might have done something for them both if I had. But both were intrinsically kind in spirit and matters seemed to come right long before Evgenia's death eight years later.

Evgenia's earlier letter to Taqui on 1st September, now in the Brotherton Collection, is a nut-shell revelation of perceived Altounyan piracy, in place of what could and should have been an idyllic relationship between Evgenia, now so vulnerably on her own, and the 'Swallows' in general.

By this time, Melkon's back and Berry Bros. were both in terminal decline. Briefly, we wondered if, between us, we could possibly branch out into selling cloth and/or cars to Syria. In this, Melkon's part was to explore "demand" in the Lebanon while I was entrusted with shipping agents. Responses were universally negative.

One evening, while staying with the family at Haws Bank, we asked Titty "how the children are taking to *Swallows and Amazons*" – only to be told that they knew nothing about it. Instead, they went to bed with *Old Peter's Russian Tales* etc.

However, in an unguarded moment over breakfast one morning, a rare disclosure was made. Titty told Judy and me how to find *The Dog's Home*, as in *The Picts and the Martyrs*.

She was not able to join us but we shot off and were thrilled and astonished to find it still existing in the woods on the east side of the lake. Judy and I had always regarded this refuge from the 'Great Aunt' for 'Dick' and 'Dorothea' as a bit of storyteller's fantasy; it wasn't. It was exactly as in the books, albeit run down and over-grown. In those days, it even had its name showing faintly on the door: 'The Dogs' Home'.

Years later, I was asked by Roger Wardale if it really existed and where it could be found. It was subsequently rediscovered and restored, digging through layers of latter-day and not always wholesome history, by The Arthur Ransome Society and Forest Enterprise, to whom it now belongs. A story in itself!

The Dogs' Home as in 'The Picts and The Martyrs' (photo by Roger Wardale)

* * *

All mention of the books and indeed the Ransomes remained taboo with Titty for several years. Then a letter arrived from her dated 2nd October 1978, about another Ransome "fairy tale" structure – but fancy asking me! This welcome change was such a reversal as to be worthy of a Hollywood-style double-take:

It's really to pick your brains, John, about "the world of Arthur Ransome". The September "Lancashire Life" contained an article [a revealing summary of how Titty felt] about the "origins" of Swallows and Amazons of all things. I hope it didn't cause Uncle Arthur & Aunt Genia to turn in their graves ... [It was] by our local writer ... on subjects of local interest (we hope) – all of them [professionally] illustrated with photographs by Asadour ... and other family photographs.

Anyway, as a result, ... the Editor has been receiving letters from readers; and one of them asks whether a certain hut mentioned in "Winter Holiday" ever really existed ... and I have a strong feeling from the way he writes about it that it really did exist.

The author, ... though a very nice person, isn't even a Swallow fan (!) and he read none of the books, except to dip into them for the purpose of his article. So he called on us this evening to ask if I could help... We all know that AR was writing about his own childhood experiences and not about those children whose names he took in vain [do we? The AR-oriented decree lived on it seems!] (and the article makes that point). "Winter Holiday" in particular is probably based on the Great Freeze of eighteen-ninety-something which he describes so vividly in his autobiography. So that hut, "built more than a hundred years ago" (I'm quoting from memory), could have existed more than 80 years ago and been destroyed long before our lifetimes ... at the edge of Windermere rather than Coniston. Melkon has the idea that you may once have discussed this (among other things) with Arthur Ransome himself. If you did and if you are willing to disclose what you learnt I should be most grateful ... Just a small point but it seems a shame not to satisfy people's interest – or do you disagree? It's a ticklish subject. I shall quite understand if you'd rather not discuss it. Anyway it's made a nice excuse for a letter ...

After this surprising *volte-face*, Judy and I vowed to gently pull her leg about it at the first opportunity. More to the point, we saw, with such pleasure, that she seemed to be recovering from the "Aunt Genia" *fracas* which had taken such toll.

However, to have questioned Ransome back in the 60s about the legitimacy of the 'North Pole' building (which is what Titty's correspondent had meant) would, even after years of "cultivating", have invited the kind of rebuke he reserved especially for "fans".

All I was able to suggest to Titty at the time was that "the old view-house" as AR called it in Chapter XXVI of *Winter Holiday*, had the ring of authority and was almost certainly near remnants of the Roman fort of 'Galava' she knew well. I added that the last time that Windermere was completely frozen over to allow full-scale skating was in February 1929, in nice time to write the book, first published, appropriately, just before Christmas 1933.

Almost fifteen years after Titty's letter, something of a revelation occurred in 1993. This related to Dowsing as in *Pigeon Post* and it was under the auspices of The Arthur Ransome Society that it took place in the manner described below.

Incidentally, I'm confident that Jeremiah was not quite referring to this type of thing when he speaks against "divinations" in Chapter14:14 and "diviners" in 27:9.

In *Pigeon Post*, 'Dick' says "the man who came to school called himself a water diviner", but the less ambiguous term 'dowser' is also used in the book. It was this ancient technology of dowsing which was demonstrated so convincingly in the effort to locate the 'old view house'. It seems that most of us can dowse with practical help and if we concentrate on what we are doing. I see it as nothing to do with inane mysticism or nauseous occult but just another very wonderful God-given facility.

The initial exploration was recorded at the time by Jim Andrews and printed in the society journal *Mixed Moss*. I summarise as follows:

> An impromptu expedition, to find the site of the building described as the 'North Pole' in Arthur Ransome's *Winter Holiday*, set off under the leadership of Dick Kelsall, on the appropriately cold but sunny afternoon of Saturday 13th March, 1993. The party consisted of Dick, Alan Wilkins, archaeologist (who had been doing considerable map-research on the subject), and Judy and Jim Andrews (whose speciality is archaeological dowsing).

> Dick had a vivid memory of being taken for a walk by an aunt in Ambleside when aged 7 [in 1929] – and clearly recalled being shown a curious little wooden building with a sort of bay-window overlooking the lake and a flagpole projecting from its roof. Dick had always thought it to be 'the Old View House' used by AR in *WH*.

Research, however, indicated that no structure had existed there since the mid-1950s, and certainly nothing was now visible on the ground. Local tradition nevertheless maintained that there used to be 'summer houses' in Borrans Park – a largely grass-covered area between the Ambleside Roman Fort and Wateredge Hotel.

Dick proceeded alone to where he recalled seeing the 'flagpole building', while the remainder of the expedition watched from afar, only joining him when he halted. Alan observed that none of the 1820-1935 maps he had so far found indicated *any* structure at that point, to which Dick replied that he couldn't be sure to within 20 feet or so, but this *looked* to be about where the building would have been. He was roughly 57 yards south-south-east of the pedestrian gateway off Borrans Road, and some 74 feet from the lake. The grass sloped gradually down, just west of a small outcrop, to a gentle shelving beach – simply *ideal* for the wrecking of Dick and Dorothea's sailing sledge ... no reaction of the dowsing rods took place on the approach to Dick, but about one foot behind his heels, the rods crossed vigorously, indicating disturbance of the subsoil and possible latter-day presence of some kind of wall.
Following the line thus found, a corner was located by the sudden re-angling of the rods, and marked by a peg. This process was then continued, until the outline of a small, thin-walled building was fully traced out.

[Jim's dowsing rods and those used most easily by other dowsers are typi-cally made from wire coat-hangers cut in two places. These are bent at right angles to form 16-inch (40cm) arms and 6-inch (15cm) legs. The legs are held vertically, free to swivel. The arms are kept horizontal and pointing forwards as steadily as possible. They tend to swing, usually inwards when directly above an underground disturbance or aquifer.] Jim's account con-tinues:

The southern aspect was in the form of a kind of 'apse', consisting of angled facets. The northern half of the structure appeared to have been rectangular, and a square shape measuring about 3ft x 3ft, perhaps a hearth-stone, had left a dowsable trace slightly east-of-centre inside the back (northern) wall.

Further dowsing (conducted with increasing difficulty owing to Jim's mounting state of excitement) revealed the presence of a post hole within the building (see plan), suggesting a pole base diameter of roughly 10ins.

A slate disk, let into the Borrans Park grass, now marks the site perma-nently – although there is still nothing, nothing whatever else to be seen on the grass.

We never did ask Titty, and its too late now, whether she, whose counter-part had been able to dowse for water so dramatically in *Pigeon Post*, had actually done any dowsing in real life. Brigit once told us how, in adulthood, "Titty did dowse quite a lot". This was not as in *Pigeon Post*, where Ransome had her using a forked hazel stick, but "with a pendulum". Apparently, she favoured a small weight of turned hardwood "suspended on a piece of thin twine". I wonder what she had in mind – *and having in mind what you are looking for does seem to help.*

Is dowsing real or imaginary? I'm sceptical by nature but Judy's brother-in-law's father, also a surgeon, spoke of finding much-needed water by this means in India before the war. With this and the veracity of those taking part in this latest find, it convinces me. This is another of God's wonderful world-wide gifts, practised, certainly over the centuries. It should be more widely recognised!

*   *   *

Mobility was becoming a problem for Titty but she and Melkon did manage to take us to Beacon Tarn. She seemed to assume that we would know it as 'Trout Tarn' – where, in Chapter 15 of *Swallowdale*, the fictional 'Titty' caught a large trout and 'Roger' fell on it. She even pointed out the nearby Beacon as 'Watch Tower Rock' – an indication of her not entire disregard for the books.

Our own exploring, with a particular fondness for woodland footpaths linking remote pubs, was never as organised as it should have been. Judy and I have always wished we lived in Lakeland and could gradually attempt to imitate Melkon who, typically, would walk round Coniston Water one way in the morning, taking a collection of local dogs who could manage the distance, and the other way in the afternoon. He once caused Titty to alert the local authorities when he failed to turn up, having "taken a wrong turning" as he afterwards explained – having passed through Ambleside, Bowness, Newby Bridge and Blawith on his "way home". He got a thorough dressing down but we were all on his side.

As a young man, this was the sort of mileage of which AR himself was capable. In *The Autobiography of Arthur Ransome*, he tells how he would start from his lodgings in Cartmel and enjoy a beer or two with the poet Lascelles Abercrombie in the *Hark to Melody* at Haverthwaite. Heartbreakingly, this is no longer an Inn but the thought keeps me in imaginary rapture.

He would then continue up the eastern side of Coniston Water to Lanehead and from there spend the rest of the day on the lake, most often visiting Peel Island, accompanied by the Collingwood girl/s, before returning on foot to Cartmel.

All this, even excluding the sailing or rowing bit of at least eight miles, was a thirty-mile excursion – and would have been so much easier on a bicycle!

*   *   *

Ups and downs continued for Titty and Melkon. By 1986 Asadour was a renowned photographer and Rahel had four lovely children. Three years later came the death of their so-loved Ani. They were strangely ill-prepared for this and never seemed to recover fully.

Titty did not manage to be present when, sixty years after *S&A* and the start of things, Taqui, Susie and Brigit celebrated with TARS in a visit to Pin Mill and Alma Cottage. It was a gentle celebration of *We Didn't Mean to go to Sea* but Taqui recalled how "We were all very keen sailors but were never obedient in the Boy Scout way they were in the book".

After the loss of Lanehead, there were inevitably times when Titty felt out of touch with the rest of the family as well as the Ransomes. Quite unexpectedly, I found myself a go-between for both parties on a number of occasions. This was not a role, or rather the need for it, which I enjoyed.

Melkon and Titty finally left Haws Bank, Coniston for Bradford in 1991, "to be nearer the children". The walls

Melkon & Titty, December 1991, Bradford

of their tiny new home became covered once more with their share of the lovely paintings from Lanehead and where to put all the books became a problem too, as the upper floors began to sag under their weight.

They had settled a mere half hour from home but this coincided with minor problems and we must have seemed slow in inviting them over. Hence Titty's *own* attractive semi-abstract Christmas card stating inside, "so near and yet so far".

Melkon and Titty's visits were an inadequate response to the happy holidays we had with them but they did evoke happy memories. Typically Titty, so appreciative in her modest way, gave special attention and encouragement to our daughter Kate's own paintings and *collage*, and so envied the large new studio we had built in the loft. She wrote of the "entertainment" supplied by our grandchildren, "there was never a dull moment."

In March 1995, I asked: "Do I detect a note of chagrin and dismay in your Christmas card, over our Ransomised Christmas cartoon?" (this was collated from a catalogue of AR book illustrations and intended as a tribute).

Titty wrote back:

My abject apologies for the Christmas card which was unintentionally formal [lacking the usual token of

Christmas card from Titty and Melkon, painted by Titty

Sincere apologies to the artists – Stephen Spurrier, Clifford Webb, Mary Shepard and Arthur Ransome

affection] ... it was obviously meant for someone else.

While on the subject of cards – though you call yours a cartoon – how right you are! I could hardly believe my eyes and I must confess that instead of displaying it I put it carefully away in a drawer. Thank you very much all the same. I can't help it, you know how I feel about all that stuff ...

Some time later, preparations were being made for the film *An Awfully Big Adventure* – a BBC2 "look at the life and work" of AR. This was not shown until February 1998 – with Taqui, the eldest, looking so young and vital, making several informative appearances and commenting that "Arthur liked people very much or hated them very much". Desmond and Dick were also included, "so at home once more where they started off and had signalled to the Ransomes across the valley from Barkbooth". Here they showed us where and how the 'Hollywood' photo references were made, for later transition into book illustrations.

For most viewers, what really amazed was their first sight of Titty. Tragically for us, she was suddenly looking more frail than we could comprehend. But had she "finally come out?" No, but I think she enjoyed saying, affectionately, what she thought of "Uncle Arthur's drawing skills". Also, for the official record, "the consequences of using real names".

Titty 13-6-97 [in rather shaky writing. I think this was after the actual filming] wrote:

... at last I am spending <u>all</u> my time "trying to paint" & that is really all I want to do... Something to do with having lived a very full & interesting, but at the same time a very frustrated life, perhaps I don't want any new experiences until I do something about the thousands that I've already had. I mean <u>painted</u> about them... there won't be any masterpieces, but that is not my aim. I shall not mind if my life comes to an end tomorrow ...

Titty's life was indeed coming to an end, and Melkon, feeling lost without her, died while in Aleppo two years later. For both of them, times of oppressive sadness were over. Judy and I now picture Titty as she really wanted to be, in glorious peace at last, painting the most beautiful scenery imaginable, with Melkon close by.

Chapter 10

The 'Swallows' (2) – Roger & Brigit

Roger, 24-10-22 to 10-12-87

Roger's character was very much that of Ransome's 'ship's boy'. Such frequent, playful and amusing remarks were so ably adapted by the author. In real life, his fictional love of steam gives way to sail.

Born in Aleppo, he was, like his sisters, schooled in England, as Ransome himself had so vehemently advised while writing *Peter Duck*, while on holiday with the family out there.

As a six-year-old, with both parents in Syria, Roger and his sisters stayed at Bank Ground Farm/'Holly Howe' Coniston. They were on their own for most of the time except for Elmast the Armenian housekeeper. With the

village two miles away by road, they felt isolated but the few locals they met were invariably "friendly natives". Notable, in Roger's mind, was the "road man". He had one eye and one arm with a hook, almost certainly a WW1 casualty, and used to greet them, whenever they returned from school or visits to Syria, with a large bag of home-made toffee, "the best ever tasted".

Roger in 'Tub', Coniston 1928 *(Photo by Titty)*

Roger first went to Abbotsholme School on the Staffordshire/Derbyshire border. Aged 8, but far away from the family and feeling teased about his Armenian name, it may not have been the happy experience it should have been. From there he progressed to college in Aleppo. But for Roger, Lakeland was the very antithesis of school and, as Brigit commented:

> To Roger, Coniston Lake and the Crake valley in which it lies was everything. On the lake and in boats he was totally happy and absorbed and *Mavis* had been his main craft ever since he was six.

> There he spent as much time as possible. Often this was while fishing and, when out sailing in the company of older sisters, their special joy was to cook recently caught fish on a primus, *while still under way*, as it tasted even better".

Just as my scout master had advocated, they were exponents of both fishing and bathing off a lee shore, as "it is only about the top yard of water which becomes warmed by the sun, and wind has the effect of piling this up on a lee shore, making it more enjoyable for fish and bathers alike".

In early days, when the children stayed at Bank Ground, Mrs Jolly, the farmer's wife, used to serve up same-type food, cooked very plainly, almost every day. Provisions for the island usually included potatoes and onions which were then baked in the campfire.

Roger and Taqui sailing *Mavis*

What I never heard about or saw in practice were the cooking facilities as first described and illustrated by Clifford Webb in *Swallows and Amazons*. I suspect these were a very rare departure from Ransome's actual-life experiences:

> Roger was there, looking at a neat ring of stones, making a fireplace with the ashes of an old fire in it. At opposite sides of the ring two stout forked sticks had been driven into the ground and built round with heavy stones, and another long stick was lying across the fireplace in the forks of the two upright sticks, so that a kettle could be hung on it over the fire.

Whenever Judy and I tried this, we found the forked sticks difficult to cut neatly without a saw. Then, they invariably split down the middle as we tried to hammer them into Peel Island's hard and stony ground. We found a

Fireside comparisons, the left side one from S&A drawn by Clifford Webb

much easier method for suspending a kettle over the fire, simply by tying three branches into what became a tripod and straddling this, robust and portable appliance, over the fire with a length of kettle-hanging chain – as did the charcoal burners as illustrated on right.

Unlike in Ransome's own childhood, the children never remembered seeing any charcoal burners, except in Syria. But happily, it was in the company of 'Uncle Arthur' that they saw a real water spout in the Mediterranean, though perhaps not with the perceived embellishments by 'Roger' as depicted in "his" *Peter Duck* drawing – with pirates and bits of ship engulfed in the upward flow!

Apart from the kettle-hanging, which I'm sure AR managed without a second thought in real life, I detect just one other impracticality in the books. In *Swallows and Amazons*, Chapter IX, the 'Swallows' are ordered to put their "Hands up!" and, thanks to falling flat on their faces, the "arrow passed harmlessly over their heads". One wonders what practical experience Arthur's generation had of such domestic playthings. After reading the book, my so-valued 9th birthday present was a bow and three arrows. These, from loving parents, were of best quality and the arrows, each with three angled feathers, had metal tips which could penetrate almost anything. Even after years of practice, I have become glad that such toys are no longer available – as arrows and my subsequent very powerful catapult, both of uncertain aim, are potentially lethal quite apart from the broken windows. In my case, handed-down air rifles were far safer except, so regrettably for a far away sparrow.

Melkon on Coniston Old Man

During each holiday, the 'Swallow' children, like their uncle Robin Collingwood when aged *four*, would climb up past the copper mines to the top of Coniston Old Man. Roger remembered on some occasions as they neared the top, having his exposed skin rubbed with snow by elder sisters, "to keep me warm!"

Years later he got to know Switzerland but, in contrast, found it "too big". Also, in the course of work, he visited "some of the most wonderful parts of the world" – yet still found "the beauty, tranquillity and atmosphere of Lakeland unsurpassed".

As in the stories, there had indeed been a tall pine 'lighthouse tree' at the northern end of Peel

Island but this was blown down before the war. In a Radio 4 'Bookshelf' programme, it was refreshing to hear Roger's voice, telling how when sailing past the island in *Mavis* one day, he was astonished to see a fully-grown pine standing there once more. He couldn't believe his eyes! Unfortunately, this proved to be a temporary stand-in lashed to a smaller tree for the making of the first *Swallows and Amazons* film. Happily, Taqui, with the persuasive auspices and company of TARS, planted a 'replacement' fir in February 1994. By then, the island being property of the National Trust, it had to be in the presence of a Forestry official.

The freezing over of Coniston Water, or 'Cuniston' as the Altounyans invariably pronounced it, was in the winter of 1939/40 when Roger found what an extraordinary feeling it was to walk on the "water" they knew so well under sail. They were actually able to reach Peel Island on foot, nearly four miles away. He told how the black ice was just like glass, in which they saw some minnows which appeared to be frozen near the surface, just as in *Winter Holiday*. They also found 'sweet little' mice on the island which had probably walked across from the mainland, only about 150 yards from its eastern shore.

I am tantalised still by the thought that, *at this very same time*, Juliet and I were enjoying much the same things just over the hill, on Esthwaite Water. If *only* we had known!

*   *   *

During the war, Roger served with distinction in the RAF, training in Rho-

desia – with two cousins of mine as we later discovered, before being posted to England as a Hurricane fighter pilot. He was an aviation expert for which he was awarded the AFC in 1944 and finished up training pilot-instructors.

Some of his leaves were spent with Dora's youngest sister, his Aunt Ursula, and her family in Troutbeck. Always fun to be with, he

Roger & Ernest, RAF & RAMC

was an especially welcome visitor in those forlorn days. He used to roll up on his motorbike, discarding layers of clothing and yards of his old school scarf.

Ursula's elder daughter, Sara, was away in the WAAF; but her other daughter, Philippa, was studying Art at Lancaster University. She told me how Roger and she would set off on bicycles to Ambleside, the motorbike having been banned by her mother. There, they caught the once-a-week bus to Coniston, where it remained all day and created a nagging dead-line lest they be stranded. Alternatively, they would cycle all the way.

Stunt man

Their usual stop was at Kirby Quay, where the Hawkshead to Coniston road first meets the lake. Here, their cousin, Janet Gnosspelius, daughter of their Aunt Barbara and her husband, Oscar 'Squashy Hat' Gnosspelius, kept her boat. Borrowing it, they would row across to the Lanehead boat-house, jump ship into *Mavis* and head down the lake under sail. They always fished, catching minnows first, as bait for perch, which in turn was bait for pike. To take a pike home for her mother to stuff and bake earned particular praise in those lean days!

As young adults, they had come to acknowledge Coniston as "tricky to sail on", with its sudden squalls and flat calms. One continues to marvel that, as children, they managed to survive!

On a good day, Roger and Philippa would speed all the way to Peel Island, to enjoy a picnic and make hot drinks over the fire. At teatime, the wind often dropped completely, the clouds would disappear and the lake become a looking-glass as they cheerfully set off to ghost back under sail or row the 4 miles.

"*Mavis* seemed to weigh a ton" and sometimes, Roger, still capable of acting the goat, would decide that better headway would be made if Philippa rowed and he pushed. Stripping down to underpants, he would leap over the side while she rowed and, from time to time, refilled and lit his pipe for him. So they "progressed" before Roger climbed back, pipe still drawing as he grabbed an oar and they made more sensible haste pulling together. On occasions, they were obliged to run all the way back to the village, to catch the bus by the skins of their teeth. Asthma cannot have been such a problem to Roger in those days!

Usually, there was no one else on the lake, but one day, when about to start for home, they saw 'Uncle Arthur' running down through 'Anna's Wood' and setting sail in his own dinghy, *Coch-y-Bonddhu*, "to see who it was that had the cheek to be on his island", as Roger put it.

Catching them up, Ransome seemed almost disappointed. "Oh, it's only you!," he said. "We'll race you back to Tent Lodge jetty!" Roger called back.

Straightaway, Arthur could be seen to cheer up, knowing that in

Roger and Hella's transport

Marriage, 1951

Coch-y-Bonddhu he had the faster boat. Nevertheless, somehow, *Mavis* arrived there first –
and his chagrin at being beaten was amplified by "a mere girl" having sailed
her all the way from Peel Island while Roger lay on the bottom boards smoking his pipe, popping up now and then to do a bit of bailing out. At this,
'Uncle Arthur' was visibly upset and, with rather scant farewells, went
fuming back down the lake!

*   *   *

After the war, Roger followed Ernest by attending Emmanuel College, Cambridge, then Medical School at The Middlesex Hospital. While studying
there he had the good fortune to stay with Taqui and family in Barnes – and
to fall in love with their charming German *au pair*. Roger married Hella a
year later in 1951, and they honeymooned on Peel Island.

This was not unalloyed bliss, as they suffered downpours worthy of 'The
Storm' in *Swallows and Amazons*. Similarly, their tent was not entirely
waterproof and Hella remembers waking to see her shoes "swilling past" her
head. No sooner had they left, than they were ordered by megaphone to
"Clear the course!" And sat amongst reeds to see Campbell flash past in
Bluebird at unbelievable speed.

Dr Roger was made Assistant Physician and Surgeon to his father at the
Altounyan Hospital in Aleppo but found it very difficult working under his
father's influence and became visibly over stressed and "virtually driven
out by local xenophobia". The trauma was brought about by having to cope
with outbreaks of tuberculosis, typhoid and tetanus. He returned to
England in 1954, depressed and disillusioned by what he regarded as his
dismal failure.

*   *   *

Roger started research at Benger Laboratories in Holmes Chapel where the Assistant Works Manager was John Pritchard, who recalled at the end of January, 1904:

> Each day about half a dozen "lesser brass" sat at a reserved table in the staff dining room and, when he was not out visiting patients, Roger was one of our number. Harry Howell was not, since he was non staff being nominally a fitter in the engineering dept., but for most days he was seconded to the works, maintaining intricate packaging machinery, and sometimes to the research department, so he was well known to us all.
>
> It was at these lunches that Roger sometimes looked round with his big appealing eyes and said "I have got an idea that I want to try out, but I need some healthy young men to help me". In other words he was looking for guinea pigs. There was never any shortage of volunteers as we always knew that Roger was not asking us to do anything which he had not already tried out on himself.

In those days, smoking was allowed in the dining rooms and as soon as the meal was finished, out came Roger's pipe and he lit up, much to the dislike of some non-smokers. Eventually, they thought of curing him of the habit and surreptitiously mixed cedar wood pencil shavings with the tobacco in his pouch – sitting back to watch results. This produced a huge cloud of blue smoke, made Roger's eyes water and invoked such a fit of coughing that we feared it more likely to kill than cure him – and at that time we did not know the extent of his asthma problem.

In 1956, Roger became Principal Research Associate with Fisons, who had now taken over Benges. His chief interest was understandably in asthma and bronchitis, of which, like so many of us, he now had first hand experience. Dyslexia was also, for him, a tiresome and demeaning difficulty – but nothing to the problems which were to come.

He had realised for some time that guinea-pigs have little in common with man "except that neither species wagged a tail". Because of this, he decided instead to experiment *on himself* and, already being allergic to guinea-pigs, he cooked up some of their hair and inhaled an aerosol of the resultant 'soup' – and promptly had a sharp attack of asthma – subject later of the film 'Hair Soup' in which David Suchet played Roger. As I remember, Barbara Altounyan was the instigator and Judy and I were able to give very minor assistance.

At this time he had been granted a disused ward in the Monsall Hospital at Crumpsall, north Manchester. This was "far out of their way" [from his detractors at Fisons] as he remarked with a grin – where he could treat extreme cases. He found it helpful to the morale of his discouraged and often distressed patients "to see their own doctor coughing, spitting and wheezing, just like themselves".

When first I met him in 1958, "a so-called world expert" had just pronounced his experiments "quite useless, unproven – and unmarketable". Being Roger, he carried on undaunted, testing two new compounds a week in clandestine development until, five years later in 1963, the first break-through came. One substance was found to afford nearly complete protection and he scribbled 'Eureka' on the spirometry chart – only to run into further indecipherable difficulties later.

Mercifully, a replacement Research Director at Fisons was put in charge and, with his far-seeing co-operation, a few months later the new drug emerged, which Roger christened 'INTAL'.

Surprisingly, the next problem was how to administer it, as some patients were unable to co-ordinate their breathing with a pressurised inhaler. At this point, having spent his war years as a pilot, Roger thought, "why not get them to inspire through a tube inside which a propellor [as he spelled it] rotates and somehow releases the drug automatically?"

Somewhat to Hella's alarm, he set up a pilot plant on the arm of their drawing-room sofa. He made small propellers carved out of thick plastic and mounted on glass tubes melted over at one end on the kitchen stove. Roger fiddled and inhaled from various models for months until, by chance, one seemed to rotate differently. Slightly out of kilter, this one vibrated and "felt like a dentist's drill. I loaded a capsule, sucked again and, Hey Presto!– a beautiful cloud!"

During the late 60s he made dozens of prototypes – and one night in the bath, rather in the manner of Archimedes, he christened them 'Spinhalers'.

A project was then set up with Roger as "chief sucker" and hundreds more variants were tested. Laboratories at Holmes Chapel really began to hum and everyone became moulded into a devoted team. INTAL was becoming everyone's child. It was an exhilarating time and Roger confidently organised three trials to be carried out by recognised experts in UK. Six months later, they declared unanimously that the drug was "inactive!"

It seems to me a sad fact of nature that, the greater any scientific revolution, the greater consequent scepticism – simply from lack of understanding and belief. Roger and George Constantinesco had a huge amount in common and must have heartily agreed!

This was a critical time for the Chairman and Directors of Fisons on one hand; and Dr Cox the Research Director and Dr Jack Howell, who ran tests with Roger, on the other. Should they, or should they not, invest huge sums of money?

It was the unquenchable faith and enthusiasm bursting out of Dr Howell and his patients which finally flattened doubts and allowed INTAL and inevitably 'Sons of INTAL' – *the start of a radical new breed of drugs*, the chance to prove themselves. As many of us are now so gratefully aware, it did so in a profoundly effective, ground-breaking and safe asthma therapy – not least for children in areas throughout the world.

Roger said, "Quite ordinary, normal people working hard in a dedicated team can still make useful discoveries ... but must have a champion to keep pushing it ahead. He must be something of a dreamer and above all a supreme optimist, otherwise he cannot hope to survive the long night of failure before dawn".

*   *   *

Visiting Roger and Hella in Wilmslow was always an uplifting experience, with five bright and lively children, exhibiting much of the archetype 'Walker Family' potential. Though not brought up on The Twelve Books, they were delightfully refreshing to a comparative outsider.

Especially, thoughts of Ransome's gracious and unflappable 'Mrs Walker' were evoked. To Hella, new challenges and setbacks must have seemed almost routine. I'm sure much must be owed to her steadfast support.

Like his father, Roger never seemed to be without some new project in hand. "Just in time!" he panted on one visit. "Take the other end will you?" and we wrestled with a wardrobe down the stairs. This was destined to become a 'dovecote' on the side of the house!

Though small in stature and, by this time, inclined to asthmatic breathlessness, I remember being impressed by his apparent power/weight ratio, little realising the extraordinary strain and physical risks he was taking at work.

On another visit, Hella explained why the dining-room carpet stuck to the feet. It seemed that Roger, a keen brewer and generous sharer of home-made wine (output 60 gallons of elderberry a year) much of it from Peel Island, was accustomed to tap the five gallon carboy of his latest brew with a plastic pen each morning before leaving for work, "to see the bubbles rise". This proved an unfortunate indulgence; there must have been some invisible flaw in the glass and during one morning ritual, it shattered and the entire contents cascaded into an inch-deep, undrinkable 'wine lake'. It had a fruity bouquet which I, at least, enjoyed for years.

I had imagined that Hella had put a stop to any further brewing in the dining room, then, 45 years later, I hear more from Roger's close friend and collaborator John Pritchard:

> Amongst the [dining table] group, Roger and I had a particular affinity. We were both music lovers (Gilbert and Sullivan etc.) amateur wine makers and had a great affection for the Lake District. Whilst I made my wine in the usual 1 gallon jars, Roger was not satisfied until he had persuaded me to allow him to acquire one of the firm's 10 gallon carboys. In this he proposed to make a monster batch using dried bananas as the raw material, having found an abundant source at a vegetarian store in Manchester.

> Unfortunately, the rest of his equipment, including the safety valve, was of the normal 1 gallon type, unable to cope with much greater pressure – and during the night this blew the bung clean out of the carboy. By morning a horrible frothy mess had oozed across the floor, crept under the door and spread over the carpet. As you may imagine, neither Roger or I were in Hella's good books for some considerable time and she forbade him to continue with the brew.

> Never one to give up easily and still with many gallons left, Roger decided to

try his hand at distilling – I warned him, being the firm's contact with the Excise Officer – that illicit distillation, upon conviction, carried a substantial prison sentence.

Ignoring my advice, Roger soon constructed a most efficient still, and in due course, I received a bottle of a most drinkable and powerful liqueur, bearing a lovely hand-painted label entitled 'Essence of Aleppo'.

Like his father, Roger was quite exceptionally good company and every one of our infrequent meetings tended to enthral. He had that thoroughly "'interested' way of looking at everything" – so like Ransome's own thoughts before him – and this did not exclude a comforting regard for the mundane.

One sunny evening, we walked over to the attractive, but sadly vacated, Gnosspelius residence. This sits on a bend with its barn facing the road on the way over to Hawkshead and its spectacular views down Coniston Water must have been a continual joy to the family. I never met Barbara Gnosspelius but was told of the telephone conversation she'd had with her sister Dora. This was a running commentary during which she remarked how she was watching *Mavis* doing a nicely controlled gybe – this when I thought I was all alone and out of sight!

The house had a substantial and very professional wiring system, the work of her husband, Oscar Gnosspelius whose expertise in mining and geology gave so much to *Pigeon Post*.

Walking back, I asked Roger if, as a frequent Lakeland resident, he was becoming saddened by the dramatic increase in visitors and traffic caused by the new M6 motorway. It was the sort of question which, in a lesser person, might have provoked an elitist response, but all he said, as we strolled past the Youth hostel, was "The more people who come to know and love The Lakes, the better".

Years later, I think of him often – while sitting in a Lakeland traffic jam!

A bit further on and quite unexpectedly, the subject of my "unusual spelling" arose. He thought this might be an inherited tendency and went on to say that he experienced the same difficulty. Sharing this problem with Roger, as already with my mother, has been an added comfort ever since!

*   *   *

Roger's facility for invention was practical and widely manifest. When Dora became bedridden for a time, he provided a weight and pulley system fixed to the ceiling. This effectively counteracted her weight on the hinged backrest – which reduced the effort of sitting up and enabled her to move about on her own.

Needless to say, *Mavis* was held centrally in the boathouse by another, particularly well-thought-out, pulley system. Later, sadly for security, he and Ernest kept her moored to a small buoy out in their little bay by yet another Roger-type device. This was an endless loop of plastic clothesline connecting one pulley offshore with one inland. It was discreetly secure, allowed hauling in and out without getting wet or resorting to a non-existent yacht tender.

Similarly, it was Roger, remembering what difficulty they had as children in raising and lowering *Mavis's* heavy iron centre plate, who
constructed the strange metal 'crane' on the top of *Mavis/Amazon's*
centre-board casing. This aided the plate's lifting tackle and I'm pleased to
see it is still in place today, though Taqui wrote:

> I do like your painting of 'Mavis' and admire the way you have tactfully
> draped the sail over the controversial centre-board pulley!

With the 1960s, it was especially good to have Judy alongside and, from our
marriage in October, a home of our own. The 'Roger appliance' she and I
most remember, might be termed his 'Fire-lighting Aid'.

In those days of open fires, he had created an airway under the floor
beneath the fire bars and the open grate. This allowed the coals to ignite far
more readily in a direct draught. Once alight and drawing, the
through-draught could easily be bypassed and thus neutralised, by opening
a 'hit and miss' vent beside the kerb.

As we had a similar 'Baxi' grate, we were familiar with the same lethargic
fire-lighting and a smoky chimney – and I set up a similar arrangement with
enthusiasm. But in my foolish way, I increasing the prescribed amount of
draft. The effect was dramatic as, with the aid of our gas poker, the coal lit
rapidly – and, if allowed, the flame soon increased and developed a roar like
a blacksmith's forge. Left too long, it devoured any number of gas pokers.

That apart, all went well for a couple of years until, one day, I was called
to the phone and left it drawing, with the room door shut – and very nearly
set the house on fire.

*   *   *

Roger and Hella were great fun and so hospitable. Judy remembers us visiting for lunch and playing ping-pong in the amicable dining room. Roger and
I played doubles against Judy and a tall Armenian gentleman. Judy played
to win and Hella who was watching "made encouraging oofing sounds"
when she slapped the ball extra hard. Roger clearly liked to win even more
and we just made it.

Another time we analysed pond life in the garden and helped to glaze the
new greenhouse. At some point, young Martin came out with an "intelligent
remark" and was given a modest reward by Roger.

Roger was aware of what he regarded as poisonous washing up detergent. They had a double sink in the kitchen and I was gently admonished for
not rinsing the dinner plates. I have been rinsing them ever since, albeit
under the hot tap, only to be mildly reproved for "wasting hot water". I'm
now told by John Pritchard that he does exactly the same, with similar
results. It does seem that Roger's influences live on!

Years later, evenings became very social, with their four or five children
each entertaining a friend in separate conversations. We left them to it!

After supper one summer evening at Lanehead, Roger, Judy and I went
up into the field above the house. The sun was beginning to sink and we had

with us a large assortment of prototype boomerangs of Roger's manufacture to try out. These were mostly cut out of plywood, each of varying bevels calculated to enhance lift and performance. Some were as large as one could conveniently throw and, as I remember, the trick was to hurl them in a vertical arc at the horizon.

This was the enjoyable bit as they could be seen in the dusk levelling out and skimming for some distance, with a slight rise on the turn. Trouble developed as, characteristically, each turned for home and could be heard, but not always seen, whistling past our heads. John Pritchard's experiences were slightly different:

> After lunch at work, if it was a fine day, Roger and I would go for a walk round the sports field and sometimes he would demonstrate his prowess with a boomerang, not always with complete success. One day the weapon veered way off course, sailed over a hedge and hit a passing police car. Fortunately, the car was being driven by a long-serving local bobby and when Roger approached him to apologise, accompanied by me, a long-serving local magistrate, the matter was soon smoothed over, forging yet another link between us.

> Some time later, Roger found a contact at the Manchester Museum and was able to inspect their large collection of boomerangs. Like most museums, the bulk of their stock was in storage but, rather to their chagrin, he had to declare that most of them were "decorative souvenirs, not actual fliers" as they had thought.

In the last issue of the 'Aventis' (heirs to Fisons) pensioners' magazine, it was stated:

> "Roger was a lovely, and a loveable man, and whilst the word genius is often loosely applied, it most certainly was true of Roger, along with another loosely applied word – hero". *[The very word which I had already used.]*

Roger was a keen supporter of Lakeland crafts and asked if we could possibly rescue a certain small business making those wooden garden baskets locally called 'swills', as the firm was threatened with closure. I so wish that this, or almost any other enterprise, had been possible – but there has always been some impediment to our settlement in Lakeland.

Like all good natives, the Altounyan families were devoted conservationists. On some expeditions, each would carry a bag and a sharpened barbecue skewer which Roger had wedged into a bamboo handle. This was to spear and collect any, thankfully rare, bits of litter along the way. I never took part in one of these forays but still imagine them developing some competitive spirit and the sort of useful *purpose* found in any Ransome story. Would that such collections, particularly of the imperishable plastics, now littering our planet, could become an international sport!

On one jolly stay, though the family roles should have been reversed, Judy and I in *Mavis/Amazon*, set off from the Lanehead boathouse and rendezvoused at 'High Peel Near' with Roger and Hella together with their children, Peter, Christine, the twins Martin and Barbara, and Heidi – and ferried them across to the landing on Peel Island. One of the island's many temptations is provided by bilberries which grow in the cliff ledges and the children were soon foraging precipitately for these.

The family's favourite picnic site, as opposed to the camping area, had always been on the flat top of its eastern cliff and, as we adults sat eating sandwiches, their small boys, Peter and Martin, went a step further and climbed up a sloping tree which hung high over cliff, rocks and water. It quite took our concentration and I looked to see if Roger and Hella were fully aware. As ideal parents, they certainly did look preoccupied – but said nothing. It was another example of the *Better Drowned Than Duffers* syndrome – and being used to active adventure, they were imbued with good sense and self-reliance, naturally surviving to this day.

[It reminds me of our own not-too-literal *Eat Off The Floor* adage put forth by Judy's surgeon brother-in-law – "to combat our super cleanliness culture and develop natural immunity".]

Anyway, when they were safely down, Judy remarked "that was very 'Arthur Ransome!'" At this, young Martin asked, to our astonishment, "What is a ransom Daddy?" Roger replied, "Arthur Ransome is someone who wrote a book about children on an island". Nothing more was said!

*   *   *

Following the sad loss of Lanehead as a holiday resort in 1967, Roger and family made their Lakeland base at Nibthwaite at the southern end of Coniston Water – close to where Ransome had spent his childhood holidays. There was the old 'quay' from which copper ore was once unloaded - and the old boathouse where *Mavis* spent her final days before restoration. The last time I sailed her was with Roger from here.

Roger was an accomplished fisherman and adept at catching char. Just a couple of doors away from their home in Wilmslow, there happened to live his very close friend, Fred Etchells, who it turned out, Roger had trained as a pilot in Rhodesia. Fred was a 'lovely' man and they made wine and fished together for about thirty years.

Brigit's husband, John Sanders, has his last memories of Roger and Fred going off in John's *Drascombe Dabber* from the little marina at Water Park, Coniston. By then Roger could hardly breathe and was obliged to fish with oxygen flask and nebuliser. Normally they rowed but, towards the end, used an outboard motor, towing a bucket to slow them down to trolling speed.

The traditional char-fishing system on Coniston and Windermere involved a long fixed rod, mounted one each side of the slow-moving boat. From these, substantial lines rigged with traces, spinners and heavy lead sinkers were lowered to the elected depth.

Arctic Char, trout-like but with a more delicate flavour, collect in shoals at varying depths and Roger used to work his lines with the lead at about ninety to one hundred feet – and five or six traces of six feet in length every six feet up the line.

A windlass which he devised and Fred helped him to make, was fastened to the gunwale with a cramp. This wound up the line to the first swivel and trace. Any fish were removed and the hooks pushed into a series of corks until all traces had been recovered. Still keeping the boat moving, the process was then reversed for another 'go'.

Char fisherman

The traditional tackle could only manage one or two widely separated traces but, with the typically Rogerian device, the fisher could cover a wide span of depths and increase the probability of reaching a shoal and making a catch. Whatever the technicalities, it was a brilliant answer to an "insoluble" problem.

Almost any Nibthwaite party night would be graced by the distribution of beautifully cooked slivers of char on cocktail crackers, so that only a few fish would feed quite a multitude. Oddly, Roger did not like the taste of char but, like Ransome, revelled in the challenges they afforded.

He had fond memories of 'Uncle Arthur' when the latter was old and forbidden to row by his doctor, but none-the-less, managing to catch char by trailing a line from *Cocky* – by maintaining a steady course and slow speed *under sail!* The problems arose when single handedly "gaffing" his catch – as sail, tiller, net and reel had somehow to be co-ordinated. Hardly the prescribed treatment one would think, for a double hernia!

* * *

In *Chimes from a Wooden Bell*, Taqui writes of Roger:

> He had that child's capacity for getting absorbed in play especially if it involved anything to do with wind or water. I can see him now coming gently down the lake before the wind, in our old boat *Mavis* with the dark brown sail well out, looking like a blowsy overloaded barge. Roger is completely relaxed at the helm, steering with a knee over the tiller, keeping his pipe alight with one hand, the other perhaps disentangling a fishing line or rescuing something just dropped overboard by a child.

> The boat is full of children of all ages, not a life-jacket between them, most of them doing things which 'Ukartha' ['Uncle Arthur'] would not approve of: trailing hands, feet, even hair in the water, leaning out dangerously and never, if they could help it, obeying orders. Roger himself took to the water when very young. There is a picture of him at hardly more than six months old sitting up fatly grinning in a wicker cradle wedged between the thwarts of the Collingwoods' old boat – another *Swallow*. And that song he was so fond of: "Take my money take my coat leave me with my fishing boat ..."

Roger was also an inveterate kite maker and flier – manifest from early days

Roger Altounyan

by making one capable of lifting Brigit off the ground as a child. It seems a pity he did not take her, airborne across the lake, towed by *Mavis* – if only to further validate the 'duffers' decree!

Kite-enthusiasm may have been inspired by their earlier days in Soukoulouk as the family sometimes used to fly kites competitively. Roger told how some of these had "desperate devices" in their tails, designed to disable or capture opponents.

In those last years at Nibthwaite, John Sanders recalls him organising the family youngsters into the production of quite large-scale kites. He was well-known in Wilmslow according to John Pritchard, not for his scientific achievements as one would expect, but more modestly for his kite flying on the common where there were some desperate combats seen in the sky for which he became the local champion.

On our last meeting, Roger told me that, somewhere high on the fells above is a tarn and, typically in the AR tradition, he had often wondered if it contained fish. The problem was that a thick belt of reeds surrounded it. To cast over these was almost as impractical as dangling lines from a helicopter. How it might be done was a typical example of what intrigued him. He devised a method by which a kite was tethered to hover over the water. From the underside of this a fishing line and tackle were deployed and controlled from the distant bank. But time for him was running out, this particular prototype never caught anything, but he and Taqui's husband, Robert Stephens, did manage a catch by playing joined fishing lines across the tarn.

At Christmas 1986, he wrote, almost illegibly, "I have just retired because of ill health ... hope to see you soon". But instead of many more happy family holidays together, Roger's decline continued and he died in an oxygen tent, aged 65 – in exchange, I often think, for the rest of us millions, throughout the world, who can now, quite literally, breathe more easily. His determination, especially during those eight years of adversity and compassion, mark him out as a National hero!

Brigit, 12-6-26 to 13-11-99

For some time after her initial introduction as the youngest of the 'Walker' family in *Swallows and Amazons,* Brigit was too small to be really useful in the books. Later she more than makes up by taking an active part (spelled 'Bridget') in *We Didn't Mean to go to Sea* – and centre-stage in *Secret Water*.

After the holidays in Lakeland and being largely brought up in Aleppo, she spent the war in Jerusalem before studying Arabic in London, then returning to take over administration of the Altounyan Hospital.

Enthusiastic about horses, she helped in training them for dressage, jumping and in the rescue of and breeding from Arab mares found among Bedouin tribes.

During the events which saw the emergence of Syria and Lebanon as independent

Brigit in Aleppo, by Dora. The organ was in Matron's drawing room

states, Brigit narrowly missed harm during an assassination attempt on Colonel Stirling, who was then *The Times* correspondent in Damascus and a long-time friend of Ernest. The experience made an impression but brought out the courage and cool-headedness which were typical of her handling of other critical situations – as we and members of The Arthur Ransome Society found so abundantly later.

It was in 1953 that she married John Sanders, a diplomat, and they saw service together in the Middle East, London, Mexico and Panama before retiring in 1980, to Nibthwaite. They had found a delightful cottage near 'Octopus Lagoon' and 'Swainson's Farm', the Ransome family headquarters in real life, where Arthur had holidayed so happily as a child. There, Brigit and John took delight in introducing their grandchildren to 'Wild Cat Island' and many other imagined places in the 'Twelve Books'.

It was the success of an appeal to restore *Mavis* to her original glory, sponsored by Christina Hardyment, that led to Brigit's deep involvement in the long-overdue formation of The Arthur Ransome Society (TARS). To everyone's delight she became its first President.

Eventually, she and John moved from The Lakes, to be nearer their family in Devon. Complete with a most enjoyable indoor swimming pool, their home stood high on the ridge overlooking Bideford Bay and out to sea to Lundy Island. Judy and I have fond memories of staying with them there, while John and Brigit recorded the small part we were to play in their video, *The Ransomes Remembered.* This faithfully recorded the reminiscences of an ever-dwindling band of relations and friends who knew Arthur in person. It was a major undertaking and involved large amounts of John and Brigit's organisational and "interrogational" skills. Her positive involvement, quiet authority and humour was everything we needed in 'TARS', and helped to pass on to a growing international membership of thousands, the very special cultural heritage endowed by AR.

Our Memorial Service for Brigit was held, as that for Titty, and later Melkon, at St. Andrew's Church, Coniston. For all three, Titty's daughter, Rahel, sang hymns in a hauntingly beautiful voice which none of us will forget and Fr Brian played a surprisingly appropriate medley of sea-shanties on the church organ. As seemed only natural, we then repaired to Bank Ground Farm/'Holly Howe', just below Lanehead. There, its present owner, Lucy Batty, gave us tea and cakes while we sat among so many grateful friends, gazing down that field to the boat houses and lake with so many precious memories. Typically, this was in glorious sunshine. It seems that nature smiles on almost anything to do with TARS – just as in the 'Twelve Books'.

Chapter 11

Dick Kelsall

Dick (born 19-6-22) played a vital part in the books in real life and became an exceptionally long-standing Ransome ally. From 1990 to this present day, his ever-youthful presence and expertise has been invaluable to The Arthur Ransome Society. We believe that parts of his character, as much as his name, appear in half of 'The Twelve Books'.

While not strictly a 'Swallow', with his slightly elder brother Desmond, he came to know Ransome as a very human friend of their family – during some of AR's most creative years.

Desmond Kelsall was a keen fisherman even as a youngster and much enjoyed Ransome's company and his stories. The practical young Dick does translate as part of 'Dick Callum', who became my favourite character, though I think that much of that (glasses, skating ability, interest in birds and science) is almost certainly Ransome himself, as a boy.

Yes, so many of Ransome's fictional characters and places are an artistic mixture, but Dick still deserves a special place here. Indeed, the whole Kelsall family were of protracted help to the Ransomes in those early years.

It was back in 1923 that Lt Colonel T. Edward Kelsall RE, having just retired from the regular Army, moved with his wife Ella and sons into 'Barkbooth' in the Winster valley, a house built in 1909 with farm buildings and twenty acres of fields, orchards and a larch wood. It lies just five miles south of Windermere and one from Bowland Bridge, where as Dick recounts, the village shop sold tempting clay pipes and multi-coloured aniseed balls.

Dick recalls how there was no electricity at that time, just candles, oil lamps and, best of all, occasional 'Aladdins' with their large incandescent mantles. Furthermore, there was no telephone, no public water supply or sewer – but it is strange how simple deprivations can sometimes concentrate the mind on more worthwhile things – and there was no shortage of initiative in this case.

The boys were gloriously free to wander over farm fields and rocky woodland, not always their own, yet without hindrance, except for the local shorthorn bull and the adders, which were more common in those days. Adders (vipers) fortunately have a retiring disposition but are quite dangerous if they feel threatened.

It must have been an ideal, slightly *"Better Drowned Than Duffers"* upbringing. Most fortunately, their parents found time to share some of the fun and games, while encouraging a sense of responsibility and instilling *sensible* discipline which made all such freedom allowable. Would that the same ways were still in vogue!

In 1925 Arthur Ransome And Evgenia came to live across the valley at Low Ludderburn; a small whitewashed cottage nearly 600 feet up on the western slopes of Cartmel Fell. It had thick walls, the stairs actually contained within them. It was cramped and lacking in headroom, particularly in the doorways, and both being so large, they quickly learned to duck when moving about.

A well, dating from Roman times, was their sole water supply. Across the yard, at right angles to the house, was a very large barn, the upper floor of which the Ransomes converted into an exceptional workroom which he described as "the best I ever had" in spite of his then financial constraints. Its south-east facing window provided superb views across the valley to the Yorkshire fells.

With Arthur and Evgenia, came something of a 'reputation'. This was based on Ransome's first-hand reporting and one-time close proximity to the Russian Revolution Leaders. There was some understandable awe and uncertainty about his views of Lenin and Trotsky – and equally misplaced, his marriage to Trotsky's secretary added fuel to local suspicion and speculation.

Their arrival created a new dimension for the Kelsall family, but the boys were instructed never to mention Russia or Mr Ransome's foreign travels in his presence. In consequence, they were apprehensive of this big man with his huge walrus moustache and tweed 'plus-fours' – but found there was nothing to fear. Indeed, he became almost one of them, with his unique way of delighting youngsters and sharing in their fun and childhood games.

Ransome was at that time writing articles on 'Fishing' for *The Manchester Guardian* and he and the Colonel, both keen fishermen, soon established a *rapport*. Dick, then aged three, was not keen on fishing but Desmond was five and became inescapably hooked. One fine day, Ransome, their father and Desmond went fishing for the small trout which inhabit the River Winster across the fields from Barkbooth. Dick was invited but wasn't really interested and later felt left out and sulked. His mother encouraged him however and said, "At least go and try on your own".

With a thin ash plant, black thread and the traditional bent pin, Dick set off with a small tin of worms in damp moss. He found another stretch of the beck well away from the professionals, and dangled his worm. It is hard to be certain what goes on in the mind of a fish and it may have been that the bent pin was not a perceived threat. It may also have been beginner's luck – for Dick suddenly landed a fair sized-trout with which he ran home too excited even to retrieve his tackle. When the experts returned it was found that Dick's fish was quite the largest. The very next day he received a delightful, personally illustrated postcard from Ransome, saying:

Congratulations on catching the best fish of the season. My best was only

7 inches. Perhaps they like thread. Anyhow now you have started on them, I suppose the trout in the Winster are in for a hard time.

At the bottom of the card was a sketch of a boy with a bent rod catching a whopper – with the caption, "RK catching the Winster Whale". This was typical of AR's kindness and enthusiasm for children's games and interests, and his infectious humour.

On another summer's day, Desmond, his father and Ransome, set off to fish on Windermere. They anchored *Swallow* just north of the east ferry landing and started by catching small perch, which Ransome then used on a second rod as live-bait for pike. In due course a small jack-pike was taken, the largest fish Desmond had ever seen. He remembers how bent Mr Ransome's fishing rod became – and his flow of instructive remarks *to the fish* as he played it in, just as if it would behave accordingly.

On 29th June 1927, there was to be an eclipse of the sun. The 'path of totality' was to pass over Clapham Common, between Ingleton and Settle. To witness this, the Kelsall family left Barkbooth at 0300 on a slightly cloudy morning in their old Morris Oxford. They were joined on the Common by the Ransomes.

Dark glasses were not then in common use, but there was enough time on arrival for Col. Kelsall to literally smoke pieces of glass over a block of burning camphor, to protect everyone's eyes. Just as the sun rose, the sky cleared fully and they had a wonderful view of the total eclipse of the rising sun.

As dawn broke fully, they could see huge crowds covering the slopes of the Common and higher ground. Dick's father, as a veteran of the horrors of the 1914/18 War, was heard to remark "What a splendid target for a machine gun". This politically heinous observation was overheard and greatly amused Ransome who, in one of his regular pieces for *The Manchester Guardian*, wrote of the event, referring to: "my friend, the man of blood", much to the Colonel's amusement.

In 1929, Ransome's doctor gave him a 'health warning', so, with Evgenia's support, he made the radical decision to give up safe employment with *The Manchester Guardian* and concentrate on what he felt would be less damagingly stressful. Far more relevant, he was recognising his true vocation – and began to write *Swallows and Amazons*.

Aged 45, things were coming together for AR as perhaps never before. The archetype family Kelsall were proving a boon and he began to bring down draft manuscripts to Barkbooth, which he read aloud to the boys and their father, to hear their reaction to his latest work. This was exciting and flattering to the youngsters and, like so many of us who have been brought up on Beatrix Potter and Lewis Caroll, it opened another unimagined world to both boys, in this case exploring and sailing. What really fascinated them was that everything described seemed so possible and "real".

Swallows and Amazons was finally published in 1930, and it was a great occasion when AR presented an inscribed copy to the assembled family. There was far more excitement when their father read it to them. This was usually in the best possible way, just before they went to sleep, their minds becoming seeped in serene adventure before blissful oblivion.

The first edition of *Swallows and Amazons* was unillustrated, but my 1935 edition has Stephen Spurrier's end-papers, "With illustrations by Clifford Webb". It was initially Webb's illustrations as much as the text which welded me to the book. They delight me still.

Clifford Webb 1894-1972

It is hard to imagine how Webb managed to achieve such quality and atmosphere, something we seldom see today! Presumably he made sketches, and almost certainly took photographic references on site. The work could then be completed in favourable conditions at home. But then there was his client!

Sadly, there were no radical cures for stomach ulcers in those days. I think it may have been in consequence, that Ransome's perceptions of people could often be exceptionally jaundiced. Typically, he could be *for* or, more probably, *downright against* someone for no apparent reason. His diary, always a favourite vehicle for letting off steam, is hugely revealing. Also, like Evgenia, what he says is seldom if ever modified. I think many of his associates, myself included, became "acceptable" only as he got to know us better. It was a mutual experience. Relations with Mr Webb, as shown by his diary, are a classic example:

10th April '31 Clifford Webb came.

11th Sailed to Blake Holme. *[This must have been with Webb in Swallow]*

12th Coniston. Sailed *Mavis* to Peel Island and to foot of lake.

13th Sailed round Belle Isle & Up & around while W made sketches of 'Swallow'.

14th C.W. left thank goodness ...

ASS. But he can draw.

In typical contrast, AR wrote, three months later on 8th July 1931:

Dear Webb,

With this is another lump of the book [*Swallowdale*]...

They [Jonathan Cape] sent me the proofs of your pictures. I think they look very well indeed and that the book as a whole will do you credit. The only one I really don't like is the picture of Titty sitting on a rock with a telescope facing the audience [not used]. I can't help hating that one, because, well, you know what authors are with their favourite characters. And my Titty is a little eager imaginative child of about nine. Not more.

But some of the new ones I had not seen are really first rate. The night scene in the Amazon River. Magnificent. And the fishing scene with Roger attached to the pike. And I very much liked the one with the lot of them pushing off the boat laden with wood. And the delightful thing of the Amazons carrying the puncheon. I'm more than ever convinced that that is the way with such things, keeping the figures such that any child can identify itself with any character, and throwing the whole energy of the artist into setting the adventure in its romantic landscape that no child can invent but that every child needs as food for its own fancy. In some of the pictures I think you are really pioneering.

Do carry on like that through *Swallowdale*.

Good luck to you. I hope all your models are doing well.

I would say more about the pictures, but I must hurry or I shall have you writing to say you are sitting and waiting.

Yours sincerely,

[Arthur Ransome]

Webb's scenery, while tending to be professionally stylised, is hauntingly beautiful, full of atmosphere and endowment; as appropriate for Ransome as E.H. Shepard was for A.A. Milne. As I had once hinted rather tactlessly to AR, Webb retains my ultimate admiration.

Moreover, his greater topographical accuracy than Ransome's wisely guarded illustrations later, provided a source of contemplation for many seekers of Ransome geography. It was only later that Ransome decided that what he wanted, exclusively, was "relevant details, with no pretty pictures to distract etc". In reality, I think complete possession of each book was also what he had in mind.

Clifford Webb, as a person, remained a tantalising mystery until nearly seventy years after his work for Ransome. Then there was an extraordinary coincidence.

Robin Anderson, a highly motivated member of The Arthur Ransome Society, was involved in the restoration of Ransome's sailing dinghy *Coch-y-Bonddhu*, *Swallow's* successor. Amazingly, '*Cocky*' had been traced by another TARS member, Chris Birt found her rotting under a tree in the grounds of a hotel in Scotland. Robin, intent on raising support funds, wrote to various possible establishments.

One kind response was from a firm building traditional sailing boats in the Isle of Wight and one of their directors, Michael Webb, revealed that he was the son of Clifford Webb the illustrator! Michael had met Ransome just once and recalled "he had an ulcer at the time and was, if my childhood memory serves me right, a bit crotchety".

He went on to describe how his father, Clifford Cyril Webb, was born in 1894 in London's dock area and died in 1972. He was of "artisan parents and an oarsman of some repute but never a sailor".

However, not only was he gifted with potential as a professional artist; he was clearly a man of exceptional calibre. He seems to have attended art classes until World War One was declared, but ten days later, aged 20, was enlisted in the Grenadier Guards and served as a private on France's Western Front. In 1915, by then an officer in The Wiltshire Regiment, he fought in Gallipoli and Mesopotamia. There, he was wounded for a second time, in the retreat from Kut el Amara. This involved "massive injuries caused by a

Clifford Webb *(Courtesy of Michael Webb)*

Turkish machine gun ..." and, as a result, though right-handed, he "had only partial use of his right arm".

During a long period of recovery in India, he took up painting in oils. In 1919 he was discharged with a small disability pension and studied at the Westminster School of Art. He was skilled in sketching, wood engraving and water colour. Later, he taught at the Birmingham School of Art where he met his future wife. Ella Monkton was of an old 'county' family, whose father owned a company producing bank notes.

Nevertheless, difficult times followed for a struggling young artist during the Great Depression, but they had jointly developed connections with the publishing world and produced a number of children's books.

This led to the historic invitation to illustrate Ransome's books. First *Swallowdale*, then *Swallows and Amazons* were illustrated for first time. Webb's models for the children were his own son and daughter, Michael and Jennifer.

He made two early visits to the Lake District and later with the family in 1936. Ransome was obviously not well during the first of these and one can only pity them both. Clifford told his son:

> Ransome suffered from an ulcer and had with him at all times a small suitcase in which were a pint of milk, a bottle of bismuth and a packet of biscuits ... he was very difficult to please.

Though Mr Webb could still row with his left arm, he could not lift either arm above the shoulder and it seems especially inappropriate that Ransome had expected him to be 'a sailor'. Early in their relationship, after seeing him off, Ransome came roaring in to see Colonel Kelsall, saying "what an idiot" Clifford Webb was. He had to land him at Bowness to catch his train and, being on a lee shore, had "asked" him, very clearly unaware of his war injuries, to jump onto the pier, first having to squeeze under the boom with his luggage no doubt.

Anyway, poor Mr Webb, not given to avoiding challenges or making excuses, made such an unsuccessful pier-head jump that *Swallow* took a nasty bump in the process; another hiccup in early Ransome relations!

I'm sure considerable mutual respect developed and Clifford Webb's illustrations, confined to the first two books, were outstanding. I believe they were a significant early contribution to international success. Then

Arthur grew to feel well placed to do the job himself and so opened another intriguing sequence.

* * *

Following the publication of *Swallows and Amazons*, it was arranged that Ransome should have tea with the Kelsalls, so Desmond went down to Hartbarrow Bridge to meet him. Walking back, AR asked if he had enjoyed *S&A* and Desmond said, "Yes, very much", and went on to ask if he would follow it with another. Ransome said he was thinking about it and, supposing that he did, "what did Desmond think ought to happen in it?

With a small boy's lack of inhibition, Desmond's reply was that he thought "John should become over-confident in handling *Swallow* and should run her on the rocks". At this Ransome gave a great guffaw and replied "That's exactly what I was thinking myself, but I haven't got any further than that at the moment".

Arthur was currently familiar with the hazardous 'Hen' and 'Chicken' rocks south of 'Ferry Nab' and one wonders if he had these in mind – or the rock between Peel Island and the east shore?

Having absorbed *Swallows and Amazons* and been invited by Ransome to have a sail in *Swallow*, the inventive young Dick decided to adapt his 'Triang' pedal car to sail. There is a good-sized level yard at 'Barkbooth' with a long sloping-down approach-lane. He acquired one of his father's strong 8ft sweetpea bamboos for the mast and his mother surrendered a white sheet for a sail. It needed a strong breeze to get up any speed but at just the right moment Ransome arrived down the road in his old solid-tyred Trojan, and with one of his great whoops of joy leapt out, full of admiration and ideas of how to improve things.

When Ransome came to write *Swallowdale*, he brought the blank 'Ship's Papers' down to Barkbooth, asking that the boys should sign them so that the handwriting was convincingly that of a child. As instructed, Desmond wrote all the names and signed as 'John Walker', Dick signed as 'Roger', also the bit about 'Gibber' the ship's monkey. In his nervousness, Dick's pen "blobbed" to his great embarrassment – but, far from being put out, AR was delighted as he said it made it so typical of what happens in real life.

The parrot which appears in the books is green and seems to have been modelled on that which belonged to AR's sister Joyce, but it was another parrot whose foot-print appears in the 'Ship's Papers', at the beginning of *Swallowdale*. Colonel Kelsall in his diary mentions that on "8-11-28, a grey parrot had arrived". This was a West African Groy and had two tones of grey with red feathers on its wings. Dick tells how it was "given by Dr Charlie Kelsall, cousin of the Colonel and a GP out in West Africa".

I wish I had been there when 'Polly', with many understandable protests, was induced to make his mark. To do this, two pieces of paper were held on a broomstick with rubber bands, one was coated in a concoction of chimney soot and oil. Polly was encouraged to first grip the black concoction and then the white. Several attempts were necessary to get the clear and very

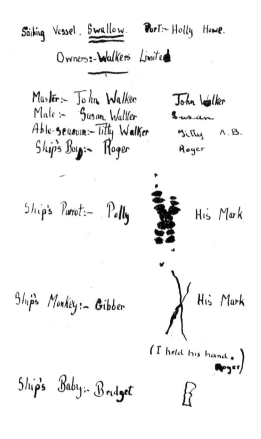

Sailing Vessel. Swallow.   Port:- Holly Howe.

Owners:-Walkers Limited

Master:- John Walker   John Walker
Mate :- Susan Walker   Susan
Able-seaman:-Titty Walker   Titty   A.B.
Ship's Boy:- Roger   Roger

Ship's Parrot:- Polly   His Mark

Ship's Monkey:- Gibber   His Mark

(I held his hand.
                    Roger)

Ship's Baby:- Bridget

The original 'Ship's Papers' (re-inked by author) from
'Swallowdale'

authentic sooty foot mark we see in the book. AR was hugely amused by the whole process and very grateful.

What with the great freezing over of Windermere in 1895, when Ransome had been a schoolboy there, the vital repeat freeze followed in February 1929 and the author's fascination with Nansen's exploits vast amounts of inspiration were provided for his classic *Winter Holiday*. I wonder if he got ideas from Dick's sailing pedal car too!

Then there was the matter of signals. In the late 1920s there were still no telephones in the Winster valley and the Ransome/Kelsall relationships seemed to cry out for some means of communication other than the children, whose frequent errand it was to run the very circuitous road between the two houses, when fishing expeditions were being planned. Also, Ransome's health was becoming a worry in this remote location and Colonel Kelsall must have asked himself "what would the Royal Engineers do here?" – and he and Ransome devised the signalling system using 'shapes', which readers of *Winter Holiday* have since become to cherish.

This involved Black signals on the whitewashed gable end of Low Ludderburn high across the valley, and White ones on the dark stone barn of Barkbooth – which was 1,000 metres away and lower down.

Originally, there were only two shapes used: Square or Diamond and Triangle, apex Up or Down – allowing up to 12 messages, as in the books. The possible combinations, in real life, were pretty good for fishing topics but not much use to Mrs Ransome and Mrs Kelsall (as they always addressed each other) since no female social topics were included in the code.

In February 1933, Col. Kelsall introduced a 2nd Edition of the code. For this another signal shape was added – the Plus or Multiplication sign – according to which way up it was hung. At last, the ladies could say, 'will you come to tea today?' or arrange to go shopping. Evgenia was delighted when she could arrange a time to be picked up and taken shopping by the kind Colonel Kelsall – simply by hoisting the appropriate shapes up the side of the house.

Ransome, in his autobiography, wrote:

> Kelsall, a great precisian, used to present me with a beautifully typed new copy of our code ('All previous issues cancelled') and pasted his own copy on one of two wooden boards hinged together to open like a book and, when not in use, kept padlocked. There was to be no leakage at his signal station. The fish never had a chance of learning beforehand what was planned for them.

* * *

In those days, there was an excellent rubber-powered 'aeroplane' made by 'Warneford' (exactly like the one with which I was sent away to boarding school. With a single stick for a fuselage, it was beautifully made with varnished silk-covered wing and tail plane. It flew splendidly and on one fine windy day, the Kelsall boys were flying theirs in a fairly responsible manner until the Ransomes arrived in the Trojan and joined in the fun.

In a natural response, the boys wound up the elastic far beyond the recommended turns and the plane soared away before the wind, for hundreds of yards. Fortunately, it remained just in sight, having landed in

A	B	C	D

1.	A.	Answer
2.	B.	Shall we go fishing ?
3.	C.	Yes
4.	D.	No
5.	A.C.	I am coming to see you
6.	A.D.	Have you any worms ?
7.	B.C.	Weather doubtful
8.	B.D.	Will you come to tea ?
9.	C.A.	Shall we fish tomorrow ?
10.	C.B.	Flagwag !!!!!! impossible
11.	D.A.	Weather good
12	D.B.	Weather bad

Original code suggested by Arthur Ransome in about 1928

'Private code' from the pocket book of 'Dick Callum' in 'Winter Holiday' (Courtesy of Dick Kelsall)

the branches of a large oak tree in the Lambhowe Plantation, high above the farm. At this, Ransome, being in his element, bundled them into the Trojan, hurried to the scene and after an organised scramble, the plane was rescued.

The Ransomes would often drop in for a yarn about fishing and the world in general. It transpired that both they and Col. Kelsall really liked bananas. On one visit, Ransome and the Colonel were settled opposite to each other, each with a banana "stripped for action" in a hand resting on an arm of the chair. At this point, Dick's father felt it necessary to warn AR that 'Smut', the black Kelsall cat, also had a passion for bananas. Ransome laughed a lot at this but clearly didn't take him seriously.

However, 'Smut' did. Lurking just out of sight, he recognised a perfect opportunity, chose his moment and, in one bound onto the arm of Ransome's chair, took a lightning swipe at his banana and knocked it away to the floor where he devoured it at leisure. Meanwhile Ransome was left with a handful of drooping skin and there were howls of delight from the assembled company, including Ransome, over "the skill and good taste of the Kelsall cat!"

Dick remembers Evgenia as a huge, cheerful woman with her hair tied back in a bun and an infectiously broad smile. She had a great command of the English language but a thick accent remained. She introduced them to her Russian version of Skittles. Using fair sized logs, she would throw these at others set up at a distance. Being only small, it was enough for the boys just to pick up the logs, not throw them!

On rare winter evening visits, Ransome would invite children to a party in the big barn at Low Ludderburn. Among those present were Peggy and Joan Hudson from Bowness who took part in the 'Hollywoods' – photographs from which Arthur later drew illustrations for the books; and occasionally the 'Swallows' from Lanehead. He would issue each with a penny whistle or tambourine etc., get out his accordion and they all sang sea shanties. He would also tell some of his 'Anansi' stories. It was one of the high spots of an evening if he recounted, in *pseudo*-West Indian sing-song tones, the enacted one about the *Pudding Tree*.

*   *   *

Having "disposed" of Clifford Webb, AR was now illustrating all the books himself; but, as he was always admitting, he could not draw figures. He started to get the Kelsall and Hudson children to "model" his characters, using any old "props" available round the Barkbooth outhouses while he took photographs. At one stage, a long wooden ladder was used to simulate a ship's shrouds which the children had to climb. Another showed Dick and Desmond with the Hudson girls "turning a capstan" constructed of broomsticks on an up-ended barrel intended for *Peter Duck*.

Also, the 'ice yacht' in Chapter 24 of *Winter Holiday* – "IT'S MOVING!": Dick remembers leaping onto their old home-made sledge in the yard at Barkbooth – on a fine summer's day!

Arthur was said to be all too aware of his reliance on photography, for

'Hollywood' of Desmond, Dick and the Hudson girls

faces and figures, to show anyone the resultant prints. Similarly, he does not refer in his *Autobiography* to the help he must have received from his undercover artistic mentors. At the Centenary Celebrations of Ransome's birth in 1984, Dick was asked by Jonathan Cape Ltd (Ransome's publishers), if he could identify "some photographs of children" in their Ransome file. It was quite a shock to recognise Desmond, himself and the Hudson girls in various actions and poses, remembering and recognising the illustrations in *Winter Holiday* and *Peter Duck* for which they had been made.

In C.E. (Ted) Alexander's book *Ransome at Home* (Amazon Publications) he writes:

> Arthur Ransome was, more often than not, a man on the move. Between his first arrival in London in 1902 and his death in 1967, he occupied twenty-five more or less snug berths in England alone, as well as other temporary moorings at home and abroad.

So, the Ransome's ten-year 'snug berth' in Low Ludderburn was unusually long and the first five books of the series completed there are tribute to the whole environment. Remarkably, towards the end of this productive period, his sixth book, *Pigeon Post*, was on the stocks and it was to Dick, by then aged 12, that he turned for help. Knowing Dick's budding interest in mechanical and electrical devices, Ransome asked if, at all possible, he "could devise a way of making homing pigeons ring an electric bell when they returned to their loft". With typical modesty, Dick describes how:

> The device was made from an empty wooden fruit box and some of my father's lighter gauge galvanised wire and staples, also I think from some of his sheet brass and wire for the contacts. I borrowed an old electric bell from

father and some wet Leclanche cells for the battery. I demonstrated it to Mr Ransome, it was crude but it worked.

This device is illustrated in *Pigeon Post*. It is an epic feature and one cannot help feeling that both Dick & Desmond are owed some kind of acknowledgement. AR clearly recognised the intelligence and potential in those boys, though he could hardly have foreseen their future achievements.

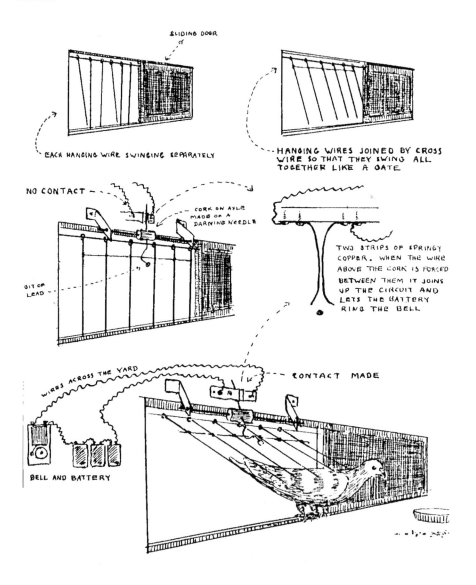

'How Dick Made The Pigeons Ring A Bell' *(Pigeon Post)*

During the war, when the Ransomes had moved to The Heald, on the east side of Coniston Water, not only were they remote from shops and village life, but food rationing was tight and many well-loved items were unavailable. By this time, Desmond was a Naval pilot with the Fleet Air Arm and, stationed in the west of Scotland, had found a source of real Scottish smoked kippers, a delicacy the Ransomes had not seen since the beginning of the war. Occasionally he was able to buy a whole box of these and despatch them to his parents, by then living in Troutbeck, near Windermere. His father and mother would then divide them into small portions and post them to selected friends, among whom the Ransomes were particularly partial to the real thing. From them a delightful card was received containing an example of AR's typed verse:

Red Herrings
Of all the fishes of the sea
The kipper is the fish for me.
God bless Mrs Kelsall!

For breakfast, dinner, supper, tea,
He is as good as good can be.
Oh, God bless Mrs Kelsall!

Who cares for salmon or for trout
When Scottish kippers are about?
God bless Mrs Kelsall!

All the best things a man can eat,
A braw red kipper has them beat
So, God bless Mrs Kelsall!

Bless her for sending us those fish,
we've scoffed the last and licked the dish.
No wonder that our heartfelt wish
Is, God bless Mrs Kelsall!

In the late 1950s, AR, now 'Dr Ransome' from 1952, wished to devise a fishing fly to imitate an elver and, somehow, he got the idea that a feather from a Vulturine Guineafowl had the ideal characteristics. By then, Desmond was working in Africa on fishery management on Lake Victoria and Ransome asked him if he could possibly get some of the special feathers from that bird which had an iridescent stripe along the centre. When used as a salmon fly, these looked like the immature eel. His theory was that, as salmon did not feed in fresh water, yet would still rise to fishing flies and other lures, they must hold memory of feeding in the Atlantic on vast shoals of migratory elver.

Trouble was, as Desmond pointed out, the Vulturine Guineafowl was then a highly protected species; yet he felt an obligation to try and help his childhood fishing friend. He had a confidential word with one of his Game Warden friends and explained his dilemma. A few days later, miraculously, a dead Vulturine Guineafowl appeared on his doorstep. Desmond posted off the feathers to AR who was delighted and sincerely grateful. Desmond fervently hoped however, that there would be no further such requests as, by then, he himself had been made an Hon. Game Warden!

Meanwhile, younger brother Dick had worked on early radar and served as an RNVR Electrical Officer. Later, it was nuclear reactor control and defence work – far more 'Winter Holiday' and related to the interests of 'Dick' and 'Dorothea' in astronomy. But by then, a bit over the top, were his department's control systems for Canada's 150ft and Australia's 210ft radio telescopes.

Chapter 12

Communications

I exchanged hundreds of letters with the 'Swallows' and Ransomes. These have spanned decades and there is much overlapping. The following are mainly concerned with Arthur and Evgenia – and, as with dear Ernest and Dora, I only wish they had been younger!

I had always been addressed as 'John' from the start by the Altounyans, but the Ransomes were very different and besides not wanting to appear a 'fan', I was determined not to appear too familiar. In these days, it seems ridiculous that it took thirteen years of signing the many letters to them as if at the bottom of a cheque. In 1971, I let myself go and signed as 'John' and was subsequently addressed as such. The 'love from' bit was to follow and, by that time, I know we meant it.

I especially enjoyed discussing the tools of his trade from early on with Arthur; and reading his diary account of it years later. At last, we were mostly in agreement though I regret never managing to wean him off a portable typewriter.

On 20th April 1960, Evgenia wrote her thanks for the weedkiller and her kind thoughts for the flame gun:

> In fact I rather wanted to borrow yours for a few days ... I am very sorry to have missed seeing you and your friend [Judy] this time especially and particularly if you both really love weeding ... It is lovely to be in the country so early in the year. We are enjoying every minute of it – we were desperately tired of London.

From Evgenia, 1-6-60: Another four pager:

> We are also very pleased with the bell which – but for you – we should never have found it by ourselves. It is very loud and the postman and all the tradespeople are delighted to make it work.

> As I said before – you are the kindest young man that ever was!

The bell was a manual wind-up affair which I got in Ambleside, it involved drilling through the front door at just the required position. This was defined by each of them pressing imaginary bell pushes with their eyes shut, to find the optimum height. It was alarmingly loud, almost worthy of that which 'Dick' got the pigeons to ring in *Pigeon Post* though, unlike the book, there was no account of broken crockery.

Evgenia wrote her usual four pages on 20th June, about Causeway Cottage and the 5 or 6 gallons consumed by the flame gun, by now on loan. Much amusement at the expense of a local gardener who, unused to the heat

FIRST-RATER

BERRY BROTHERS LIMITED

70 JOHN WILLIAM STREET
HUDDERSFIELD
EST. 1880

HUDDERSFIELD
WORSTEDS

TELEPHONE
OHU4 32189

as from Grasmere Road.

13th March 1960

Dear Dr and Mrs Ransome,

    I did enjoy my visit !.

    I enclose the weed killer which I think, with respect, may find gainful employment in your shrubbery.

    Following our conversation about Carbon Paper, I wondered if you would like to try the enclosed samples. We get boxes and boxes of (free) carbons to try and I would be delighted to send whatever is required.

    Incidentally, I'm trying the new Olympia we discussed, an Elite type example with Black/Red silk ribbon. I find it more sophisticated than the old Remington Portable but dislike the long travel on the keys and consequent lack of wallop. I find the standard machines in our office very much easier - and I seriously think (split infinitive ?) an office machine may be far more suitable for your requirements - if portability is not essential.

    I hope you are sharing our lovely weather !

        Yours sincerely

generated, welded "his best pair of crepe-rubber soled shoes" to the drive. She continued:

> 'You are too young and romantic to envy people living on board boats! Having a nice house near sailing water and a very small sailing boat is a much sounder proposition, believe me!'

*   *   *

When first we were married, I had mentioned to Evgenia that Judy and I possessed just four "Chippendale" chairs and an antique wardrobe. She said we were wise never to submit to 'Hire Purchase'. What amused them was that, on return from honeymoon, we had to borrow a bed, kitchen table and lived out of suitcases. All went well until the day when mother-in-law opened the

Telephone: <u>NEWBY BRIDGE</u> ~~ØXXX~~

452

April 19.1960

Dear Mr.Berry,

Haverthwaite,

near ULVERSTON,

Lancashire

↙ These bits in RED

When you give the postman a choice between Newby Bridge
and Finsthwaite, **both being wrong,** a slight delay in deliver
is not only possibbe but probable. However,your letter and
carbons and food for weeds all arrived in due course and I
have already made some experiments which, with apologies for
my bad typing, I now send for your inspection.

    I think that on the whole the best is RED BOX 321. But
it may turn out that the lightweights do not stand up so well
to steady typing. But I do not usually need more than one
copy. I am sending you an original sheet and the eight
resulting specimens of carbon copy. The four Ellam's Plasbag
seem to me about identical and all four are quite good enough

    Allow me to say here and now how much I admire your
office stationery with the first rater at the head. And, of
course, your typing lives up to the stationery.

    It really is enormously good of you to take so much
trouble on my behalf. I am enjoying the **Splendid 99** and
suspect that my typing would be less inefficient if it did
not tempt me into driving too fast.

    I hope all pestilences will have blown over before your
next visit. We look forward to seeing you and to meeting
your friend.

                    Yours sincerely,

                    Art Ransome

From teday on I shall be giving a trial to the carbons,
beginning with Red Box 321 which is so good that I cannot
imagine myself wanting a better.

wardrobe doors – only to find my 'workshop' with racks and racks of tools. I
think this confirmed her worst fears and I felt obliged to build a garage
extension to house workbenches and tools.

Evgenia 28-10-60: (another four-pager)

    Let me wish you "to live happily ever after" … I am enclosing a cutting from
    the Westmorland Gazette in case you are still interested in Causeway End. I
    think it ought to be possible to buy it for £1,200 – 1,500 but I am also certain

that the agents will ask a lot more. Do bargain with them like a horse dealer, offer them half or – at best two thirds of whatever they ask.

I am, of course selfishly interested in having kind neighbours in that house ...'

Evgenia wrote, on 29th December, 1960, "Thank you for your charming [Christmas] card ..." and responded by drawing a very competent piece of holly in red and green on their card. On this is mounted a photograph of them both on the terrace. Two pages follow about the Flame Gun.

> ... and then my own arrived and there they sat [the two FGs] – side by side – in the garage, eating their heads off in idleness.

The Ransomes at Hill Top Cottage on Midsummer Day 1960

With our card the following year, we told them of our map on the chimney breast at home. This was a composite version of all the Lakeland book end papers and gave a picture of diverse activity. Evgenia replied:

> We do admire your very cosy and really "living" room with the cat and all your tools living in it too. Lets have your kitchen next time, with both of you stirring the Xmas pudding and the Pussy cat helping. From Arthur & Evgenia Ransome

"Living" room, our Christmas card of 1961

I never discussed my sad loss of Ernest with the Ransomes and, anyway, their minds were fully concentrated on the first filming of *Swallows and Amazons*. The early version of this is described in his following letter to their staunch friends, with East Anglian connections, the Busks:

```
                                Haverthwaite,
                                near Ulverston,
     April 29,1962.            Lancashire.


        My dear Busks,
             Isn't the year working up to its climax of arriving
        Busks?  I like to think it is.
             It has been a rotten year so far. The journey north
        was a horror, winding up with G being dreadfully sick ,
        poisoned by petrol fumes.  I wasn't sick but would have been
        thankful if I could have been. Then came the worst cold
        I can ever remember up here., and Genia made her own
        cold much worse by heroic stoking of all the fires. I am
        less mobile than ever.  We were able to move into the cottage
        on April 17 and have seen Tree Creepers,Long-tailed XXXXXX
        tits, buzzards, roe-deer.  The thinning of the trees below
        us has enormously improved the view .
             Meanwhile business crises finally getting the Television
        Contract  in the late afternoon of the last day that would
        allow a dollop (a welcome dollop )of cash  to be divided between
        two financial years. And on the top of all this we are half
        inclined to think that we ought never to have agreed to let
        TV work its wicked will at all. I find it very difficult to
        follow  Alastair Sim's sound advice  ("Take every bawbee you
        can screw out of them ....and then forget all about it."-  I
        only wish I could.  I cannot  help foreseeing every kind of
        disaster, with horrid children with loathsome voices and
                                                        why
        so forth. They say that it will mean that a lot of brats
        will make their parents buy the book.  I don't see why they
        they should not warn their parents off any such action.
        They are supposed to be coming up here in a gang to perform and
        be filmed while so doing. Well ! Well !!  And how are they
        going to find the brats to be filmed while sailing?  And
        where will they find S xx  and A, the two boats.  They
        have already plumped for the wrong island   (with no
        harbour)  In fact general prospect of horror.
```

                                        Haverthwaite,
                                        nr.Ulverston,
September 23.1962   Lancashire.

Dear Mr.Berry,

        Thank you for your (and your wife's) kind sympathy
over the misfortunes of my book. I wholeheartedly agree with
your remarks and wish to goodness you had been here all
this summer so that,being immobilized myself, I could have
asked you to keep a stern eye on these scoundrels.

        I entirely agree with your remarks, though I think
they would have been more disgusted if you had seen theXXx
script.

        I t XXX looks as though we should be going to London
pretty soon. But I fear it is too late now for a rescue.
All we can do is to lay in a stock of motor-horns with
which to make a nasty noise when the thingx is actually
shown. Alas, with TV the scoundrels will never hear it.
I hope a few people will be enraged by it and write letters
complaining .   The awful thing is that "my agent" has
given them an option on SWALLOWDALE and PETER DUCK.

        I here hand over.

                    arthur Ransome

Judy and I had prescient dread that the film would not be worthy; and nothing would satisfy the author. Anyway, we all must have a different picture in mind from the written word.

Dora Altounyan, 27-9-62:

> I went with Janet to see the Ransomes the other day, and heard the full story of the film about the Swallows. It is a sad tale. It might have been a splendid show, but they seem to have bungled the whole thing.

Evgenia, 25-10-62:

> I wish I could see your hearth. And I wish I'd remembered where my hoard of blue stones was at the time you were here. It turned up the other day and I am sure these are much better than the ones you took away. ... please call for more blue pebbles.

> [The 'blue stones' were remnants from an old mound at the back of Hill Top garden, they are a dense Russian blue "glass". Years later, Dick Kelsall told me they are actually the slag which was formed by an iron smelting forge – of which Leighton Forge at Arnside is a classic example.]

Our Christmas card, 1962

Fox's favourite Christmas dish
Is rabbit served on toast
But Rabbit's special party trick
Is copyin' them wot boast. (by Judy)

Evgenia, 22-10-63:

Your letter sent [as requested by the ARs] via the BBC has not reached us yet. If it ever will I shall let you know. We got 3 letters selected by the BBC as typical, they all praise – but who cares for: "We liked S.& A. very much. We always watch children's television and like <u>all</u> the programmes"!

Dora, 2-2-64:

'How our weather is made', Christmas card 1963

The more I look at your Christmas card, the more I find in it to chuckle at and make me wonder, John, how you learned to <u>draw</u> so well!

This was one of the last times we heard from Dora and her general encouragement and advice over the years has buoyed me up ever since.

Titty, 10-4-64:

> We are all very pleased to hear what Bosun found for you under the goose
> berry bush and of course are longing to see her... if you ever feel like a
> weekend away you could have my mother's best bedroom ...

Evgenia's reply

John in 'Secret Harbour'

Evgenia 11-11-64:

> Tthe Wild Cat harbour with you in a yellow jacket is one [print] I very much wanted and I very much like the one of the boat [*Mavis/Amazon*] sailing against the very blue hills ... I have the cheapest [Brownie] camera ...
>
> I don't know about letting you take a film. It all depends – Dr Ransome is not at all well and his moods are unpredictable.
>
> You might find it more rewarding to film the cats. The kittens are 5 months old and as big as their mother. The three of them together are playing most wonderful and noisy games.

Our Christmas card for that year, showing Peel Island and our efforts, with the help of Bo'sun, to introduce Elizabeth to *Winter Holiday*. It was partly intended to amuse Dora and thank her for past encouragements but arrived too late.

On Christmas Day 1964, 'The Race'. Introducing Elizabeth to 'Winter Holiday'.

Judy: "A glorious day for the race!"

John: "What race?"

Judy: "The human race silly!"

Evgenia, 25-3-65:

> I see that you are bothered by the question of how does one get a plot for a story. I am afraid nobody can answer it. There are undoubtedly some people whose brains are bristling with plots – they are the lucky ones. But the majority of plots, I think, are the results of using one's imagination to develop and expand some well observed incidents, events or situations and to fit in suitable characters or to project well observed characters into imaginary situations and work out the probable consequences.
>
> My husband did not find plots easy to invent but he never started actual writing until he had worked out a skeleton for his story; he also often wrote the middle or the last Chapters before the earlier ones which meant a good deal of dovetailing, revising and general tidying up at the end. But other people having, no doubt, their plots firmly in their minds start by putting down the title and then proceed from page 1 Chapter I right through to the

last page of the last Chapter without revising or changing a single word of their manuscript. (Hugh Walpole wrote like that). And some people (Enid Blyton says so of herself) need only a clean sheet of paper in the typewriter before them and the words as well as the story just pour out without any conscious effort on the writer's part.

But however the writers arrive at their plots and whatever their individual methods of writing – the great majority of them have the irrepressible urge to write at a very early age. You, have already reached your thirties [37] and yet not intending to write immediately, are decidedly a late starter. But don't let it stop you from trying. In fact unless you try and try and try again you won't be able to tell whether you can do it. And don't put off the start too long.

With kind regards and best wishes to the whole family ...

[I must try to start!]

Both the Ransomes were, for a time, in (different) hospitals.

'Exercise' by Evgenia

Evgenia 10-12-65:

It is most correct and proper to ask for permission to quote anybody in your own publication, however small and private, and I am glad you asked.

Of course we have no objection to your quoting the bit from WINTER HOLIDAY on your Christmas card [ie. *Softly, at first, as if it hardly meant it, the snow began to fall.*] I hope it is as nice a card this year as yours usually are.

We are looking forward to seeing it in due course.

Yes, a short article about Dr.Ransome appeared in last Sunday's OBSERVER; to be exact – hardly more than a long caption to a large coloured photograph of Lakeland scenery, annoyingly inaccurate in most of its statements.

I am sorry to say that Dr Ransome is not very happy in Hospital. But he is so feeble and helpless that I cannot cope at home singlehanded any longer though I am much better now than I was two months ago. There is no hope of his getting any better, And there is not the slightest hope of getting any domestic help.

With kindest regards to you all ...

Evgenia, 7-3-66:

> We did like your Xmas card and the most peaceful domestic scene it represented. But I must admit that I personally for some reason expected a rather snowy landscape.

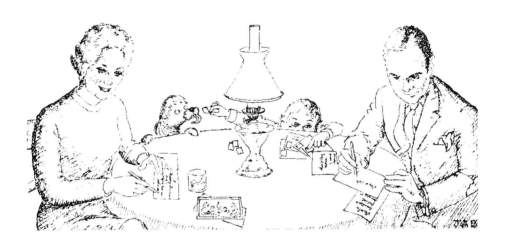

While drawing our 1965 Christmas card, which contained the quotation from 'Winter Holiday': "Softly, at first, as if it hardly meant it, the snow began to fall."

The Ransomes had become inured to regular 'reports' and, after Arthur's death on 3rd June 1967, nothing seemed quite the same but, Judy and I kept up with Evgenia and were fairly regular visitors at Hill Top. Usually this was on the way home from Lanehead. The drill was to rush round the garden with a hoe before an enjoyable chat over tea.

I told her how, in August 1963, my friend Peter Smith, had kindly asked if I would like to join his father-in-law in bringing his six-tonner, *Salote*, home to Pin Mill from Flushing. Needless to say, I couldn't wait and was especially keen to see the port so vividly described in *We Didn't Mean to go to Sea* and Evgenia's description of Arthur's exploratory voyage from Pin Mill in his own *Nancy Blackett* before writing the book.

After a long train journey, the three of us had a night aboard *Salote* before casting off at 0630. To my lasting sorrow, we had to by-pass Kanaal Street and the inner harbour as seen in *WD*. But so started an exciting voyage and a brief illustration of what those children must have experienced, unable to turn back in the high winds and seas. In our case, the best course we could lay was Ostend where we arrived five hours later and had to stay for another three days with adverse winds up to force eight. We had to return by steamer but celebrated by revisiting all the old haunts, the yard at Pin Mill, Alma Cottage and beer at the Butt and Oyster.

I told her of another life-long friendship with my cousin, another 'Peter'. Apart from weaving nearly all the cloth we sold, he and I, after "Naval Control of Shipping" courses at Admiralty, took part in mine-sweeping exercises.

He was leading a rather parallel life to my own, albeit as an experienced yachtsman, fine craftsman and our "best man". We were deeply saddened when, while tired out and cutting patterns at the mill, he accidentally cut off his left hand in a gimping machine. Being Peter, he carried on as usual and six weeks later, during a Cowes race off the Isle of Wight, coped with a violent storm and a raw stump. As I told Evgenia, the rest of the crew were being sick below when he brought them safely home, quite literally, single handed.

Chapter 13

Droppings In & Movings On

B ack in 18th January 1964, Arthur had his eightieth birthday. Unfortunately, long before then, he had become noticeably limited and inward
looking, changing from day to day. Though so geographically isolated, there
was no obvious recourse to radio or newspapers at Hill Top – even after the
recent arrival of electricity, television was fiercely eschewed – and had to be
viewed with a tolerant neighbour on occasions. With fewer surviving
friends and visitors, the regular calls and support by Janet Gnosspelius,
daughter of 'Squashy hat', was especially welcome.

They were still enjoying their natural surroundings, and the deer,
buzzards and redstarts were a delight. But after exceptionally active lives,
their remoteness, house-bound infirmity and extra time for reflection was
taking its toll. Also, with Arthur's increasing dependence, Evgenia's strong
character was becoming more evident, and his own, proportionately subju-
gated.

During our own visits to Hill Top, conversation tended to polarise
between the good and, far more often, the bad. So it was with the Herdwick
sheep. These could often be seen making frantic attempts to scale the wire
netting which extended above their boundary walls – and were attributed to
the long-deceased Beatrix Potter who, at worst, could have been blamed for
her gift of their surrounding acres to the National Trust.

Sometimes, when I got him on his own, I would try to encourage Arthur
into bringing out some of his reminiscences but he wouldn't easily be
drawn. At such times there would be mumbled and ambiguous acquies-
cence which revealed nothing. It was far better to leave him to open conversations but this took time.

What became far more rewarding was his response potential to my own
nautical "swinging the lamp". This seemed to awake interest and was first
revealed when I told him how father had joined HMS *Princess Royal* as an
ordinary seaman in 1916, often coaling ship but gaining an RNVR commis-
sion and finishing up in charge of 13 armed trawlers.

I told how getting involved a second time, aged 41, in 1939 was very
different but at least he finished the last few years cruising the Firth of
Clyde, playing lots of golf and enjoying himself immensely giving away
surplus equipment, as "Port Amenities Liaison Officer".

This was on the staff of Rear Admiral Horan RN, brought back from
retirement, in HMS *Warren*, which was actually the plush Hollywood Hotel

in Largs. As was his tradition, giving orders down the bridge voice pipe, Rear Admiral Horan kept words to a minimum. One morning, father was called to his office:

> *Horan:* Signal from Admiralty on the blower PALO, I'm to reduce staff by 25%. Question is, HOW, without loss of efficiency? Any bright ideas?
>
> *Father, after some concentrated thought:* Well sir, I'm a bit of a gardener and, if I was pruning an apple tree, I wouldn't start with secateurs. Oh no, I would start with a saw!
>
> *Horan:* I follow your drift Berry; carry on.

Father carried on, feeling quite indispensable as always – only to discover the following day that it was he and his small staff of helpers who were being "sawn off" and allowed to go home – as indeed, he had really wanted. Arthur was still intermittently chuckling about this when I had to leave half an hour later.

*   *   *

The Altounyan family had long been a subject we bypassed at Hill Top. But the time came when I felt compelled to say how much I owed to them in many different ways. From Ransome there was no comment, just a very welcome sigh of compliance.

Much more is known now about Ransome's extraordinary life than I knew at the time. Today I am struck by how much my own experience of 'Lanehead' and its influence is a remarkable, albeit very modest, echo of his own.

I told him how it was partly owing to *his* influence, notably because of the visual communications and nautical air which pervade the books, that I had chosen to train as a conscript Visual Signalman, and how shocked we all were the day we "passed out" after twelve months training in summer 1947, to hear that "the use of Semaphore is to cease forthwith".

This announcement took place in the lovely house and grounds of HMS *Mercury* at Petersfield and I asked if he knew it. He did, apparently from much earlier perambulations, but as the home of Lady Peel, going on to recall the extraordinary "X"-shaped staircase. He appeared to dry up at this stage and I think he was reminded of rather mixed earlier days.

Half a lifetime later, I read from Ted Alexander's *Ransome at Home*:

> Arthur's and Ivy's first home together [in 1909] was a cottage 800 feet up on the top of Stoner Hill, looking out over what Arthur describes as 'a precipitous drop' down to the plain of Petersfield to the South Downs. ...

> Towards the end of September Ransome walked from Petersfield to London, a distance of almost sixty miles. He got as far as Guildford on the first day and completed the journey on the second. Four days later he was back at home

Weeks later, Arthur's interest in the area became more apparent and triggered the best response I can remember when I described HMS *Mercury's* parade ground lectures.

Typically, these would start with examples of how *not* to do things and the fictional participants were almost invariably named 'Bloggins' and 'Spifkins'. Recounting what they got up to in very polished, almost theatrical performances, as relayed to Arthur, kept him in stitches.

The story he enjoyed most involved the elderly .303 Lea Enfield rifle. It was a lecture given by an archetypal Gunnery Chief Petty Officer visiting from Whale Island whose style and studied delivery had become something of a byword, even the subject of some mimicry on the BBC. It went something like:

> *CPO:* "... And now we comes to the butt of the rifle. The butt-o-the-rifle is usually made from either Helm, Hash or Ickory ..."
>
> *Bright spark at the back:* "I say Chiefy, surely you must mean Elm, Ash or Hickory!"
>
> *CPO:* "I means wot I sez, HELM, HASH OR ICKORY and . . hif I may continoo, the butt-o-the-rifle is also sometimes made of a very-ard-wood, wot is called Lignum Vitae.
>
> Now LIGNUM VITAAHH is also wot-is-used for makin' Piles for Piers - an wen I sez PILES FOR PIERS – you silly "billy"-at-the-back-there – I means PILES FOR PIERS and not bleedin' EMORROIDS FER HARISTOCRATS."

Ransome had been giggling long before the punch-line but then, with me little realising quite how close this was to home, he let out a huge GUFFAW! ... Evgenia, peering round the door, merely bit her lip.

He seemed transformed and almost expansive when next I called. He asked if I had read John Wyndham's astonishing science-fiction novel *The Day of the Triffids*, "worthy of H.G. Wells". This had clearly left a deep impression. He went on to describe how the grotesque 'triffids' grew to over seven feet tall and, though initially encouraged for their yield of high-grade vegetable oil, had multiplied and become an appalling menace. They could "walk" and *take firm root* almost anywhere into *earth*, ready to ambush passers by. To be slashed by their dreadful stem meant almost certain death.

Ransome stopped there and I shall always remember him becoming visibly embarrassed, seeming to ponder whether, or not, to continue ... After a very long pause, obvious shamefacedness and my encouragement, he decided to go on.

I was taken by the elbow to the front door, he opened it and pointed outside to the troughs which lay, one to each side. These were like deep ceramic sinks, full of earth and flowers. In continued humiliation, he went on to say that the book had been so convincing that after reading it, he had become positively "unable to go out without first checking, left and right, for dug-in 'triffids'".

He and the author had been in touch and, as I suggested, "You have become a bit of a fan". He admitted this – with even more reluctance and shame.

It turned out that he had acquired two copies and wanted me to have the spare. I have suffered from the same susceptibilities ever since!

* * *

With the Ransome's congratulations and best wishes on our engagement, came a kind invitation to visit. However, since fitting the wind-up door-bell at Hill Top, I had, on one occasion, been "hoist with my own petard" – by ringing it while poor Arthur was all alone (in the far-distant bathroom). This occasioned the only-ever rebuke I received from Evgenia and it had become the customary courtesy to telephone before subsequent arrivals. We made a point of this for Judy's first visit and, with the prospect of meeting her for the first time, they most kindly urged us forth.

Our passage from Lanehead, along so many leafy lanes, had made Judy concerned about the cottage's sheer remoteness now that the Ransomes were becoming dependant on transport by local taxi. Her eyes were wide and mouth almost agape as we walked up the drive and she paused to admire the flower-filled sinks and my handy work on the bell. By this time I may have put some tape round the actual gong but the loudness in that slate-floored interior remained alarming even to us outside.

As usual, it was Mrs Ransome who opened the door and though I had described her to Judy before, she was startled by Evgenia's size, still nearly six feet tall, Amazonian and with ebullient charm. Ransome was in his study above the garage so we climbed the steps to find him, characteristically sitting at the cloth-covered table, but by now, behind our much-debated *portable* new 'Olympia' typewriter. He rose, welcomed me and received Judy most courteously. We chatted for a while about this and that and there was an air of contentment and friendliness that was a joy to see. None-the-less, I was puzzled to see the blank sheet of paper in front of him. It was almost as if he had run out of ideas or was waiting for some inspiration, a complete change from what had gone before. Evgenia, sensing my curiosity as she guided us down to the garden, admitted he was becoming "less active".

By now, thoroughly at ease, Judy wondered if she might take photographs but quickly realised that it would be a violation even to ask.

By then, thanks to father's 'flame thrower' the garden was pleasantly free from weeds. Clearly, after Arthur and their beloved tabby cat, this was Evgenia's main object of devotion. It was down one of several paths that we met their friendly 'Sally'. With her, we had a little chat and she began to purr quite effusively. Judy then wandering ahead and came across a tobacco pipe which lay almost out of sight on the path. Picking it up, she said to Mrs Ransome, "I think Dr Ransome has dropped his pipe". "Oh no" she said, "that's mine," and popped it into the pocket of her overall dress. [The pipe was small, curly and with a silver band – exactly like the one with which we are now familiar in the photograph of Evgenia and her sister in 1918, as young women, complete with pet snake, on page 208 of Hugh Brogan's *The Life of Arthur Ransome*.]

Before our marriage, It was one of the list of understandable concerns from Judy's father, that I was ten years older than she. I had mentioned this *en passant* to the Ransomes and had been greeted with amused uproar – and assurances that the same discrepancy had worked "perfectly well" for them.

As an absurd formality, we invited the Ransomes, the Altounyans and Constantinescos, to our wedding and of course each in turn declined for very obvious reasons.

Ernest Altounyan, 10-10-60:

> [Following Wedding apologies] Dora and I can only hope that later on, when we have the house to ourselves, you will both be able to come and stay with us and perhaps choose, as a wedding present, one of her pictures... Be sure that we shall both be thinking of you, very sincerely, on the Great Day.
>
> The boat is of course yours to sail at any time.
>
> Yours ever and ever
>
> EA

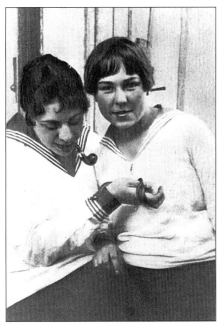

Evgenia Shelepina (with snake) and her sister Iraida, summer 1918

So it was that we had our first shared stay at Lanehead – one of the happiest ambiences I have known. Just being there would have been more than we could have wished – but then came the almost *carte blanche* choice of one of dear Dora's paintings. From such a wealth of superb Impressionist-type oils, the school I most admired, this might have been overwhelming, but there was just one which encapsulated our fondest associations too: Dora's, 20"x14" oil, 'Afternoon at Coniston'. It was painted from 'Holly Howe', starting with the boathouse and, across a glistening lake, sombre banks rising to delightful patches of bright sun setting over Banisteads. The 'High Tops' Ransome describes is in blue/purple shadow, crossed by transient rays of light. It is a challenging, changing subject, painted in consequent lush looseness and verve, almost certainly at a single sitting long ago. How I should have loved to be there!

Fully restored and within a dark frame, as Dora had insisted, it now occupies a special place in our sitting room. It reminds us daily of especially happy times but I experience just occasional pangs of guilt; that we, "not family", have something so redolent as the view from Lanehead and the way down to so much delight.

Our second combined visit to the Ransomes at Hill Top was as a married couple and, very kindly and unexpectedly, they gave us a gold-embossed 'Telephone Numbers' book, and a blank recipe book, which now contains our favourite dishes. Both are in regular service over forty years later. So sensibly, they were not wrapped but, regretfully, no gifts were ever inscribed except later, for a soft-back copy of *The Theatres of London*, rather sparingly, "To the Berrys from the Ransomes".

I think the ARs had developed an aversion to things being cherished for the wrong reason and renounced all "value-added" mementoes.

Over tea and buns, we discussed favourite writers and conversation took a bizarre turn when Ransome declared, so far as we can remember though it stretches credulity, that "Shakespeare had some difficulty in writing". We assumed this conversation stopper was tongue in cheek, but then Evgenia, in all apparent seriousness, agreed with him. He went on reassuringly to say how much they admired Enid Blyton as a writer for children.

I think it was not till 1942 that, with wartime restrictions and surrounded by deer at 'The Heald' that Arthur became a practical shot. By August 1962, aged 78, he was still nourishing that sporting instinct. From a window overlooking the garden, he showed us two, much-perforated, cardboard targets nailed to a tree stump on the far-away bank. This could conveniently be fired at from the house and he showed us how he aimed, by resting the .22 rifle on the window ledge. His 27-6-62 diary records:

> Police 'Sergeant' brought form? for my rifle (firearm) certificate. A very nice chap but I was horribly insecure in talking with him.

And two years later, rather sadly:

> Janet [Gnosspelius] here, shooting very well (I shot very badly) target .22.

* * *

About this time, our kind friends, the Jackson Smiths, had transferred *Rilla*, with the help of young Peter and a pilot, via the Firth of Forth and Clyde to Tighnabruaich in the Kyles of Bute. As before, they so-kindly included us in their new cruising ground. It was also an area the Ransomes knew and we hoped to trap them into going much further and discussing Lewis and *Great Northern* book territory but they seemed to sense this and very nearly branded us as 'fans'.

Instead, we described our summer holidays in1963 when a cruise in Loch Fyne included Lochgilphead and we berthed in the basin leading to the Crinan Canal. Somehow, everything appeared especially spruce. This was our second visit yet the grass appeared remarkably green and the geese especially white. We asked at the pub what was going on and learnt that the Royal Sailing Yacht *Bloodhound*, was expected next day.

Judy and I got up early and saw her peak appear over the horizon and later, entering the lock where we looked down on a very young Prince Charles, Princess Anne and Prince Olaf of Sweden as they busied themselves protecting *Bloodhound*'s immaculate sides with the largest inflated fenders ever seen.

As they moved up into the basin, we thought of dipping our red ensign but exchanged friendly and informal waves instead. As it happened, we were the only other craft in the tiny basin, our cockpits stern on and an air of happy freedom existed which would seem impossible today. Our usual 'drinks before lunch' were echoed with lemonade next door as they prepared for the canal passage out to sea and the Sound of Jura. We felt to be so much a part of it and, with surreptitious glances, to see them so enjoying themselves

Teatime aboard *Rilla* with Clare and Jackson Smith
(photo by Judy)

as, with studied nonchalance, we strove not to intrude.

* * *

We visited Dora, Titty and the children at Lanehead with our Elizabeth when she was only six weeks old – and got it on film. As always, it was a lovely occasion but we were shocked to see how frail Dora had become. After lunch, we visited Hill Top and the Ransomes seemed touched by being introduced to one so young, yet welcomed her quite formally as one would an adult.

"To celebrate" we retired to the greenhouse and Evgenia gave us lots of geranium plants, with instructions on how to propagate. We have been tending their offspring ever since.

Elizabeth appeared to take it all in and responded by smiling patiently but, for her, it had been a long day and circumstances had got far beyond her control. Not fully *au fait*, Evgenia and I went to look for a chamber pot.

Left alone with the great man and Elizabeth, Judy felt slightly in awe but he beamed like a benevolent uncle and commented appreciatively about the shape of Elizabeth's head. He claimed to be a phrenologist and pronounced that she would become "an intellectual".

He went on to say that he came from Leeds and, for such an obvious countryman, this so surprised Judy that she neglected to tell him that she came, not from Huddersfield as he supposed, but from Nailsworth in Gloucestershire. Years later she regretted this when reading Alexander's *Ransome at Home*, which describes AR's extraordinary life and escapades – with long walks from Stroud, just four miles from the Nailsworth he must have known so well.

By the time Judy and Evgenia finally got Elizabeth to the bathroom, a full valeting service was necessary, but we need not have worried. Evgenia took charge and could not have been more kind and helpful.

We have since wondered if Elizabeth, now very happily married to David and with two lovely daughters, both Ransome fans – will ever tell them about *once being bathed "by Trotsky's secretary"*.

* * *

From early married life, the nearest we got to owning a *Swallow-* or *Amazon*-type boat was our very early 10ft Mirror dinghy. As this was sponsored through *The Daily Mirror*, we naturally named her *Alice* and either trailed her or, as usual accompanied by our caravan, carried her everywhere on the roof of successive estate cars.

We experienced the most delightful freedom, trailing and sailing all over England, Wales and Scotland. This was whenever we could escape and at minimal expense, sometimes on canals, a helpful nursery for the children but mostly in The Lakes, Broadland and sea.

The Ransomes insisted on being kept informed, especially about 'The Broads', but for a change over tea and buns one afternoon, I told what happened to a tailor customer of mine.

* * *

Each weekend, he and "three of the lads" took his small cruiser exploring the canal system around Walsall and Dudley. This was just after the war and their declared aim was to "reopen British Waterways".

So, on one precious weekend exploring in a new direction, they reached a collapsed notice reading 'Closed Tunnel' and felt obliged to see why. They went into it at slow speed with searchlight full on and ran into a dead sheep and a railway sleeper before squeezing out into daylight and the highly raised canal beyond.

It was "quite an experience to be gazing down on fields and the backs of cows twenty feet below" as they sat drinking beer and listening to gramophone records on the hot cabin roof, a much gentler version of Ransome's 'Hullabaloos' in *Coot Club* as the ARs readily agreed.

Anyway, all went well until they came to a bend and a new experience as the cruiser brushed against the coypu-riddled bank. Without warning, this gave way and they, huge rats and torrents of water sluiced down into a cabbage field far below. Mercifully, the boat stayed upright, afloat again as water continued to cascade.

Meanwhile, the secured gramophone played on while, with beer tankards raised in trembling hands, they pondered "what are we going to tell our wives this time?"

* * *

The last time I saw Arthur was a shock. In spite of Evgenia's tearful warnings as she pushed me towards the stairs, I felt unprimed. I was not prepared for such decline.

I found him sitting at his rug-covered table as usual. But this had been pulled right up to the window, was clear of all implements and supported only his elbows. He acknowledged my presence with a nod and vague smile as I sat beside him, then replaced his elbows on the table, chin in hands. He remained silent and was seemingly absorbed by the view across the valley of Rusland Pool and the woods and hills far beyond. For quite some time we shared the view in utter quietness and I wondered if we saw the same things – and what it meant to us.

We had shared such an enjoyable relationship in later years, yet it occurred to me that I still wanted to know so much of what he thought of things. It was clearly too late for that now and, somehow on reflection, it no longer seemed to matter. After years of study and reflection, I knew so much already.

I have wished since that I had offered to read to him for a while – much in the way that, long ago, Juliet and I had been captured and eventually lulled into sweet dreams by passages from the books ...

Emotional gestures were "not the thing" in my day, but I suddenly found my arm squeezing round his shoulders and saying "thank you, thank you, for all you have given to us" – but already he seemed in a different world – a consistently happy one I did so hope!

*   *   *

Arthur was in hospital the next time Judy and I called. We ate one of Evgenia's delightful curries and I'm told that she and I talked and talked – while Judy and two-year-old Elizabeth spoke of other things.

Arthur died on 3-6-67. We missed the funeral but called on Evgenia days later. She seemed strangely ill-prepared for a life inevitably on her own. A time of unimagined loneliness was to follow. It was a merciful release for Arthur but everything had become negative. She was neither willing nor able to carry on at Hill Top, yet had no idea of where to go. There was also the awful necessity of reducing possessions, essentially thousands of Arthur's books – which were stacked in the garage and a nearby barn. I wish I had been more help!

There were few contemporaries left. Yet, still many friends wishing to remember:

Hella Altounyan, Roger's widow, wrote to us on 12-6-67:

> I tried hard to get hold of you ... Granada television brought a tribute to Arthur Ransome by way of making a film of Coniston – Peel Island with an interview with Titty and Peter – in place of Roger sailing the *Amazon*. Only 10 minutes but rather fun. ...

Evgenia, 5-7-67:

> I feel great relief at his suffering being over. But after nearly fifty years together there is an awful emptiness – now that he is gone.

> I have been very unwell and went myself as a patient into the hospital where he was four days before he died and stayed there after his death for nearly a fortnight... But it has not restored me enough to think that I could go on living here all alone much longer. But I can't move just yet and I don't know where to go.

Evgenia, 19-7-68;

> It is a very long time since I had any news of you. I hope you are flourishing.
>
> As I have been steadily getting more and more lame and less and less able to keep this house and particularly the garden the way I would like to see them kept it made me very miserable and I have decided to give up the struggle.
>
> A week ago I have sold the house and am now in the throes of preparing to hand it over to the new owners. There is a most dreadful amount of junk collected in the garage, the barn and the house itself. At the moment it does not seem possible ever to sort it all out by August 7th when I rather hope to move to my new home at AYNHOE PARK, Nr. BANBURY, OXON.
>
> I wonder if you are actually on your holiday and, if so, where? Sailing somewhere I presume.
>
> With kindest regards to the whole family

Evgenia, 19-12-68:

> Selling Hill Top and moving to Aynhoe Park made me more ill than ever ... The better I feel – the less I like this flat country and its climate. After all, I have lived in the Lakes for 45 years and got used to the views and clear fresh air.

While visiting tailors in that direction, I found Evgenia in the most beautiful and historic surrounding at Aynhoe. Her flat was on the ground floor of the east wing and the substantially reduced but precious nucleus of Arthur's old library was housed in the disused ovens and fireplace there. This huge and high ceilinged room had a spare bedroom in the recently added 'minstrel gallery' though she was self contained on the ground floor. She had become quite slim and elegant in these cloistered surroundings.

Not uncharacteristically, she complained of the flat countryside and "severe climate", subject to extremes she explained, being the furthest point inland. Nevertheless, she seemed to have a resigned contentment at last.

Teatime with Elizabeth and Kate, Christmas 1970

Evgenia, 12-6-70, prior to another visit:

> … congratulations on the arrival of Kate, I hope that Elizabeth is pleased to have a little sister, but she has been too long the only pebble on the beach, she might have been rather resentful of Kate's arrival.

> … it is very kind of you to suggest taking me out to dinner but I would much prefer you sharing my supper here, if you don't mind …

> I am much looking forward to seeing you on the 16th.

> With love [a first] to all the family.

Elizabeth and Kate

Evgenia, 23-12-71:

> Dear John, [another first after 13 years of defensive formality.]

> I was awfully pleased to get the picture of Berry family studio, in full blast. I don't agree with your title for it. I would have called it "They bit off more than they could chew". The model has proved too strong meat for the artists. I give the first prize to KATE – THE OCTOPUS; it has got a lot of feeling in it ; the pure enjoyment of the sitter and the absolute exasperation of the painter. I wish you all the luck in your Art Society.

> I can't remember what I told you about writing in general; I was probably talking through my hat. What do I know about writing? I have never written a thing nor have I ever suffered from ambition to be a writer.

> I rather admire your leisurely approach to either branch of Art. You are not in a hurry to get there but quite happy to be going along in that direction. Quite

"Eye of Beholder card," Christmas 1971

unlike one of my husband's friends who put in his diary EIGHTEEN TODAY AND NOTHING DONE !

Kind regards and best wishes to the whole family

Yours sincerely

Evgenia Ransome

> *[Over thirty years later, at 75, I hope Evgenia and Arthur will forgive me for Discovering Swallows and Ransomes.]*

On Evgenia's 1973 Christmas card:

> Many thanks for the portrait of the artist and his family.
>
> Please continue to be solvent. St Anne's [Windermere] is a jolly good school and renewing your ties with the Lake District would do you a lot of good.
>
> I think you got it a little mixed about 8 years is too soon for being introduced to *Swallows & Amazons*. A.R., like myself, thought that no child is too young to be read aloud to – but it is <u>up to the reader</u> to find what really interests the child most. It is also very stimulating in making the child want to read for itself. But one must be prepared that what interested and excited the parent may never at any age be of any interest to the child. Very disappointing but true. But in reading S. & A. series it is best to begin with the first. If you have any volume in Penguin edition they give the chronological order in which the books were published.
>
> There was a film of *Swallows and Amazons* made this Summer but it will start being shown <u>in cinemas</u> only at Easter 1974.
>
> And yes, thank you, I do manage to keep reasonably well and warm, if not too mobile. My only complaint is the quite unreasonably bad cook we've got at present.

Judy about to read 'Winter Holiday'. Christmas 1973

Evgenia's last letter to us is as follows. In response, we agreed that the excellent Ronald Fraser was wrongly cast for the almost impossible part of 'Captain Flint' – and one imagines him emerging from the lake, chest heaving

Aynhoe Park
Banbury
Oxon

January 4.1975

Dear John, Judy, Elisabeth and Kate,

I am very sorry I have not sent you a Christmas
card. But I have been much afflicted by some nasty germ
all through the second half of December and was quite
unable to cope.

But I am sending you now my most sincere good
wishes for a very Happy New Year.

As for depression, inflation, strikes etc. I am
very much in the same boat as everybody else. But I don't
see any good in trying to complain louder than other
people.

I had many letters from people who saw the film.
The prevailing verdict was: the scenery - excellent;
some of the actors - a bad choice; John - very feeble,
Captain Flint - an absolute pain in the neck. (This is
just what I think of Ronald Fraser playing Captain Flint).
But a good many of these critics also said that on the
whole they liked the film well enough to want to see it
again. I believe that in spite of the producers intent-
ions of advertising and showing the film as widely as
possible over the whole country the distribution and the
length of time it was shown at different places were so
uneven that there are quite a number of disappointed
people who have not seen it - though badly wanted to.

Thank you for your Christmas card. It is the most
eloquent protest of a parent against the relentless
energy of the young offspring. Still, I don't think you
must grumble; after all you are included in the party on
equal terms. And if you know your George Orwell you must
see that it is only reasonable that the leaders are a bit
more equal than the camels of the party. You see, you

P.T.O.

might have been refused admission all together on account of your senile old age. 40 ? 45 ? or whatever it is now.

Now that Elizareth is at St.Anne's and you are visiting the Lake District often - I wonder if you have been to see Arthur Ransome's memorial "corner" in Abbot Hall Museum in Kendal? If you haven't, please, try to do it sometime. I should be very much interested in your comments.

For various reasons I am leaving Aynhoe Park at the end of next February and moving into Flat 3, GRETTON Court,
OB3 OQN Girton, Cambridge. It is a much smaller flat than I have got now and I shall badly miss my enormous sitting room, but otherwise I hope I shall be more comfortable there than I have been at Aynhoe Park lately.

Best wishes for the New Year

And more power to your drawing hand!

Yours sincerely

Evgenia Ransome

behind a wet nylon shirt, just as other scenes were not entirely in keeping. It had taken Richard Pilbrow nine months to persuade Evgenia – that he really intended to stick closely to the book yet it was an impossible to encapsulate so much in a short film, still less to expect Evgenia to feel responsible for it in her last days. It was almost as if she knew that correspondence was coming to an end.

On 19th March 1975, a Pickfords' van had arrived at Aynhoe Park and packed up all her belongings for removal to Gretton Court. Then a taxi arrived to take her there but had to be sent back. Evgenia had already passed on.

* * *

Back in 1971, after a lecture from Titty, I had joined The Huddersfield Art Society and I felt gathered together with kindred spirits at last.

Now, the oil paints and scrubbed-down brushes "given" to me by our long-deceased Auntie Katharine really came into their own and I often thanked her as I squeezed out precious dollops from indecipherable tubes onto her huge and highly polished pallet.

Summer evenings were spent painting landscapes, subsequently exhibited in pubs, restaurants, hospitals, banks and shops. This provided a very small erratic income. Pubs were a favourite subject and I recall trying to complete an oil of one which, in those days, was surrounded by a number of roundabouts, known locally as 'the silly isles'. Painting from life often presents a hurdle, in this case especially, it was inquisitive passers-by sharing the pavement.

In order to prevent them having to squeeze past amongst the zooming traffic, I stepped over a low wall and set up my easel on an area of rough grass and relative tranquillity. All went well until an elderly gentleman climbed over too and stood resolutely beside me. He would not be shaken off and had an irritating way of asking questions and tapping me on the shoulder. In some exasperation, I told him that dusk was falling and that I must be allowed to concentrate. "I understand that," he replied, "but I think you ought to know, you're standing in my garden."

* * *

From 1973, I had been getting modest local portrait commissions but was hugely impressed by the inspirational style, colour and potential of an artist who, so fortunately lived in Holmfirth nearby. Judy and I became determined to ask Trevor Stubley to paint an oil of our 9 year old Elizabeth, before he became too expensive. Fortunately, he was unaware of my own aspirations and I was allowed to sit in and see how it was done.

This involved poor Elizabeth in weekend sittings on a throne of bricks supporting a table top in the bedroom of his four small sons. She never complained but it was clear that she was not really enjoying the hours of silent inactivity. All went well until, with the growing licence which passed for freedom in those days, Trevor's eldest son, while swinging above us on a trapeze, accidentally (?) hit Trevor in the middle of the back while finishing Elizabeth's portrait – causing him to splat over what had been a beautiful left eye.

Trevor was not amused and, amid the first signs of delight from Elizabeth, the culprit was horizontally evacuated. Moments later, Trevor's artist wife, Val, yelled up the stairs "The donkeys are out". These were a valued part of a menagerie of dogs, goats, pigs, ducklings and cats and we set off chasing them across the moors, Elizabeth in fits of laughter all the way.

We came to a quiet reservoir with somnolent fishermen grouped like statues round its glass-like surface. Here, the donkeys had stopped for a drink, then a family dog caught them up and jumped in for a swim and, while trying to retrieve him, another son fell out of a tree into the water with a considerable splash. The scene was transformed and, to Elizabeth's increasing delight, we were all chased away by irate fishermen.

Her portrait became one of those submitted to the Royal Society of Portrait Painters and Trevor became Yorkshire's Royal Portraitist, later to paint The Queen, become Vice President and much more.

Having been promoted to a higher and more active plane and there being no one else available at the time, I took his place as a portrait demonstrator for annual exhibitions and Art Societies around Yorkshire. This increased my meagre commissions too and, thanks to him, life became more rewarding in every way.

It did occur to me however that, apart from earlier Life classes and unwitting "demonstrations" by Trevor, I had no formal Art College training and I feared to appear unprofessional. But, just as I have imaginary chats with mother and the Almighty, I developed an extra habit of "conferring" with the late dear Dora Altounyan concerning profession portraiture and, by

carefully laying out each problem, she did seem to invoke most practical solutions. During such congress, the sitter sometimes appeared in utter bewilderment, as I gazed into eternity.

I have always admired the work of Edwardian painters and in 1976, one of my earlier endeavours at portraiture was in this vein, a 24"x 36" oil of Elizabeth and Kate on their school trunk complete with a Berry Bros. barrow as on a station platform. For this, the children had to be requested, bribed and ordered into sitting still, their countenances assuming such abject misery that instead of naming the picture 'Arrival' as planned, it became 'Departure'.

Trevor Stubley's portrait of Elizabeth aged nine in 1973

*   *   *

When mother died in 1978, Juliet and I felt irretrievable loss. She had been our main influence in early life and her ever-loving and selfless thoughts will remain with us forever.

After 100 years, in 1980, Berry Bros. was forced to close. Father, aged 81, when not playing golf, was still "indispensable" but mounting losses in both suitings and

Departure

trimmings were unsustainable and our affectionate staff became redundant. After his 68 years of service including two world wars, father had indeed earned a rest but, without mother, this lasted for just two years.

In the meantime, I found myself unemployed, something I thought only happened to other people. Queuing up at the Labour exchange – with Judy and I sometimes visiting Kate at boarding school in the same week – was quite bizarre.

We were not entirely without capital but determined not to just spend it on the cost of living. Also, the genetic culture of 'work' remained except that I found myself not in universal demand. Fortunately after my interminable tax contributions, I found that having tried, the State was obliged to support us for a whole year and I began to recognise a golden opportunity to do my own thing at last.

We decided that a studio must be built in the dark and draughty roof space. Fortunately, the house had a ridge roof and this would later allow room for an additional staircase over the original. Work was started with Judy handing five-metre joists up through a trapdoor in the landing ceiling and these were made to double up with the ceiling joists from an internal central wall to both front and back eaves.

The whole project went on each day and night for a year and the floor, once boarded, was lit by four huge Velux windows. Then the rafters were insulated, sheathed and planked, the walls snowcemed to reveal a brilliant twenty-foot-square floor space with huge lockers under the lower purlins. Almost at once an easel and portable throne appeared, a stove, bookcases, beds, sofas, a washbasin and desks etc.

Among the many places to sit, one has been added and regarded as a rather delicate subject and permanently rug-covered. It is the product of years of development and now ripe for marketing – a prototype WC with, 'for hygienic purposes', an easily-fitted small handle to both lid and seat (as used every day, by every one, elsewhere in the house). The only thing to remind overnight visitors is that this one is not plumbed in.

The 'Studio' with its south and north 'lights' has spectacular views and has been an invaluable work and social gathering place ever since. I liked to think it compares with AR's workroom at Low Ludderburn, which he called "the best I ever had".

All I needed then were more portrait commissions and, in the meantime some paid employment. The trouble was, aged 53, I had no viable aptitudes or experience. In desperation, I consented to be a Double Glazing salesman and, by perverse fortune, sold all the front windows of a house on the first evening out – but nothing more during the dismal twelve months to follow. It transpired that, to wear a tee shirt and lean in doorways was the way to create real trust and demand in Barnsley.

My portrait of Kate aged nine in 1979

Fortunately, dear old Huddersfield Art Society came to my aid. One established member was married to a property restorer in the Colne Valley and after stringent tests on his garage wall, I was promoted to become a builder's labourer. To be paid for working "with hands" and seeing how building should be done was what *I* had always wanted.

I was part of a team and our first project was to pull down a dear old cottage in Marsden, and "restore it in keeping". The local authorities were endlessly doctrinaire as always, but knew little of local history and failed to recognise its prime feature, a historic 'wuzzing hole' in full view beside the little lane.

This was about an inch-wide cavity which, with considerable effort, one or two hundred years earlier, had been cut into a large stone. As with many others which remain in the area, it had clearly been used in the process of drying raw wool after scouring.

The procedure was to insert a strong stick into the hole and from this a basket containing the wet scoured wool was dangled. Then, by "wuzzing" it round and round as fast as possible, centrifugal force spun off moisture.

What a sight it must have been! As always, the hole was sited about hip level and wool workers, especially the children, were much smaller in those days.

The rest of our team lived locally but appeared not to recognise its value, so I drew special attention to it before we started pulling down and carefully laying out different thicknesses of stone into their respective 'courses' in a field across the lane. Days later, my top half suddenly stuck horizontally and, paralysed with age-old lumbago, I was laid off for a week. I returned to find the front wall had been "restored" and that the precious wuzzing hole had been replaced – well above our heads.

For months I found it impossible to stand upright and lift heavy loads. Instead I was relegated to pointing walls and houses in the Colne Valley towards Marsden. My initials remain on them still and I'm often reminded of Uncle Clifford, aged 13, desperately pushing his barrow along the same roads.

*   *   *

It was about this time that Titty spoke up and told me to "stop messing about". Almost in answer, my Trevor benefactor, now in high demand for private commissions, handed over his employment with a National Portrait institution in 1984. This involved painting pupils in private schools as part of a team all over England. It turned out to be a most absorbing experience which required up to four frantic pastel portraits, or two half oils every single day. As if electrifying tension was not enough, we then had to mount and frame, making it an unofficial twelve hour day.

In November, after a "day's work" at a famous girl's school, the lights suddenly went out at 8pm and, unaccompanied, I found myself locked into the science block with all windows locked and no apparent means of escape. In utter darkness I fell down a stone staircase and only after much banging was I let out. I naturally spoke to the caretaker but exactly the same thing happened the following November.

Even when working as a team, we often went without lunch to keep up and for the first time ever, I became so mentally exhausted at times that I could not even work out how to open the car door.

But the sheer joy of portraiture amply made up for everything and it was especially rewarding painting as a group and witnessing some classical style. The evenings were even better, discussing what each of us had done over compensating amounts of food and drink.

We had such interesting sitters too, boys and girls from all over the world, some with great natural character and beauty to the occasional amusing junior royals. They had plenty to say and, singly or in groups, we enjoyed them all.

The River Stour at King's School, Canterbury, with its punts and rowers, ran around the historic wall of one "studio". Among my sitters was a boy called Chaplin. He turned up as a pie-frilled chorister and could not sit still but reluctantly confessed to being a recognisable grandson of Charlie Chaplin.

There were hundreds of subjects over the years and we visited a wealth of locations including manor houses and castles.

*   *   *

In May1985, I was able to visit Titty and Melkon in Coniston and swap progress reports. Her ideas were most helpful and encouraging as always. Meanwhile, a team of us was spending the happy week painting portraits in the stable block where Kate was still at School in Windermere.

She and her pal 'Tor' supplied us all with lunch and tea. On our first day it was pouring with rain as they brought our delicious roast beef and Yorkshire puddings down the long drive with the greeting, "don't break off Dad, its cold already".

Both Elizabeth and Kate have behaved beautifully and remain very loving to this day. Even as grownup mothers after meals, they tend to ask absentmindedly "may I get down" – but much earlier, Judy and I were quite unprepared for that "certain age!"

But, just as Evgenia had told us, the school was excellent in every way and, during Elizabeth and Kate's twelve overlapping years, we had been on most friendly and Christian name terms with the headmaster.

Then, in Kate's last two weeks, came the first of three letters – "Dear Mr & Mrs Berry, I have to tell you that Kate has been found on the roof ... if ever this happens again ..." (Years later, it transpired that "smoke dispersal" was the reason – an expellable offence!)

The following weekend she was home for an exeat and got a suitable dressing down from Judy. Then, as we prepared to take her back on Sunday evening, she asked if she might take back "a bottle of your lovely home-made wine Mum, to share with my friends for the very last time". At this, Judy was visibly touched, overcome by visions of Kate and her band of twelve contemporaries sharing a thimble full each – not each of them securing a bottle in rather the same way and holding quite a party in the field above.

Most fortunately, Judy's wine had not fermented and Kate was able to help matron to put the rest of the girls to bed – though still obliged to write a letter of apology to her long after leaving school. Sensible discipline was widespread and accepted as essential in those days – of lasting benefit, even for the offspring of them both!

But her last day at school coincided with a very special event, when everyone was assembled on the terrace for what, after twelve years, was also to be the headmaster's last day at school. It was a lovely sunny Sunday morning and over the sunlit conifers could be seen the sparkle of Lake Windermere and the snow-capped Langdales beneath a deep blue sky.

The headmaster, aside from being tall, dark and handsome, was highly respected by all and there was a reverent hush and much beating of womanly hearts as he took his stand and prepared to address them for the very last time.

But just then, though certainly not scheduled, was the sound of high heels clip clopping up the steps from the car park – as a 'Kissagram Girl' from Bowness, hired by Kate and Tor, suddenly appeared.

Dressed in a formal hat, an invisible body stocking and abundant lipstick, she clip clopped across the terrace, mounted the dais, grabbed the headmaster round the neck and gave him a resounding and very sticky kiss across the cheek.

There followed a shocked silence and heart-stopping bewilderment. What could possibly follow this unprecedented breach in a school devoted to high academic achievement and exemplary conduct?

But he rose to the occasion and answered in the only possible way ... giving the girl a resounding kiss in reply.

*   *   *

As a child, I never dreamt that yet another of my oldest friends, this time from primary school, would become a portrait artist. But after 27 years with the Palm Beach aristocracy, painting the Duke of Edinburgh and Princess Anne, he settled on these shores and shared our Christmases before his death in 2003.

Annual turnover from my own commissions appeared minuscule in comparison with John Orr's and even painting the odd nobility and foreign royal was through schools and the race horse 'Silver Buck', thanks to a kind relation of Judy's. I was starting from scratch and there was too much "resting". I wondered how to appear more established.

In a desperate measure to increase turnover, I turned to *Who's Who* and wrote to a number of well-known locals, offering them a free sitting. The response was unexpectedly positive, every single one accepted and the task took many fascinating weeks to complete.

I decided to start on the list of six acquiescent bishops, notably the former "Most Revd. Archbishop of York" and Titty, reading my eventual "Sitters Include CV", laughingly suggested I was "becoming a bit of a fraud".

After a fortifying pub lunch round the corner, I parked our yellow Citroën Dyane in the Bishopthorpe Palace yard and walked, laden with equipment, to the garden entrance as instructed. There, leaning unexpectedly up against the arched gateway was a large notice – with the intriguing inscription "Real Ale round the Back".

At this I pictured some heavenly alehouse down by the river but there was no time to look. Instead I reported to the office exactly on time and was shown up to a huge and delightful room on an upper floor. This looked over the Palace gardens to a wide expanse of the River Ouse.

While setting up, His Grace appeared and turned out to be unexpectedly helpful. Conversation was relaxed and pleasant, an uplifting experience as we chatted away and, thanks to his striking features, a pleasing pastel drawing was achieved.

Meanwhile, a table was being laid and we had an enjoyable afternoon tea with his wife and family. During a rare pause in conversation, I mentioned the sign board in the garden and asked if there was "a tavern down by the river". "Oh no," he said, "I was having my usual gaze at it this morning and saw this large panel of wood floating round the corner. I rushed down to the jetty and caught it with the boat hook. It's waiting to go back to The Red Lion".

*   *   *

In 1986, I was asked to paint HMS *President* – where she lay alongside the Thames Embankment above Blackfriars Bridge. Not an engaging subject it seemed yet this was for the highly respected London Division of the RNR, to mark their scheduled transfer to St Catherine's Dock a year later. Gradually the brief, though not always the fee, was extended and extended – to include "The Lord Mayor's Show" which, apart from thousands of onlookers includes an annual procession covering about a five mile course and extraordinary mobile 'floats'.

The first year I attended, the tide was out and the ship lay on the mud twenty feet below, almost out of sight. Foolishly, I stood on the embankment wall high above trying to get some idea of how she would look, but there was a surge in the crowd and I was very nearly pushed over.

A year later, the tide was up and everything was happening on a perfect day. But while making sketches and frenetic photo references, I was knocked down by one of the mobile floats, lost my security tab and was arrested by a police officer for "wandering about". Thankfully, this turned out to be a minor diversion but one which my patrons later insisted "must be included in the painting". Apart from this, the finished work shows The Lord Mayor's gold coach and, with some artistic licence, the moment it stops alongside the ship.

This actual scene is repeated in much the same order each year. It shows the Lord Mayor receiving his tot of rum from 'The Queen / God Bless Her' rum barrel, toasting the considerable crowd on stands nearby and before proceeding, being ceremonially kissed, by a long-suffering Wren, the same one if not the same Lord Mayor, year after year.

Twelve months later, Judy and I were invited to a banquet in the spacious new Divisional Headquarters ashore beneath the suddenly floodlit Tower Bridge. We sat agog at the wardroom top table, surrounded for the first time by more jovial admirals than I knew existed. They kept us in fits of laughter.

Then came the unveiling and I was kindly asked how I "managed to catch so much detail, at just the right moment?"

"With very great difficulty!" I briefly replied.

*   *   *

We had to wait till 1990 for the founding of The Arthur Ransome Society (TARS) and some of our happiest years. Sharing Ransome-type experiences

HMS *President*

and values with fellow enthusiasts has given us an enriched participation and such like-minded friendships we never imagined. Some of our entrenched members still read the exceptional twelve books one after another, year after year. We tend to do the same, while challenged with the remarkably characteristic audio tapes by Gabriel Woolf. The essence of these keep us rivetted on journeys, lunch and tea.

One jolly experience was being invited with Judy to stay in a woodland cottage while painting an 18ft long x 14ft tall background for *Amazon* where she now rests in the Windermere Steamboat Museum. This shows her grounded between the narrow entrance amid the rock face, boulder and shingle of "the secret harbour". Later, Kate joined us and we spent another delightful week in the flat above the museum. Here were fascinating views across the lake, with swallows and house martins doing extraordinary aerobatics. Each day, Kate and I painted another Lakeland backdrop. This was twenty feet long by eight foot high, today sadly faded, for the fully restored *Coch-y-Bonddhu*, Ransome's successor to *Swallow*. I'm sure Arthur would approve of the whole 'Swallows and Amazons' ambience. It is another tribute to all he gave to us.

Chapter 14

Many Happy Returns

As a northerner, I feel we must concede that special parts of East Anglia are second only to Lakeland as a Ransome heartland. On top of that, all Broadland visits for me are a celebration of that memorable holiday with my parents and Juliet in 1939 – her 'Log' of that other *'Mavis'* culminating in the initial contact with Ransome and so much that was to follow. The Northern Broads have ever since been held dear, more than ever from 1960, when pilgrimages could be shared with Judy.

Amusingly, the Ransomes had always seemed interested and more prepared to lower their guard and discuss activity in this area – perhaps because real place names are used in the Broadland books and, in consequence, he was spared from the geographical where-about questions by fans.

Evgenia, 4-10-61:

> Thank you very much for *Let's be Broad-minded* [a most amusing book by Dennis Rooke – brilliantly illustrated by Alan d'Egville]. It brought back to us all the fun and pleasure we got out of sailing on the Broads – so many years ago it feels now. .

For us, religiously, after every few years of Broadland deprivation, Judy and

Horning village pump in 1939

I have made our way to the exceptional Horning and relived memories, so infectiously encapsulated in *Coot Club* and *The Big Six*. Almost always while they were alive, we reported back to the Ransomes with details from the ship's log.

The village remained as lovely in 1994 as I remember it 55 years earlier, except that the village pump on the green, where Juliet and I used to "water ship" with the milk churn carrier, has been replaced by a less characterful tap.

Alas, Banham's boat yard, once immediately down river from the staithe, has been replaced by the first row of desirable riverside residences, and Percival's by the second.

It was from the loft window of Banham's [rechristened 'Jonnatt's' by AR] that 'Pete', youngest of the 'Death & Glories', lost his jiggling tooth – with the aid of fishing line tied round it and the thrown-out brick to which it was attached.

Thankfully, a third shed was built just before the war and this remains, now known as Southgate's. From here we managed to hire their last available dinghy – very GRP, about two thirds the length of *Titmouse* and sporting a bright purple terylene sail – whatever would 'Tom Dudgeon' think?

"Then we hove our ship to, with the wind at sou'west boys," Spanish Ladies.

Our idea of setting out against the wind, actually more to the sou'east, was simply to be sure of making it back to the yard before closure at 5 o'clock.

So started the single day and night we had so looked forward to and carefully planned for weeks before; a leisurely sail to Ranworth, grog and grub at the Maltsters, and a gentle potter up the hill to dear old 1370 St Helen's church, to marvel once more at the 15th century lectern, service book and glorious 14th century rood screen depicting the twelve apostles, climb the worn and winding steps up the tower to take colour snaps for the grandchildren of those faraway white sails crossing, so majestically and mysteriously, the distant woods and fields in the sun ...

Trouble was, the wind was fitful and shielded as usual by buildings, ever-expanding vegetation, the rising ground behind the village and a just-detectable flood tide. Far more crucially, the hire-boat's wooden centre-board had an unstoppable way of floating back up its case, which our old friend, the foreman had joked was 'only natural'.

So it was that, half an hour after hoisting the single lugsail, we were still tacking crab-wise, back and forth, between the same bits of bank, within easy hailing of the yard.

"We've found the perfect name for your boat," I called.

"What's 'at then?" replied the foreman.

"Piglet."

"Why *Piglet*?" he questioned obligingly.

"'Cos' she's a *proper little swine*," I called in local parlance.

With that, we downed sail. I took the oars, Judy the tiller and we waved goodbye.

Down river we went, past the idyllic cottage and garden. I always imagined this belonged to 'Mr Tedder' the village policeman and this time it even had a perfect *Death and Glory* of a small 20ft (60m) lifeboat conversion moored alongside – but no sign of 'Joe', 'Bill' and 'Pete' aboard or digging for bait for that matter.

Then, further downstream, we experienced the usual rising excitement as we moved towards where we thought, but could never be sure, was the delightful ambience of 'Dr Dudgeon'. Once more, Judy read aloud the relevant bit from *Coot Club*:

[Tom] sailed past the staithe and the boathouses till he came to the little old house with a roof thatched with reeds, and a golden bream swimming merrily into the wind high above one of the gables.

However much we scrutinised, nothing looked quite as it should. We have

'Tom Came Sailing Home' from 'Coot Club'

come to acknowledge that the home of Tom remains anonymous. Perhaps 'secrets are secrets' for a very good reason. It would not have done to have Ransome devotees turning up for real or imagined treatment at a supposed doctor's surgery, for the rest of time!

Then, past the pleasantly converted 'smock' windmill, we approached the now populated "wilderness" and wondered once more which of the intriguing dykes and little backwaters had sheltered the *Death and Glory*. Round the bend was The Ferry Inn so tragically changed in real life by war-time bombs in 1941 and, later burnt down from sparks on its thatched roof in 1967. It now bears little resemblance to those relatively innocent *Coot Club* times of 1934 but remains a welcome stopping place.

Nearby, on the same side, the trap for 'George Owdon' had been laid while a bit further, on the south bank was 'No.7', the coot's nest, a later generation no doubt but certainly there were no white feathers on the ones we met.

Here, and in almost every reach, we were made aware of the increasing number of really monstrous and expensive "plastic bathtubs" slithering up and down river. At least they made hardly any wake, were less polluting; and the local wildlife seemed to regard them as non-threatening, even as a rightful source of nourishment.

But what had become of the once-preponderant sailing-yachts? We were reminded of so many happy voyages under sail in the earlier days, before the so-welcome arrival of Elizabeth and Kate, when we used to keep the ARs informed about our plans.

After one such report we were astonished to receive the following reply:

Evgenia 30-4-62:

We are so pleased you are going for your holiday on the Broads in two small boats instead of one big one and we hope you will see the difference in the same way we always did.

Funnily enough the first names that sprang to mind were *Winsome* and

Welcome – but then I thought that they must be so old by now they are no longer in the running.

Please take some nice photographs of your cruise ...

Do come to see us when next you are next in the Lakes.

This was to be our first voyage in *Welcome* and our friends Anthony and Jennifer were to join us in *Winsome*. Out of the hundreds of yachts available at the time, it seemed extraordinary that, by chance, we should choose the same crafts that the Ransomes knew so well 32 years earlier, but then, our tastes were similar in so many ways!

As we later explained to the ARs, Anthony and Jennifer were new to sail and, to begin with, we had lots of fun at their expense. Typically, with help from the gimballed cockpit stove, we would roar past to windward while nonchalantly sipping tea and studying the map or morning paper. Also, each morning after breakfast, we rather pointedly, gave them a good start.

But the northern Broads are an ideal nursery for sail and our companions were improving much faster than anticipated. One morning, after washing up, they were completely out of sight. Confidently, we set off in pursuit, only to be stopped by one vessel after another coming the other way – to whom they had passed on spurious concern for our well-being and conveyed rudimentary tips on how to make sail and cast off.

It was years later that we learnt more detail of how the Ransomes, them-selves, fared. This was from an unpublished bit of his Autobiography. They first hired *Welcome* in the spring of 1931 and with them, in *Winsome*, were Ted Scott of *The Manchester Guardian* and his son Dick.

> Our first boat on the Broads was one of the last two built by old Walter Woods of Potter Heigham... She was Una-rigged with a gaff sail and her mast stepped close to her bows. She drew so little water that she could make her way up any ditch, and in her we explored thoroughly the whole of the Broads north of Yarmouth. Our favourite time for the Broads was immediately after the Easter Holiday, when, in those days, the motor cruisers were for the most part lying unused and waiting for the summer. It was also the best time for birds. We could see the bearded tits, the big hawks over Hickling and Horsey, hear the booming of the bittern and sometimes see one flying low over the reeds, and very soon found that the birds have made up their minds that sailing boats are harmless. A rowing boat or a motor boat will frighten them from afar, but slipping silently by in a sailing boat or dinghy we were able to photograph great crested grebes on their nests and watch, from only a few yards away, the parent birds swimming with the young ones on their backs, shrugging off first one and then another to take a swimming lesson.

Dick Kelsall's father was encouraged to 'come sailing' with the ARs. On 29th April 1933, he, Desmond and Dick, aged 11, left Barkbooth and the Winster Valley at 6am, arriving at Herbert Woods Potter Heigham at 5.40pm. Their *open* Morris 'Oxford', maximum speed 50mph, covered the 310 miles at an average speed of 26mph according to the scientific Dick.

They picked up *Welcome* from Woods and sailed down the Thurne to the Bure for the night, just as we quanted her 30 years later. The ARs had picked up their more roomy *Fairway* from Wroxham and they rendezvoused at the Horning Hall landing, everyone flying a recognition flag in place of the normal burgee.

Dick remembers "the excitement of sailing in such wild flat places, the quietness and seeing many trading wherries with their dark brown sails, laden with reeds and other cargo".

It was clearly Colonel Kelsall, 'the great precisian', who wrote the log. It gives a military accurate account of all arrivals and departures but nothing of what actually happened. Dick remembers the life he glimpsed aboard the *Fairway*: "There was much appreciated tinned 'Goblin' pudding, and to save washing up, poached eggs in soup eaten together! My mother was rather horrified at this lapse!"

*   *   *

Judy and I tended to observe Evgenia's Broadland edicts and one of these was "Sailing boats are really best in early spring before there are leaves on the trees". In response, we rather overdid things the following year, and set off in our now favourite hire-yacht *Welcome* from Herbert Woods at Potter Heigham – in early March.

Between their basin and the river was a footbridge which forbade the passage of a raised mast. So, after some enthusiastic quanting, we suddenly found ourselves out in the River Thurne, being driven down stream in a light snowstorm.

As the mate suggested, the sensible thing to do here was to moor and raise the mast and sail at leisure. But by the time this had registered, there were no public facilities in sight and early signs of dusk were appearing. "To save time", I decided to quant on and, with Judy at the tiller, raise the mast and sail while under way.

I think I was confusing ourselves with a wherry we had once seen shooting Acle bridge. To do this, the helmsman had left the tiller and passed, seemingly at leisure and extraordinary composure through throngs of children on the side deck, lowered its huge sail, then the mast within feet of the bridge, passing through, still in mid channel and raising mast and sail again, all while still under steerage way.

With this in mind and in open water, I reasoned that the raising of *Welcome's* mast and sail, even under slower passage through the water, would be easier and much as we had done so often before – albeit moored to the bank.

Unfortunately, what with catching shrouds on corners of the cabin roof as the mast rose, being hopelessly out of practice and forgetting the incomparably greater momentum carried by a wherry, we finished up losing all steerage way and circled, with bow then stern towards the bank. Worse still, our mast protruded far beyond the stern and the final embarrassment came when this engaged with an empty dustbin and pushed it noisily across somebody's lawn.

Once the mast and boom were safely back in their crutch and aided by a

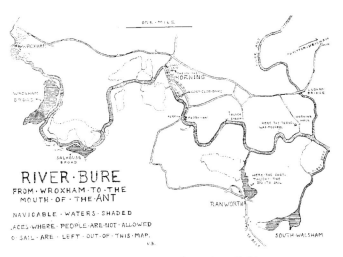

RIVER·BURE
FROM·WROXHAM·TO·THE
MOUTH·OF·THE·ANT

NAVICABLE·WATERS·SHADED
.ACES·WHERE·PEOPLE·ARE·NOT·ALLOWED
C·SAIL·ARE·LEFT·OUT·OF·THIS·MAP.
N.B.

'River Bure' map from 'Coot Club'

billowing NE wind, I quanted till dark and we berthed inevitably on a lee shore at Thurne Mouth in the Bure.

By now it was near freezing but once the awning was rigged, all was made snug below with the potentially lethal paraffin heater we had brought from home. After eating huge amounts of soup, bread, cheese and apples, we played chess before turning off the stove and collapsing into hot water-bottled bunks where, after a page or two of *Coot Club*, came blissful oblivion.

It was certainly less populated at that time of year and the leafless trees allowed some excellent sailing as we visited all the usual haunts in unusual freedom. The second week brought exceptionally high winds causing any number of accidents. We tried to keep well clear of anything moving but, while moored for lunch one day, a bowsprit suddenly appeared in the cabin, we had been inexplicably rammed amidships. We felt mortified as *Welcome's* beautiful flush-planked top strake had suddenly acquired a hole. Most fortunately, our assailants, being sailing types, were honest and apologetic as we swapped particulars, they admitted full responsibility and the yard was completely understanding. They had clearly braced themselves for more-than-usual Saturday repairs and a patch was expertly let into *Welcome's* side while we were packing to go home.

We had not the heart to tell the Ransomes of this but still marvel at the service and pleasure this simple, honest craft had given over at least thirty-two years and, as illustrated, not always in the most capable hands!

To the ARs 14-5-64:

Elizabeth is six weeks old today ... Judy expects her to manage a jib sheet before long ...

Evgenia, 7-9-64:

We were interested in the Yachting magazine – we never see any now – but we wished you knew the Lakes – Windermere and Coniston in particular before motor boats were invented...

[I had also sent them a copy of 'Jenny', the Clyde Puffer.]

... So I enjoyed once more the trip to Glasgow on a Scottish tramp.

I am interested to hear about your going on the Broads next month – the motor cruiser at that time of year and considering your bringing the baby and the puppy with you is better than a sailing boat – but remember that it is the end of the season and most boats need an overhaul. Make sure that your calor gas cooker ... [is] in good working order ... We had a lot of trouble with gas cookers & stoves when we used to take a cruiser in the autumn as being more comfortable to fish from than a small sailing boat.

She wrote later:

"I expect you are preparing a detailed log with plenty of illustrations."

To the ARs, 8-11-64:

Most of our time on the Broads involved domestic chores though the younger end, which included our poodle puppy, Bo's'n enjoyed every minute and became extremely salty. Elizabeth, being under eighteen, was obliged to spend some time in The Maltster's flower bed and, as the bar has been turned into the prow of a boat with "port holes" overlooking the broad, we felt more comfortable outside anyway.

*   *   *

By 1994, river traffic had multiplied once more. It was mostly power driven, large, expensive-looking and in convoy, usually with fenders dangling, sometimes in the water. It follows that we were aware of fewer obvious-Ransome-oriented types. Typically, 'Dad' would be up forrard, alone at the wheel, while thirty feet away, 'Mum' would be pacing the galley, a distant look on her face, their children, or 'kids' as we are now expected to call them (with that implied margin of over-tolerance) appeared in the vast cabin space amidships watching television, apparently unmoved by their surroundings – until they saw us enjoying ourselves with some *purpose* in life – and we all started waving happily.

I can just imagine Arthur saying "Enjoyment is in inverse proportion to size and sophistication", or Ernest saying, " What about *Amazon's* sixty years service at an initial cost of £15!" Sadly, we are told by locals that *size and sophistication* is just what is in main demand, a guarantee of huge expense and boredom in consequence, as it insulates us from all that Broadland has to offer.

How different it could have been under sail, with only two to a boat, as the ARs advocated – not to mention being imbued with Ransome awareness from an early age!

But what has become of all the dinghies which abounded in earlier days? Before and after the war, these cost ten shillings (50p) a week to hire or, if one could afford it, double this with a sail and rudder. They were of primitive clinker construction with limited windward ability but we loved them dearly.

Towed astern, they could be a bit of a nuisance, but really came into their own after tea. Not only did they allow us to moor virtually wherever we pleased, sometimes to a mud weight in some tranquil broad or, more often, to the bank, conveniently far from an over-crowded staithe but with lovely walks ashore. They also gave access to the remotest dykes and backwaters, which were seemingly untouched by man and especially packed with fish and natural interest. Paradoxically, this literal 'sculling about' in the dog watches was almost always our happiest time of the day.

*   *   *

Early morning freshness would usually start with a swim and, in those earlier days it was well to remember that raw sewage was not tanked aboard but discreetly pumped into the water. This had a way of building up under moorings and the trick was not to dive too steeply – as I once did, so memorably, from Ranworth staithe.

Not for modern youngsters would be the challenge of quanting a thirty-foot yacht from Potter Heigham to Horning as I tried to do in '39 with the help of Father. Auxiliary power was unknown to us and while still under sail, we particularly relished every casual breath as, with Mother at the tiller we would ghost along reach after reach with no apparent wind. More than once we were asked "Have you got an electric motor?"

On idyllic evenings we caught sizeable roach with new bread simply pressed over a hook dangled in the clear water. These were often our delicious supper.

After that there were bird books or local history, the swapping of yarns and bits of the books after a paraffin lamp-lit evening meal. (As I boasted to Ransome, *Mavis* relied on paraffin, unlike the *Teasel* which used batteries in *Coot Club*.) Then came the test of 'land legs' with a well-earned run ashore – down that bat-swooping lane towards the 'wilderness' where we invariably chose our favourite residence with inland moorings alongside. Then, the Ferry Inn, before returning and falling into our bunks with so-precipitate sleep.

On our 1994 excursion in the rather awful *Piglet* dinghy, audible warning of approach to other vessels was maintained by our port side rowlock which rendered an appropriately pig-like squeak. The starboard side, though silent, soon exhibited a more serious end-of-season characteristic by coming adrift. No sooner had I screwed it back as best I could with bare fingers, and resumed rowing, than a grotesque 'Mississippi paddle-steamer' listed over us as passengers on both decks crowded the rail and it became quite a challenge for Judy to acknowledge their vociferous goodwill. I noticed how, while intent on maintaining course, she was absentmindedly keeping a hand raised in reply, rather in the manner of a royal wave or benediction!

Further down stream we passed flotillas of different "makes" of bird, mainly coots, ducks, crested grebes, occasional swans – the moorhens charging about everywhere. Not a single coot, a possible offspring of that in *Coot Club* had a white wing feather.

Some reaches appeared especially favoured. There was much darting about with seemingly robust attacks on the opposition, yet all were clearly enjoying themselves in the sparkling light and there was no apparent malice. The larger birds could so easily have menaced yet there seemed to be recognised rules of fair play, almost tolerant affection.

After two enthralling miles of twisting river, we sighted Horning Church at last and the lush green lawns below it busy with so-fortunate Soay sheep. Here we swept 180 degrees to starboard and moored in a shallow bay on the opposite bank, what bliss!

Essential stores were landed and, while I "laid the table", Judy could not resist exploring a rough pathway along the raised inner bank. How content she felt in the warm sun, surrounded by such beauty and birdsong ... the sky seeming to have developed promising windy bits of cirrus among the blue ...

All at once there was a cry and muffled splash, moments later she emerged, scratched and covered in mud – having tripped over a hidden tree root and taken a spectacular header into rotting reed bog and nettles. For a moment she looked quite "decomposed" but recovered bravely and there was a general sense of revival as we tucked into our beer and sandwiches while sunning peacefully on our borrowed nylon life jackets.

Exploring a rough pathway

We gazed on the hauntingly remembered panorama across the river, the top of Horning Church and Vicarage tucked on its mound among the trees and the large early-twenties thatched house, known locally as 'Storey's', with its complex waterway approaches and lawns down to the water's edge. It all appeared so inviting and there was the same old heron resting on one leg, looking incredibly like garden furniture.

One lawn was colonised and muddied by the mixed blessing and comparatively new phenomena of a huge flock of Canada Geese, a handsome creature which has expanded out of proportion and we hear is rather good to eat. At least they left alone those 'black' sheep with their devoted lawn-care, close-cropping the grass so assiduously, yet managing to feed and water it at the same time. What human gardener could do more!

Occasionally, we were obliged to break off to acknowledge passing traffic. Strange how it was the crews of massive "gin palaces" sweeping by in their opulent splendour, who seemed to envy us most.

All this time, the south easterly wind was freshening visibly in the willows among the dense osier bushes and reeds upstream across the river. It was a shame to leave without more exploring – but time to hoist sail. Secretly, this was another moment we had both looked forward to.

But it was Judy who was most prepared. She leapt in first and grabbed the tiller, saying it was time she showed how it was done.

With much initial rudder-waggling and whistling for wind, *Piglet* was coaxed along in the lee of woodland and reeds until ripples appeared and we were obliged to lean out abruptly to windward as she leapt forward, a bone in her teeth and fairly galloping away, all sins forgiven.

Piglet was in some ways a dark horse, for back up those hard-won reaches we now leapt and scampered with aplomb. The strengthening wind too could not have been more obliging, seeming to follow us round corners. There was hardly ever the threat of an unwanted gybe as, when necessary and unhampered by shrouds, Judy simply released more and more sail. It was now our turn to wave at cruisers as *we* swept past *them*, to port or starboard, creating more fun for boats and bird life with our embarrassingly boisterous wake.

We became quite a spectacle as we shot past the Ferry and were soon in the home straight. At this, *Piglet* really raised her skirts and began to plane as, with joyous shame, she must have exceeded the 4mph speed limit. This was an apparent source of shared enjoyment and one fisherman even appeared to 'present arms' by raising his rod in clear acclaim (we liked to think).

All too soon, the Swan Hotel appeared alongside and we circled into wind to starboard for a perfect soft landing beside the lawn. Here we bagged a table which commanded that fascinating bend in the river where one can see so clearly up and down and everything possible always seems to be happening at once.

The Swan does a splendid cream tea and we sat there glowing in the lowering sun, enveloped in complete contentment, with just nice time in which to return *Piglet* to her sty, a perfect ending to our day.

* * *

It was also a time of relaxed contemplation as we debated where exactly it had been that 'George Owdon' had committed himself so decisively. Judy foraged for the chart once more and the revelation in *The Big Six – but could not find her glasses.*

These were the only pair she had and we clearly remembered her wearing them to navigate on the way out. We looked for them everywhere, especially in the boat and rucksack ... until, at last, a chilling thought occurred. Oh Horrors, no not that! But still, I felt compelled to ask ... "Did you put your spectacles on for diving into the undergrowth dear?"

*   *   *

All semblance of serenity evaporated as we approached Southgate's and, saying a little prayer, asked if we could "borrow something with an engine". "But it's 5 o'clock and closing time," said our friend the foreman, but then relented on hearing our plight. Visitors can often be a source of well-concealed irritation, but he knew us from previous years and seemed prepared to make allowances.

The task of moving half their stately fleet of real yachts proved complicated before he was able to release all that was left – the ugliest GRP launch with 'go-faster stripes' ever seen. In this, we proceeded downstream at a very properly governed 4mph – just hoping we should not meet anyone we knew.

By 5.30pm, familiar scenes hove into view – but what was this? Across the very mouth of our verdant retreat, with no possible landing access, lay an opulent latter-day *Margoletta* motor cruiser, arrogantly and securely moored as if she owned the place. What cheek!

We felt thoroughly exasperated. For a foolish moment, I was tempted to do a very mild 'George Owdon' by slacking off one of their mooring lines to squeeze ashore ... but instead, leaned over and knocked on the cabin door.

Long moments passed. Then, surprising sounds of Mozart, the welcome smell of cooking and there in the cockpit glow stood the 'Hullabaloos' – just two seemingly sober and surprisingly "nice people like us!" As we tried to explain, they even asked how they could help, took our lines and handed us aboard as if we were old friends. Gosh!

Along the narrow raised path we went, managing not to trip but finding that one crushed bed of reed and nettles looks much like another. Hurriedly, we selected what Judy thought was the likeliest and gradually, on hands and knees, we worked across its six-foot width, lifting one thatch of rotting vegetation after another. The further we got, the deeper it went as, with bare and bleeding hands, we dug almost to water level through some very pungent and abrasive compost.

It was October and progressively dusk under the trees, the situation more desperate by the minute and we were feeling more foolish all the time – and time itself was running out!

More and more earth, reed and nettles were torn up and flung aside, regardless. It almost developed into a game as decorum went to the winds and we became more and more splattered with rotting thatch – when all at once, against all probability in the increasing gloom, the tiniest glint of gold appeared.

With diminished expectations, we could hardly believe but dug further with much more care and managed to extract Judy's precious, only and expensive spectacles, surprisingly clean and intact – miraculous!

Filthy, but sighted and rejoicing, there was an undignified scramble back to our civilised new friends in the '*Margoletta*'. The 'Hullabaloos' had even waited about and kindly helped us across their immaculate decks with every assurance that "it will all mop off". We left them with grateful, very contrite hearts and managed to reach port only thirty minutes after the ultimate deadline.

We were dishevelled, bleeding and utterly whacked but, after a glorious bath, we took our table at the Swan and, in jovial company over copious amounts of delicious food and drink, all tiredness and discomfort simply melted away.

Over coffee, we told new friends how little we had achieved of our long-planned itinerary, yet this did not seem to matter. We had been in Ransome country again, the focus of so many happy times. Perhaps most of all, we had been *involved* and though this had included minor tribulation, it was almost as in any Ransome story, where adversity is gradually overtaken by *purpose and achievement.*

Our room looked over that sweeping bend in the Bure and, feeling slightly light-headed, we gazed at the entrancing moonlit scene below before falling into bed and quickly losing consciousness. I just managed to mumble, "It's been rather a hard day" – but was not a bit surprised when Judy mumbled back, "I would not have missed it for worlds!"

And so it goes. In spite of 'the rapid approach of middle age', Ransome-imbued awareness remains, not to mention love, faith and hope, as we live in the new millennium ...

THE ARTHUR RANSOME
SOCIETY (TARS)

> **"All dates before 13 June 1990 should be prefixed BT (Before TARS) to signify the inauguration of The Arthur Ransome Society at Windermere Steamboat Museum, for that day was a watershed in the affairs of men, women and children." – George Wray**

The Arthur Ransome Society was formed in 1990 for enthusiasts of all ages who, typically, have enjoyed the famous 'Swallows and Amazons' series of books. TARS in the UK is split into six regions, each with it own programme of events: a wide range of social activities, including literary matters and research, sailing, fishing, camping, walking, climbing and exploring – bringing together all those who share the values and spirit which Ransome fostered. Highlights are the AGM weekends and bi-annual 'Literary Weekend.'

Membership covers thousands of men, women, students and children in over thirty countries. Australia, New Zealand, the USA, Canada and Japan have thriving local groups of their own. The Society regularly produces high-quality magazines and journals for members. In addition, 'Amazon Publications' publishes a book each year. There is a much-appreciated 'Society Stall' at some meetings with huge displays of books, video tapes, audio tapes and other Ransome-related extras.

The Society is based at the Abbot Hall Museum in Kendal, where there is a special Ransome room with his desk, some favourite books, typewriter and personal possesssions on display. Alongside is a children's playroom with games and activities on a *Swallows and Amazons* theme. TARS has close links with the Windermere Steamboat Museum at Bowness and financed the restoration of two of the original dinghies in the stories. *Amazon* and *Coch-y-bonddhu* are on permanent display there, *'Cochy'* still being sailed at TARS events. There is also the Ruskin Museum at Coniston – founded by Ransome's mentor, W.G. Collingwood.

A separate Trust of TARS members has purchased the 1931 Hillyard cutter *Nancy Blackett*, the original *Goblin* in 'We Didn't Mean to Go To Sea'. Now fully restored, she is seaworthy and cruises the coast making appearances at numerous Festivals of the Sea etc.

For further information on TARS, contact:

The Membership Secretary, The Arthur Ransome Society,
The Abbot Hall Gallery, Kendal, Cumbria LA9 5AL

Telephone: 01539 722464 or email: tarsinfo@arthur-ransome.org

Or visit the Arthur Ransome web site: www. arthur-ransome.org/ar/